How Schools Make Race

SERIES | **RACE** AND
EDUCATION

Series edited by H. Richard Milner IV

OTHER BOOKS IN THIS SERIES

How Schools Make Race

Teaching Latinx Racialization in America

LAURA C. CHÁVEZ-MORENO

HARVARD EDUCATION PRESS

CAMBRIDGE, MASSACHUSETTS

Paperback ISBN 9781682539224

Library of Congress Cataloging-in-Publication Data

Names: Chávez-Moreno, Laura C, author.
Title: How schools make race : teaching Latinx racialization in America / Laura C. Chávez-Moreno.
Description: Cambridge, Massachusetts : Harvard Education Press, [2024] | Includes bibliographical references and index.
Identifiers: LCCN 2024016135 | ISBN 9781682539224 (paperback)
Subjects: LCSH: Race awareness—United States. | Hispanic Americans—United States—Ethnic identity. | Educational equalization—United States. | Education, Bilingual—United States.
Classification: LCC BF723.R3 C43 2024 | DDC 305.23508900973—dc23/eng/20240701
LC record available at https://lccn.loc.gov/2024016135

Published by Harvard Education Press,
an imprint of the Harvard Education Publishing Group

Harvard Education Press
8 Story Street
Cambridge, MA 02138

Cover Design: Endpaper Studio

The typefaces in this book are Sabon and MyriadPro.

I dedicate this book to the educators who, against numerous obstacles, have stood firm in their political commitment to teach about and against race and racism.

And, as always, to my students—you have taught me so much.

Contents

Preface

On Friday, June 16, 2017, Amlie High School held its graduation ceremony.[1] I had attended other high school graduations, including my own in Douglas, Arizona, a town bordering México, and five graduations as a public high school teacher of Spanish in Philadelphia. But this was my first in a midwestern city, and I wondered how different it would be. I arrived at the large sports arena where the ceremony was to take place, ten minutes before the 7:30 p.m. start time. After going through the metal detectors, I entered the stands, the usual "Pomp and Circumstance" march echoing and competing with people's buzz of anticipation, and I was surprised that the lower sections looked packed. I had not expected so many to be early, indicating to me that I was late compared with the proud families. I sat close to where one of my study's teacher participants had texted me that she would be sitting. Not finding her, I looked through the printed program pamphlet, now looking for acknowledgment of Amlie High's bilingual education dual-language program, which I had been studying for more than a year. This commencement included the dual-language program's first cohort of graduating seniors, who had started twelve years ago in Somos Bilingüe Elementary School. It was a notable accomplishment for the students, Amlie High, the Oakville Urban School District, and for Oakville's Latinx community, who had fought to establish dual-language education as a means to improve Latinxs' education.

Seeing that the pamphlet did not mention the program, I glanced over the 350 robed graduating seniors sitting in the middle of the arena. Everyone excitedly chatted until 7:37 p.m., when an announcement called us to rise for the US national anthem. Then Amlie's principal addressed the audience, with an American Sign Language interpreter nearby. The speech acknowledged the disparities of economic status and of opportunities within Amlie High's student population. "Some of you have been homeless, some of you have competed in championships," said the principal, adding the customary commencement comments, "If you work hard, believe in yourself, the world

is yours." Next, select student speakers went up to the podium individually. The fifth student to speak shared:

> We are so lucky to have attended a diverse school. We have students
> who are different races, religions, . . . I even went to a quinceañera and bar
> mitzvah. . . . I learned a great deal from classes but also lots of my class-
> mates who opened my eyes. For some of us, it means we will go to places,
> universities with less diversity. We have to seek diversity.

The mention of diversity struck me because all the speakers, including this
student, were White. Amlie High's racial makeup was approximately
41 percent White, 23 percent Black/African American, 21 percent Latinx/
Hispanic, 10 percent multiracial, 5 percent Asian American, <1 percent Native
American, and <1 percent Pacific Islander.[2] This racial composition made
Amlie one of Oakville's "less White high schools." Yet not until 8:16 p.m.
did a Black student break the trend. After her, another White student speaker
came to the podium. She was the only one to note that Amlie's dual-language
graduates were a district first. Her remark prompted applause and cheering
in scattered places throughout the crowd, including behind me, causing me
to turn and see a Latinx family with young kids and a crying baby. Her
remark also eased my disappointment that the ceremony had not formally
recognized this community's or the individual students' bilingual education
accomplishments. The ceremony ended without featuring any Latinx student or even the token inclusion of Spanish.

This surprised me. During the years I had spent at Oakville for the
research study that is the catalyst for this book, many repeated the idea that
Amlie's diversity was its strength, making it stand out from Oakville's
other (better-achieving) high schools. While other schools also promote this
narrative, it takes on special significance when we note that Oakville's
Latinx community made possible the racially diverse Spanish-English dual-
language program. While some people expect that bilingual education is a
space *for* Latinxs—where they have a chance at meeting their needs and
have a voice on par with their dominant peers—the ceremony upended the
idea of the dual-language program providing opportunities and representation that uplift Latinxs even when outside of the program. The district's
educators, policymakers, and community members portrayed this program
as for the educational attainment and benefit not only of Latinxs, but also
of *all* students. The district used it to address the needs of Spanish-dominant
Latinxs who would otherwise be placed in subtractive English as a Second
Language (ESL) courses.[3] Oakville's Latinx community, along with others,

regarded the program as an intervention for ameliorating racial injustice, for providing Latinx students a linguistically and culturally relevant education. The district also used it to curtail White flight by attracting White families looking for bilingual education, a scarce resource in public schools.[4] This made the absence of Latinx honorees at the graduation ceremony all the more apparent.

The absence might also lead some to question whether dual-language education can provide educational equity to students who are racialized as Others.[5] This book tackles this equity issue by showing how these patterns and other practices convey ideas about race and Latinxs in schools. It uses Oakville's secondary-level bilingual education program as an example to show how schools *make* race.

By "make race," I mean how schools convey ideas about race, whether intentionally or not, and contribute to society's ongoing redefinition of racial categories and hierarchies.[6] Societies construct race through historical, legal, political, economic, discursive, and/or other practices that discriminate and mark—and thereby *make*—racialized groups in relation to other groups.[7] Scholars call this *racialization*—the process of socially forming racialized patterns, meanings, and the boundaries of racialized groups. This process also involves placing these groups in a hierarchy and distributing resources along racial lines.[8]

Schools, as institutions in society, make race by contributing to racialization. Schools inform people's ideas about race, sometimes by teachers providing explicit lessons on race or racism. But more often than not, and usually unintentionally, schools make race through their practices, policies, and discourses. For example, curriculum and pedagogy can implicitly convey ideas about race, and whether curriculum and pedagogy are culturally relevant for students can affect student achievement outcomes.[9] These outcomes often reflect the way schools distribute resources, demonstrating racial patterns that in turn shape perceptions about race. Schools also make race by informing and reinforcing boundaries of the different racialized groups. Through all these means and more, schools play a key role in society's construction of racial ideas and racialized groups.

In this race-making role, schooling is a *racial project*.[10] "Racial projects" are activities or actions that produce societal ideas about race and distribute resources along racial lines.[11] They can include institutions like prisons, immigration laws, housing financing programs, advertising campaigns, entertainment, religion, health care, sports, and schools. Schooling is a racial project in that it, intentionally or not, teaches people to make sense of race and distributes resources along racial lines. While schools cannot escape being a racial project, people can contest how schools function as such. For instance, bilingual education can be viewed as a racial project aimed at promoting equitable resource distribution among Latinxs, as I will illustrate in these pages.

In this book, I examine how schooling makes race by looking at how a schooling community's bilingual education program imparts lessons about race, even in instances that do not explicitly touch on race. I focused on a bilingual education program, but not because bilingual education racializes more than mainstream or monolingual schools. As a racial project, bilingual education—just as much as other schooling—perpetuates societal ideas about race and thus cannot help making race and making the Latinx racialized group. Rather, I centered a bilingual education program due to its commitment to offering Latinx students a linguistically and culturally relevant education and its perceived role in ameliorating racial injustice. All schooling, including this program, should provide a linguistically and culturally relevant education to students, and bilingual education is one of the more widely available approaches for doing so.

But whether bilingual education (and, for that matter, schooling) can accomplish these goals hinges on how it functions as a racial project. People, including those racialized as Others, wield influence in shaping racial meanings and how schooling functions as a racial project. Educators' practices in and outside the classroom play a crucial role in determining whether schooling actively confronts racism and provides students with opportunities for engaging in anti-racist action. Consequently, purposeful instruction on race is essential, given the uncertainty around whether schools—or even bilingual education—can serve as a racial project that challenges racist ideas.

BOOK OVERVIEW

In this book, I tell the story of Oakville Urban School District's bilingual education program's successes and tensions in providing an equitable education—a racial project that equitably distributes resources and develops youths' critical consciousness about race. The story focuses on teachers and the program's policies and practices, and it also includes the perspectives of youth, parents, and other adult community members. I demonstrate how schools make race by centering on the dual-language program's making of the Latinx racialized group and of Latinidad (two concepts I describe in the introduction). Specifically, I delve into how the program conveyed ideas about race, the Latinx racialized group, and Latinidad through its practices and policies—such as recruitment, testing, tracking, awards, pedagogy, and even absences in curriculum—and the distribution of resources. I present the interplay among these aspects of schooling and reveal how they contribute to shaping and making the Latinx group *in relation to* other racialized groups.[12] Some vignettes presented here illustrate how the bilingual program confronts racist ideas and practices. But most examples paint a less ideal picture, mirroring the prevalent reality of schooling within a racialized society.

The book's general question is: How does Oakville' dual-language program function as a racial project that contributes to making race and the Latinx racialized group? To address this question more specifically, I ask: What ideas about race and "Latinx" did the program convey to students? What ideas did the program convey about Latinidad and the Latinx racialized group in relation to other racialized groups? How did the program's racialization practices and structures affect Latinxs' material consequences? The answers will provide education practitioners in bilingual and nonbilingual education alike examples of the racialization process and how to strive toward the worthwhile goal of making bilingual education (and schooling) a racial project that contests racial injustice.

I answer the three questions in three sections, each focusing on one question and each exploring a different aspect of racialization and Latinxs in schooling.

Part 1, "Teaching Racialization," introduces some of the ideas about race and the Latinx category that the program conveyed. Chapter 1 takes us into the dual-language classrooms to see how the teachers' pedagogy and curriculum conceptualized race and how students made sense of these ideas. Chapter 2 illustrates how program participants made sense of race, including questioning whether Latinx should be categorized as a race. It also presents notions about race and Latinxs that contradict the simplistic idea of race being about skin tone and appearance. The section reveals how these practices, however ambivalently, led to constructing Latinx as a racialized group.

Part 2, "Making Latinidad," illustrates how the program's teachers' practices, ideas, and discourses assigned meaning to Latinidad and to the Latinx group by relationally positioning them with other racialized groups. Chapter 3 focuses on how Latinidad is constructed in relation to Indigeneity and Asian-ness and how the Spanish language binds the Latinx racialized group. Chapter 4 continues to show how the program assigned meaning to the Latinx racialized group through Spanish while adding a focus on Latinidad's relational positioning with Blackness. This section demonstrates how the program made the Spanish language the *signature boundary* of what delineates the Latinx racialized group.

Part 3, "Racialization's Consequences," reveals how the district's dual-language program, at the structural level, reflects and reinforces race and racial hierarchy, practices that—intentionally or not—affected Latinxs' material outcomes. Chapter 5 presents the structural practices and policies that produce patterns that perpetuate the common sense of racialized distinctions and inferiorities. Chapter 6 describes how structures and patterns maintain the white-supremacist racial hierarchy and inequitable material outcomes. The section advances a relational analysis of Latinidad with an emphasis on whiteness, which in turn sheds light on the Latinx community's lack of power and the effects of racialization on Latinxs.

As a whole, the six chapters show how schools make race through the various aspects of schooling—such as program policies and practices, curriculum, and pedagogy—and by producing and reproducing racial patterns. The chapters reveal the complexity of how the dual-language program conveyed some contradictory ideas about race, the Latinx racialized group, and Latinidad, affecting how people make sense of race. For example, the program's participants indicated that race was about skin color and labeled "Latino" as an ethnicity and a shared culture and language. Nevertheless, they also perceived race through more intricate, interconnected perspectives that unveiled how they framed "Latino" as a racialized group, regardless of its visual diversity. The program regarded "Latino" as a racialized group by situating it in relation to other racialized groups, and the program's educational content underscored the experience of racism within the Latinx community akin to that experienced by other racialized groups.

Delving deeper into the story, I found that other factors also contributed to the concepts of Latinx and Latinidad. The program's teachings conflated Latinxs with Latin Americans, even though Latin America has its own racial diversity and categories and its people do not commonly use "Latino/Latina" as their identifier. This conflation misleadingly implied that race and "Latino" are stable concepts, consistent across various times and contexts. Moreover, the program's portrayal of Latinidad as rooted in the language and cultural practices of Spaniards and Latin Americans, rather than those of Latinxs, cast Latinxs as perpetual foreigners. The program generally did not challenge the boundaries delineating the racialized groups or even the white-supremacist racial hierarchy. It constructed Latinidad in ways that worked to separate Latinxs from Blackness, Indigeneity, and Asian-ness. However, by emphasizing Latin America's colonial history and the contemporary racial discrimination Latinxs face in America, the program also constructed Latinidad as distinct from whiteness.

While the dual-language program was established as a district reform for improving Latinxs' education outcomes, some of its contradictory roles and lessons resulted from structural restraints, which limited the program's potential as a racial project that advances educational equity. For instance, its testing and tracking practices relegated many Latinxs to remedial classes with substandard learning opportunities. It favored youth whose parents possessed the wherewithal to keep their child in the program, compared with bilingual Latinx children from families with lesser means or political clout. It celebrated bilingualism, but restricted who was officially acknowledged as biliterate, overlooking many non-dual-language Latinx students. In short, the program continued to distribute resources in ways that disproportionately benefited White middle-class students, consequently displaying racialized patterns of achievement that perpetuated racial categorization and often placed Latinxs below other racialized groups.

In the conclusion, I offer recommendations and elaborate on the racialization of Latinxs. These recommendations address the tension between the program being a racial project that perpetuates dominant ideas or that advances critical-racial ideas about race and racism. Ultimately, my argument is that since schools already make and teach about race—even if unintentionally and implicitly—they should intentionally adopt teaching approaches that promote anti-racist ideas and the ambivalence about race.[13]

Introduction

This story is situated during the nation's change from what some claimed to be a "postracial" America under President Barack Obama to a hyper-racial period fueled by the racist demagoguery of President Donald Trump.

It also unfolds against the backdrop of national demographic change. In recent years Latinxs have been the principal driver of US population growth.[1] In 2003, Latinx/Hispanic became the largest "minority group" in the United States.[2] This national demographic change was felt in the state of RedRock (and in the South during the same time period), which experienced a marked increase in its Latinx population from 1990 to 2000.[3] Nearly half of RedRock's Latinx population were immigrants to the United States. RedRock's Latinx population more than doubled in those years, which a state demographer called "unprecedented." From 2000 to 2010, the Latinx population again increased by 74 percent, attributed to RedRock's good economic conditions and available employment in the agriculture, forestry, printing, food-preparation, and meatpacking industries. These industries attracted many migrant workers from other states who stayed rather than followed seasonal opportunities. These demographic changes made RedRock a "new Latino destination," a term that highlights that the destination does not have large-scale and long-standing histories of Latinx communities.[4] While RedRock had a significant increase in the Latinx population, it is noteworthy that Latinxs have lived in this area since the beginning of the twentieth century and that the land has a long, rich history and continuing presence of various Indigenous nations.[5]

OAKVILLE, REDROCK

Oakville was a metropolitan city made up of scenic neighborhoods with nicely paved bike paths, lakes, and parks. In warmer months, residents hosted festivals and farmers' markets and enjoyed botanical gardens and outdoor restaurants. During the winter months, outdoorsy residents ice fished or skated on the frozen lakes. People were accustomed to the harsh winter; consequently, Oakville's schools did not usually close schools due to snow.

Oakville was known for having good jobs and schools and a vibrant middle class—a depiction that mostly comes from the (White) collective imagination. The image was most representative of the city's lakeside section, with white-collar (mostly White) family houses and above-average-performing schools. Oakville had earned a reputation for being more liberal on social issues than most places in RedRock because of its voting patterns and many left-leaning protests and political organizations.

Despite its liberal reputation and ranking as one of the best US cities to live in, Oakville suffered racial disparities that ranked among the worst in the nation. These disparities appeared in the county correctional facilities, where Black, Latinx, and Native American individuals were vastly over-represented. The Indigenous tribes' history and presence in the region is mostly erased except for some streets bearing names from the Indigenous nations. Along the streets housing the largest number of racially minoritized residents, one could find many payday loan companies and fast-food businesses. These streets also housed all the schools performing below the city's average.

Even though Oakville was relatively more racially diverse than other parts of RedRock, the state's changing racial demographics significantly affected Oakville. Between 1999 and 2014, there was a 17 percent increase in the share of Latinx children in low-income families. During the same period, the poverty rates among Oakville's Latinx population rose sharply, increasing from 17 percent to 28 percent, given that the increase in the Latinx population was particularly of low-income individuals and/or families. This demographic shift led to Oakville's Latinx community experiencing lower incomes and higher poverty rates compared with the city's average.

Of Oakville's Latinx residents, almost 75 percent identified their origin as from México, 10 percent from Puerto Rico, 5 percent from Central America (Nicaragua with the largest percentage), 5 percent from South America (Colombia with the largest percentage), and 3 percent from Cuba.[6] It was unclear how many of RedRock's Latinxs identified as Indigenous. Seven percent of Oakville's Latinxs/Hispanics also identified as multiracial, and approximately 2 percent identified as Afro-Latinxs (Latinx/Hispanic *and* Black/African American).

Despite the evidence of stark racial inequities, this city's residents were not racially isolated, meaning that racialized groups had contact and encounters with other racialized groups through public institutions like schools.

OAKVILLE URBAN SCHOOL DISTRICT

The Oakville Urban School District was experiencing much of the state's shift in population and saw a surge of Latinx relative newcomers compared with the Black and White students it historically enrolled. Latinx students surpassed Asian American students in the early 2000s and surpassed Black students in the 2013–2014 school year to become the largest racialized-Othered group in the district. The district also experienced the out-migration of Whites and an increase in the number of racialized-Othered students (see figure I.1).

To show the increase in another way, in the 1990–1991 school year, Latinxs were almost 3 percent of the district's students. By 2015–2016, Latinxs composed over 20 percent of the student population. From 1990 to 2015, the district went from being a predominantly (80 percent) White school district to one where Whites were less than half and racialized Others comprised 57 percent of the district. (See figure I.2 for a comparison of the population percentages by group.)

Following trends in other new Latinx destinations, the school district was known for its more favorable educational indicators, such as higher rates of high school graduation and college enrollment on average, along with a smaller proportion of students from low socioeconomic backgrounds and fewer minority student enrollments.[7] Yet it also followed the larger trend of not meeting the needs of racialized-Othered students.[8] For example, there was a marked stratification between Latinx and White students in enrollment in college-preparatory math courses. Additionally, possibly due to Oakville's Latinx community being less established than its Black community, as an active member in local Latinx organizations, I heard from Latinx community members that they perceived themselves as having less political power than the Black community.[9]

The district also could not keep up with bilingual staffing demands to meet Latinxs' linguistic needs. It struggled to improve the outcomes of students designated as English language learners (ELLs). Many Latinx parents and community members pressed the district to improve the achievement of its Latinx students and Latinx students designated as ELLs. They called for implementing dual-language programs instead of the existing subtractive English as a Second Language programs, which they critiqued for providing substandard learning experiences, segregating students from their English-dominant peers, and not developing ELLs' home language(s). The district responded by forming, along with the community, a racially diverse

FIGURE I.1 Number of students by racialized group in Oakville Urban School District, 1990–2015

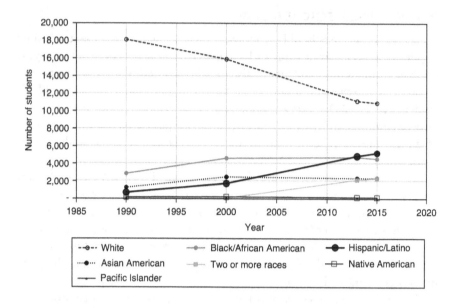

FIGURE I.2 Percentage of students by racialized group in Oakville Urban School District, 1990–2015

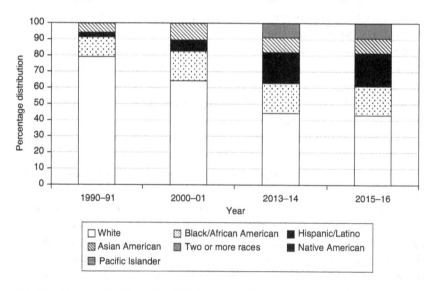

Note: The groups "Pacific Islander" and "Native American" are not clearly distinguishable in figure I.2 because their percentages are each less than 1 percent.

dual-language Somos Bilingüe Elementary School. This intervention expanded into providing dual-language strand programs at other elementary schools and eventually at some secondary-level schools.

THE SCHOOLS AND THEIR DUAL-LANGUAGE PROGRAM

We will find out more about the two schools in the following chapters, but here, I share how Amlie High School and Borane Middle School formed a sort of community.[10] The two were within a short walk of each other. Upon graduating from Borane, students usually attended Amlie. These two racially diverse schools were in the news for having exceptional students and award-winning teachers. But they also faced challenges such as high teacher turnover and occasional newsworthy transgressions such as students drinking alcohol on campus or tragedies like shootings. The schools were located in a blue-collar area, and people described them as less desirable in comparison to the academic rigor and status of the district's other middle and high schools, which were also more White and middle class.

While Borane and Amlie shared many characteristics, they also had some differences. Only Borane received Title 1 funds (federal financial assistance to schools with high percentages of children from low-income families). Borane was among the highest-poverty schools in the state based on free and reduced-price school lunch data (approximately 64 percent low income). Amlie's White student population, approximately 41 percent and predominantly middle class, was higher than Borane's 31 percent. Still, both schools grappled with the effects of disinvestment in public schools, as seen in the inadequate facilities, and they struggled to address the needs of their students from disadvantaged backgrounds.

Both schools offered the dual-language program, which attracted students who had been in the program since elementary school. The district described its schools' dual-language program as having "every student in the classroom [be] a model of their native language and a learner of a second language." To accomplish this, the program, like other such endeavors, classified its students as either English dominant or Spanish dominant. It then used this classification to create dual-language classrooms comprising an equal balance of native English speakers and native Spanish speakers "integrated for instruction so that both groups of students serve in the role of language model and language learner at different times."[11] The district described this student makeup as "essential for the design and success of the program" and conducted a lottery process for admission into the program at first grade to ensure that "classrooms are built at a 50:50 to 60:40 ratio based on language background." This classification and balancing aimed for all to learn from the mainstream curriculum and become bilingual by serving as language models to their peers.[12]

In the Oakville district, this linguistic balancing resulted in a racial composition of mostly Latinx students for the Spanish-dominant half (who were almost all labeled ELLs) and made the English-dominant half mostly White youth, with two to three Latinx students who were not ELLs, one to two Black students, and even fewer Asian American students. For example, one dual-language eighth-grade classroom of 24 students had 14 Latinx, 9 White, 1 Black, 0 Native American, and 0 Asian American students—a racial distribution that was typical in the program.[13] While ELLs and Latinxs usually attend schools with high racial segregation rates at the national level, in Oakville, the popularity of the dual-language program, particularly among some middle-class (especially White) families, racially integrated ELLs and Latinxs with other racialized youth.[14]

This means that this dual-language program was an educational space where Latinxs could possibly receive an "integrated" (with White students) and culturally/linguistically relevant education.[15] Most of the district's educators, practitioners, policymakers, parents, youth, and community members saw the program's biliterate and bicultural focus as offering an equitable education to Latinx youth and Latinxs labeled as ELLs. Many saw it as departing from racist practices like segregating Latinx students and demeaning their culture and language.

WHY STUDYING RACE MATTERS AND ITS CONTRIBUTIONS

While Spanish-English bilingual education, like other forms of schooling, constructs ideas about *all* racialized groups, one of this book's main contributions lies in showing how schools racialize through examples of how a bilingual program positions the Latinx group in relation to other racialized groups.[16] We will see how the program constructed Latinx as a racialized group through its relative position to other racialized groups, thereby situating these groups in a racial hierarchy. Additionally, we will learn about the material consequences of these dynamics, especially for Latinxs in the program.[17] We will delve into how dual-language education, with its growth and popularity among White middle-class families, conducts its race-making work. Specifically, we will see how it perpetuates and challenges the construction of the Latinx category by its participants—and thus by our society.

Why does it matter how educators, students, and scholars conceptualize race and Latinx? It matters for several reasons. First, it matters because Latinxs constitute the largest racialized group "of color" in the United States.[18] Understanding how our society thinks about the Latinx category is a crucial component of understanding how our society thinks about race, engages in racialization processes, forms intraracial coalitions, and offers solutions to inequities.[19] By demonstrating how schools teach about the racial category "Latinx," I hope to inform teachers, students, and all readers how schooling informs people's ideas about race and racial categories. Simply put, learning how schooling constructs the Latinx racialized group provides valuable insights into the processes of racialization within education.

Second, though people generally recognize that schools are an important societal institution, most do not necessarily recognize that educational institutions contribute to how we make sense of our racialized society and the social outcomes of groups, including Latinxs. If we recognize that our society is structured by racism, then it becomes crucial to examine the role our schools play in perpetuating this racist structure, including in how it affects Latinxs.[20]

A third reason why the conceptualization of Latinx matters has to do with the often-overlooked reality that schools teach about race, even if it is not immediately apparent or explicit. Because our society is organized and founded on racial narratives and practices, schools invariably impart ideas about race and racism, typically in subtle, implicit ways.[21] While many schools may not teach about race as explicitly as they do an algebraic equation in math lessons or a metaphor in English classes, racial ideas are still conveyed through policies, curricular decisions, and conversations. Teachers, students, and other individuals in schools inevitably talk about race, even if tacitly.[22] Thus, it is essential for educators to recognize that "mainstream" schooling, which often avoids direct discussions of race, nonetheless perpetuates racial ideas. Moreover, challenging race-evasive ideas is crucial because these ideas downplay the significance of racism in material conditions, as exemplified in explanations that attribute "Latino academic underperformance" to "Latino culture."[23]

Before I share the last reason why the racialization of Latinxs matters, let me connect the idea of "making race" to contemporary debates around so-called "critical race theory" (CRT) in schools.[24] At a time when many states and districts across the United States have prohibited the teaching of critical race theory and/or ethnic studies, it may seem oddly unhelpful to highlight a case of how a bilingual education program teaches about race.[25] Notably, this book does not employ nor is it about CRT in the way that I define CRT, as a theoretical lens to examine racial injustice.[26] Still, CRT has influenced my way of thinking about racial issues, perhaps most relevantly by inform-ing my view that CRT scholars must not shy away from critically examin-ing cherished civil rights victories like bilingual education.

My statement that schools teach about race and "make race" does not mean that schools are teaching CRT. Rather, by "make race," I suggest that *all* schools (even if they are not explicitly teaching racial stereotypes, histo-ries, etc.) teach about race and racialized groups and perpetuate racialized outcomes. For example, schools "make race" by ignoring African American history or banning books. It is better to recognize that schools are always conveying ideas about race. Therefore, it is essential that educators approach teaching about race intentionally, competently, strategically, and ambitiously, and in anti-racist ways.[27]

That takes me to a fourth reason why conceptualizations of race and Latinx matter. As education scholar Bettina Love argues, theory gives people a "deep understanding of oppression and how it works structurally."[28] In terms of educators, what theories and stories they know matter because these stories and theories influence how they make sense of our world and how they teach. Thus, *how* educators understand race matters. Teachers' under-standing of race will be reflected in their pedagogy. For example, when teach-ers understand race through the lens of bigotry and mistreatment from some individuals, their anti-racist teaching may promote inclusive multicul-turalism and could preclude teaching about structural anti-racism.

Educators can help create schools that challenge racist ideas. They can do this by enhancing students' critical consciousness about race and racialized groups.[29] This is significant because critical consciousness—which involves questioning and acting against oppression—plays a part in how individuals relate to others' struggles, form coalitions across racial categories, and work toward justice.[30] Educators can work with students to imagine and move toward a different society.

For scholars, conceptualizations of race and Latinx matter because this research can influence teachers' understanding of these ideas. Seeking change through delivering top-down ideas has serious limits; thus, my theory of change recognizes that teachers learn through taking an inquiry stance.[31] Nevertheless, scholarship does affect teachers' understanding of concepts like race. For example, in my tertiary studies and teacher training, I gained a deeper and nuanced understanding of race and of how structural oppression works from reading scholars' writings.[32]

This book challenges taken-for-granted notions of race and the Latinx category and highlights their constructed and dynamic nature. It does not present Latinx as a united or already constituted group.[33] Rather, I show that the bilingual education program at Oakville provided inconsistent teachings about race and Latinidad, contributing to the incompleteness and instability of the Latinx category. While at times the program tried to promote Latinidad as bound by a shared culture and the Spanish language, in reality it constructed "Latinx" through multiple contradictory ideas. By examining how bilingual education helps to make "Latinx" a racialized group alongside other racialized groups, I aim to better understand the specificity and complexity of Latinidad.

In the chapters that follow, I reveal how the bilingual education program contributed to socially constructing the Spanish language as the *signature boundary* that delineates the Latinx racialized group from others. I use "signature" instead of "identifying" to emphasize that my theoretical claim is not centered on individuals' or the group's identity or a real feature, but rather highlights how society associates and distinguishes the *group* in relation to other groups. This claim does not suggest a conflation of language and race. Instead, I contend that the dual-language program reflected and reinforced the significance of the Spanish language, even as people celebrated linguistic and cultural differences, in binding the Latinx racialized group and setting it apart from other racialized groups.

The notion that bilingual education contributes to establishing the Spanish language as the signature boundary that delineates the Latinx racialized group is significant because it sheds light on how schools contribute to the construction of Latinx as a racialized category. It is crucial for understanding how Latinx fits into the United States' racial imagination, especially considering that the formation of the Hispanic/Latinx category has been well-documented, even though the boundaries, or what defines Hispanic/Latinx, may remain ambiguous.[34] This theoretical claim also has practical consequences that I explore throughout the book.

DEFINING TERMS

Before describing examples of how schools racialize, I define what racialization is, starting with the more common terms *racism* and *race*.

Racism and Race

Racism consists of the practices, policies, and ideologies in institutions and society that normalize and produce injustice and domination based on race.[35] For many, the word *race* evokes images of varying skin tones and other physical characteristics, referred to as *phenotypes*. Some interpret these differences as indicative of biologically distinct human lineages, even though basic science confirms that biological races do not exist.[36] Yet this fallacy has long pervaded society, influencing how people think and act.[37] The concept of biological race has evolved, with some people now alluding to race by referencing "culture."[38] Thus race continues to be a social reality, manifesting in lived experiences and material consequences.[39]

Social science, cultural studies, and history show how European elites invented race as a category in their colonial and imperial projects to justify their domination of others.[40] As a European-originated classification system, the purpose of race is nefarious: racial ideas enforce the false notion of (biological) "human lineages," dehumanize certain groups, and position the groups into a white supremacist racial hierarchy, where mostly elite Whites materially benefit at the expense of racialized Others. (I use "racialized Others" instead of "people of color" to challenge reducing race to phenotype and to refer to the racialized groups Asian American, Black/African American, Native American, Latinx, and Muslim/Arab and those at the intersections who are Otherized.[41] "White" is also a racialized category, even though Whites' racialization serves fundamentally to label other groups as unworthy and inferior; thus I do not refer to Whites as "racialized Others.") Racial ideas sort people into groups by essentializing and ignoring their intragroup cultural diversity; these ideas also socially construct differences to delineate and mark the groups.

To illustrate how our society reinforces the misconception of race as biological, consider the example from sociologist Karen Fields and historian Barbara Fields.[42] They point out that air pollution tends to be worse in areas with disproportionately high populations of racialized Others. Breathing in contaminated air, taken together with the fact that racialized Others also have substandard health care, results in racialized Others having higher levels of asthma or other health problems. But when people report this pattern using racial terms—for example, "Black folks and Latinx folks having higher levels of sickness compared with White folks"—this sometimes leads to the faulty reasoning that there is an inherent inferiority of racialized Others that makes them susceptible to asthma or other diseases. Simply put, in our racialized society, these patterns misleadingly reinforce the idea that human biological races exist.[43] Fields and Fields point out that our society is steeped with patterns that naturalize race in ways that present racialized categories as fixed and that obscure the process of racialization.

Much like in the previous example, education outcomes also produce patterns that perpetuate the illusion of race as biological and its accompanying ideas of racialized Others' inferiority. Inadequately funding schools with high numbers of racialized Others results in these students having subpar educational outcomes.[44] These lower outcomes feed into the commonly accepted falsehood that inherent intellectual differences in races exist. When scholars do not expose these practices as contributing to the process of racialization, they further reinforce race as a natural grouping.

Racialized Group and Racialization

A *racialized group* refers to a group of people who have been (mistakenly) perceived as a biological race and/or have undergone a historical, social, cultural, legal, and contextual process in order to be understood as a group.[45] Racialized groups are mainly identified by or delineated from other groups according to artificial and arbitrary differences such as skin tone, phenotype, and language. I prefer the term "racialized group" over "race" to emphasize the dynamic and constructed *process* of this categorization.

Racialization encompasses a historical, social, cultural, legal, and contextual process that involves the development of concepts surrounding race, such as the notion of distinct biological differences between humans.[46] It includes the categorization of individuals into racialized groups, even when conflicting interpretations are attributed to these groups and categories. These designations have tangible and significant impacts on people's lives. The racialization process demarcates a group's boundaries *in relation to* other groups.[47] It includes marking a racialized group's boundaries through the distribution of resources along racial lines.[48] (*Note:* Because my focus is on the making of groups, I do not mean racialization to refer simply to racial discrimination [racially discriminatory acts] or an individual's racial identity.)

Racialized Categories, Ethnicity, and Culture

Racialization includes the process of essentializing and placing people into racial categories that ignore the diversity in cultural practices. Racializing, for example, Salvadoran, Honduran, Cuban American, and so forth into one group—Latinx—ignores the complexities that make people fully human. Through racialization, Mexicans and Dominicans may be lumped together in one category even if they do not feel they share cultural practices. People resist this, of course, because acknowledging cultural practices and these differences point to being part of a community and being fully human. Thus, Latinxs may hold on to the nation-state descriptors—"I'm Mexican American" or "I'm Salvadorean"—because they associate this with their community and with being recognized. Using nationality differentiates them from other Latinxs and may signal their ethnicity.[49]

Categorizing people and defining group labels is a contentious matter that involves power, politics, culture, and the struggle for recognition and representation. This is also true for ethnic categories. It is useful to contrast racialization with the social construct of *ethnicity*, which I use to highlight the similarities and differences in the cultural practices of various communities and groups.[50] An ethnic group is a community of people *who make similar meaning* from their *shared routine cultural practices* and is perceived as different by the dominant group within their society.[51] Ethnic categories spotlight different groups' distinct cultural practices but not necessarily with the nefarious intent of racialization, that is, with the implication that a group is innately unhuman or biologically different.

Many ethnic studies scholars and social scientists of race have inquired into the construction of different racialized categories, noting their fluidity. Some scholars who focus on the Latinx group have noted that this group has been racially "stereotyped as having a particular physical appearance characterized by olive or brown skin and dark, straight hair."[52] But this stereotype is too broad to mark the Latinx racial category. After all, some Latinxs do not fit this stereotype, and people from parts of, for example, the Middle East or Asia could also fit this description, yet US society does not identify them as Latinx.

Latinx phenotypical diversity contributes to scholars' debate over whether "Latinx" is an ethnic and/or a racial category. Some scholars argue that the group is primarily ethnic, based on shared cultural elements like the Spanish language and Catholicism.[53] Others note that, despite the US census labeling Latinx as an ethnicity, the label functions as a racial one in some ways.[54] Some maintain that Latinx is one of the United States' racialized groups, separate from and a middle tier in the Black/White racial hierarchy.[55] Still other scholars describe Latinx as *ethnoracial*—both ethnic and racial.[56] This debate includes the idea that some Latinxs are "White," with some researchers showing that categorizing Latinxs as White has been used to marginalize some Latinxs.[57] Arlene Dávila notes that Latinxs are simultaneously subjected to processes of racialized othering and whitening; therefore, describing Latinxs based on one or another process is reductive.[58] A number of social science researchers argue that Latinxs in the United States should be seen as a racialized group because doing otherwise constructs the group as perpetual foreigners.[59] Others note that despite Latinxs' phenotypical diversity, they are still racialized by their "Latinidad," a response that leads some to ask what comprises Latinidad.[60] This leads some scholars to point out that Latinidad is used to erase Indigeneity and perpetuate anti-Blackness.[61] What has gained increasing consensus is that because racialized differences and categories are socially constructed, the boundaries delineating groups change and vary depending on context.[62]

In this book, my analysis focuses on the racialized group category and the complex racialization processes in the bilingual program, rather than on comparisons concentrated on distinct cultural practices within or across groups. Consequently, I choose not to use the term "ethnoracial" in this book. Moreover, if that term were to describe the Latinx group, it would also apply to all other groups, as the Latinx racialized group encompasses all the fluidity, complexities, and contradictions inherent in the other racialized categories that the United States has historically, legally, and socially constructed.[63] I emphasize the difference between "racialized group" and "ethnic group" because I believe that we require a richer vocabulary to describe our social reality, rather than simplifying it by synonymizing. Consequently, I oppose using these terms interchangeably, even though they may share some commonalities.[64]

Latinx and Latinidad

Language is a contested field where colonial subjects and communities struggle over recognition and self-determination. While participants in my study often used "Latino" and "Hispanic" interchangeably, I prefer "Latinx." This word attempts to reject—albeit inadequately—the glorification of Spanish colonialism, which is present in the term "Hispanic." Still, the term is inadequate, as it retains a European reference, linked to Latin America—a name imposed by Eurocentric elites to assert their claim over the region and counteract British and US imperialism.[65]

I use the US term "Latinx" to refer to a racialized category for incorporating people into the settler colonial white supremacist nation-state. In this conception, "Latinx" refers to a racialized group that resides in the United States, is imagined as having a connection to the Spanish language, and suffers the effects of multiple colonialisms, specifically Spanish colonialism, American colonialism, and American imperialism.[66] The Latinx term also is used to form and mobilize coalitions against oppression.

I prefer "Latinx" over "Latino/Latina/Latine" for several other reasons. First, it aligns with the efforts of queer communities who introduced "Latinx" to challenge gender binaries and patriarchy. Secondly, it avoids stigmatizing US Spanish, which is often criticized for not conforming to the rules established by "native" Spanish speakers, as invoked to support "Latine." Finally, the use of "X" symbolizes a rejection of the term "Latin," highlighting the need to challenge its European referent.[67]

As an ideology and discourse, Latinidad serves a particular function in our society. Much like Blackness and whiteness, Latinidad varies depending on context, and it changes over time.[68] While it does not encapsulate the essence of "Latinx," its ideas and practices are associated with Latinxs because being identified as such can grant access to the discourses and to learning the ideologies that Latinidad conveys. In my investigation of how Oakville's dual-language program constructs the Latinx racialized group and Latinidad, I uncover the ideas the program conveyed, implicitly or explicitly, about the ideological work Latinidad performs in our society. This includes notions of what it means to be "Latino" and the real-world impacts of these ideas.[69]

Next, I return to the question of how schools make race, the Latinx group, and Latinidad.

LATINXS, RACIALIZATION, AND DUAL LANGUAGE: WHAT RESEARCHERS KNOW

In 2018, Hispanics/Latinxs comprised 27 percent of the US public-school student population, the largest racialized group.[70] In 2014–2015, they comprised more than 75 percent of those classified as ELLs in the public school student population.[71] Long-standing educational debates on improving education for Latinxs have predominantly concentrated on strategies for providing linguistically accessible or bilingual education.[72] While some research has delved into the linguistic and/or racial discrimination faced by Latinx students and the resulting challenges, education researchers have largely not examined how bilingual schooling racializes, let alone makes Latinidad.[73]

But researchers know that schools are sites of racialization. They understand that schools function to distribute resources in society along racial lines, such as underfunding schools in Latinx communities.[74] They have revealed that schools convey racial lessons through their formal, informal, and hidden curricula and practices.[75] And they know that students' skin color, language, names, culture, and socioeconomic status all contribute (although in different ways) to a person's racial identity (both ascribed and self-imposed).

Sociologist Amanda Lewis studied a Spanish-English dual-language program that included many Latinx students.[76] In the English classroom she observed, she found that Latinx students' actual skin tone did not correlate entirely to their racial identity. She suggested instead that "people seemed to understand race less coherently," and that possibly "racial boundaries were operating more fluidly here so that race mattered differently if not less."[77] She noted that language was particularly important, although her analysis was not meant to provide specificity to Latinidad.

Linguistic anthropologist Jonathan Rosa provided a specific window into Latinidad. He compared Mexican American and Puerto Rican youth and their ideas of Latinidad in a predominantly Latinx Chicago high school and community.[78] Rosa documented how dress, music, language practices, and interactions all contribute to creating ideas of the groups and of pan-Latinidad. He cogently showed that colonial logics about racial and linguistic hierarchies have made Latinidad seem "natural" instead of a socially constructed category.

A NEW LATINX DESTINATION: WHAT RESEARCHERS WANT TO KNOW

Context matters for racialization and the forming of racialized groups. Consequently, new destinations for Latinxs have piqued the interest of some scholars because of the racial implications of such changes.[79] This book offers an example from a midwestern state that has experienced recent and substantial increases in the Latinx population (majority immigrant and Mexican or Central American) in the past two decades. The story documents a specific time and place, offering a "comparative inquiry of the social construction of Latinidad."[80] In doing so, it lends itself to future comparisons of racial relations and ideologies with other periods and locations.

Education scholars also have called for studying the changing, understudied new Latinx destinations, like the US Midwest.[81] They argue that scholars, educators, and policymakers need to better understand these contexts' dynamics if they are to provide better educational opportunities.[82] In education, understanding how schools respond to the challenges and opportunities brought by population changes can lead to improving the educational processes that affect Latinx students' experiences and outcomes. Studying schooling, especially the secondary level where students make sense of common-sense ideas about race, provides vital information to understand regional racialization.[83]

With its specific focus on schooling, this book highlights the potential consequences that this racial demographic shift has for the equitable education of students, particularly Latinxs. Accordingly, it contributes to understanding how the schooling of the growing Latinx populations in new destinations differs from sites where histories of anti-Latinx racism as well as infrastructures to contest marginalization are more common.[84] The shifts happening throughout many parts of the United States amplify and/or spur new interpretations of racial stereotypes and highlight challenges in language education policies for Latinx and bilingual youth.[85]

(CON)JOINING CONVERSATIONS ON EDUCATION EQUITY FOR LATINXS

Bilingual/language-education research has traditionally studied linguistic questions.[86] But in the last decade, critical scholars have focused on how power imbalances, racism, and other -isms affect the equity potential of bilingual and dual-language education.[87] Some bilingual education scholars debate whether equity for linguistically minoritized youth can be achieved through a dual-language model because of its embedded ideologies, linguistic practices, and classroom power imbalances.[88]

To provide insight into these questions, we may look to education-race scholarship for guidance. Education-race researchers have been attentive to schools forming ideas about race, with some focusing on how schooling engages in racialization.[89] But the predominant way the education field studies "race" is by examining the *racism* a certain racialized group faces in the classroom.[90] This includes a focus on racial discrimination against the more commonly studied groups, such as Black youth and Latinx youth.[91] Few theorize race or conceptualize and study schools as *race-making* institutions.[92] One of the ways the education field undertheorizes and reifies race is by the field's prevalent practice of stating "race is a social construction." But this statement is simply perfunctory when the racialization process is not exposed.[93]

The bilingual education field may benefit from avoiding education-race scholarship's oversights in its uptake of racial issues. Education-race expert Zeus Leonardo argues that educational scholarship on race surprisingly leaves the concept of race undefined, which "is a problem not merely of definition but about setting conceptual parameters and analytical clarity."[94] Leonardo further points out that undertheorizing race reifies race as natural and perpetual, thus calls for engaging with racial formation theories.[95] Like Leonardo, education scholars Lesley Bartlett and Bryan Brayboy have called for education researchers to "analyze the ways that schools themselves affect the constantly shifting terrain of racial formation."[96] Similar to Leonardo's critique about education scholarship needing clarity and parameters about the concept of race, the education field's general lack of attention to the process of racialization may contribute to fossilizing racialized categories and conflating race, racism, and racialization.[97] Yet schooling's role in racialization makes it crucial for education scholars to reflect on our language and clarify the nuances of our central concepts.[98]

Current education research on race and bilingual schooling has begun to explore how bilingual education contributes to the social construction of Latinidad and racialized categories.[99] Most scholars of education and race, including Latinx education, have investigated individuals' identity and have not focused on how schooling changes and/or teaches the construction of the Latinx racialized category, even if this scholarship may be expansive in terms of including, for example, Afro-Latinxs, Indigenous Latinxs, and White Latinxs.[100] Understanding how bilingual-education educators engage in this work influences the prospects for providing an equitable education, particularly to Latinx students.

This book also contributes to connecting sociology to the education field's understanding of racialization as a sociocultural process and a product of schooling that shapes the category "Latinx."[101] By engaging in an inquiry on the relational positioning of Latinxs in bilingual education and drawing on sociological theories of racialization, this book answers sociologists' calls for studies of school processes, practices, politics, and outcomes that inform the construction and transformation of racial boundaries and hierarchies. In line with Lewis's book, my book contributes a relational racialization analysis with a focus on the construction of Latinidad in relation to other racialized groups.[102]

In the chapters that follow, I draw from research showing how people's visual and auditory judgments combine to form ideas about race and racialized groups.[103] As I argue in this book, groups' racial boundaries are shaped based on different criteria, not just skin color, and language plays a significant role in the racialization of Latinxs.[104] In this way, I connect a relational racialization lens with emerging theories in raciolinguistics to offer a critical perspective on how bilingual schooling works to produce relational racialized marginalization and to construct Latinidad.[105]

A RELATIONAL ETHNOGRAPHY ON HOW BILINGUAL EDUCATION RACIALIZES

Prior to starting my formal data collection for this book (February 2016–June 2017), I knew there would be much to learn from studying this racially diverse program. I wanted to examine how it provided a culturally relevant, equitable education to its students—which, to me, meant it had to be race-conscious and anti-racist.[106] I focused on secondary-level instead of the more common elementary-level dual-language program/school for one main reason: I believed the topics of race and racism would be more likely to be taught explicitly in the secondary levels than in elementary grades.

Because far less research exists about secondary-level compared with elementary-level dual-language programs/schools, especially qualitative ethnographic research studies, I designed the study as an exploratory ethnography.[107] While I did not begin the study with the intention of exploring how the program constructed the Latinx group and Latinidad, engaging in an exploratory ethnography enabled me to identify interesting leads. Many of my observations and questions directed me to this approach and transformed this "into a relational inquiry."[108] One of those leads pertained to how the program positioned its Latinx students in relation to other racialized groups and how it taught Latinidad.

A relational racialization lens, as historian Natalia Molina and other scholars argue, aims to understand racialized groups as socially constructed and always in correspondence to and in conjunction with other groups.[109] Studying racialization relationally means examining the common sense of "race" and the racializing of groups and how these understandings are embedded in society's social and institutional structures, policies, and practices. Thus, a relational racialization study focuses on how policies, practices, and people put racialized groups in relation to other groups. Examining racialization from a relational perspective reveals both the similarities and differences in how various racialized groups have been integrated into society. This approach also demonstrates how structures of white supremacy have adapted to the unique conditions surrounding each group's incorporation.[110] The *effects* of how racialized groups are positioned, discriminated against, and relate to each other contribute to forming the boundaries of racialized groups.

Studying racialization from a relational perspective involves moving beyond the commonplace comparison of racialized groups to whiteness or the Black/White binary.[111] Decentering whiteness might be disconcerting to some, given the importance of not obscuring white supremacy. However, employing a relational racialization approach moves away from focusing only on the relations between Whites and racially minoritized groups to allow for a more nuanced examination of the relationships and differences among these various racialized-Othered groups. In doing so, this approach thereby deepens our understanding of how these groups are constructed. This enables a focus on how and where the Latinx group falls in a hierarchical structure in relation to other racialized groups.

Although research using a relational racialization perspective is growing, especially in ethnic studies, it has primarily been employed in historical approaches to inquiry.[112] Applying this lens with a qualitative ethnographic study to the field of education, in particular bilingual education, contributes to the lively interdisciplinary conversation about the fluidity and position of Latinxs in the US racial imaginary.[113] Additionally, studying the relational connections between racialized Others can benefit the field's understanding of racialization. While it may be easy to accept that bilingual education, as with all forms of schooling, shapes ideas about race and racialized groups, we need to better understand *how* this process works. As we will see in this book, the relational racialization lens provides unique insights into the racialization of Latinx students, particularly around issues of equity.

The study at the heart of this book is not particular to a bilingual education program per se. It could have been in a different type of program or schooling context. To personalize anthropologist Clifford Geertz's saying that "Anthropologists don't study villages . . . they study *in* villages," I did not study a dual-language program, I studied a *process* in a dual-language program.[114] My object of analysis was the process of racialization of Latinxs, specifically how the program teaches through its practices and policies to understand what Latinidad means, the positioning of Latinx individuals in relation to other racialized groups and power dynamics, and how these advance or thwart an equitable education for Latinxs and other marginalized youth. While students' sensemaking was not the center of analysis, I did examine how students understood "Latinx" relative to other racialized categories, including by accepting, adapting, negotiating, or rejecting these ideas as they made sense of race in their own way.

Even though the dual-language classrooms I observed were composed of at least half Latinx students with the other half comprising mostly White students (and zero to two Black or Asian students), this book does not replace America's Black/White binary with a Latinx/White one. Rather, the book shows the relational aspects of the invention of the Latinx racialized group through an interrogation of different racial ideologies and racisms. I describe how Latinidad was differently positioned in relation to Blackness, Indigeneity, and whiteness. I unpack what makes the Latinx racialized group by looking at its boundaries, what it is compared to, and how attitudes, practices, and policies directed at one racialized group affect others. My analyses help to explain how racialization maintains hierarchies and relational processes that perpetuate tensions between racialized groups.

A BRIEF (RACIAL) HISTORY OF BILINGUAL EDUCATION

While some may not see bilingual education as a racial intervention, it is entwined with racial struggles and has a historical role in forming Latinx as a racialized group. In the 1870s, Mexican elites used bilingual education to distance themselves racially and linguistically from other groups, namely Indians, Whites, and lower-socioeconomic-class Mexicans.[115] The 1960s and 1970s, Chicana/o Movement activists and scholars fought for community control of schools and saw bilingual education as a way to address the needs of their youth, teach about culture and racial struggle, and uplift the community.[116] Their work grounded bilingual education in ethnic studies and strove to make it a project for anti-racism, anti-imperialism, and anti-colonialism.[117] Some viewed bilingual schooling as an alternative to deficit-oriented English as a Second Language programs, which provide remedial instruction that normalizes whiteness.[118]

But as bilingual education became institutionalized, policymakers and activists advanced competing visions of its purpose and approach.[119] The federal 1968 Bilingual Education Act, which offered funding to public schools for establishing bilingual programs, supported bilingual education as a mechanism to correct Latinxs' supposed linguistic, cultural, and racial deficiencies through technocratic approaches and instilling pride in the Spanish language.[120] This framing of bilingual education mirrored multicultural education's focus on inclusion, tolerance, and pride in "many cultures" and rarely interrogated structural causes of inequity.[121] This distanced bilingual education from the struggle for ethnic studies in schools.[122] It also diminished bilingual education's race-radical approach, which included economically uplifting the Latinx community, reframing language education issues into the principal racial injustice the Latinx community faces instead of addressing poverty.[123]

In 1974, the US Supreme Court's case *Lau v. Nichols*, brought by Chinese families of children learning English, ruled that teaching students in a language they do not understand was "a mockery of public education."[124] Policies and rulings like these, along with community activism, prompted civil rights laws to require public schools to remove the language barriers that prevented students from accessing instruction. While these acts do not mandate bilingual education, some schools did institutionalize this approach, making it more widely available.

Starting in the 1990s, anti-Latinx and anti-immigrant racism led to several states restricting or outright banning bilingual education, reinforcing language education as a chief concern for Latinxs.[125] Despite the restrictions, the number of dual-language bilingual education programs across the United States surged from 39 in 1991 to 422 in 2011.[126] Changes in the perception of bilingualism and bilingual programs influenced this rise. While "bilingual education" connotes classrooms for ELLs—that is, "at-risk" racialized Others—dual language was not weighed down with these negative connotations.[127] Instead, it was marketed as a way for all students to become bilingual. Consequently, dual language became politically palatable in part because it provided a "bilingual advantage" to English-dominant children, prompting some affluent (White) parents to demand dual-language programs.[128] Additionally, media touted the brain benefits of bilingualism, and some scholars announced the "astounding effectiveness of dual language education for all."[129]

With dual language being branded as "for all," calls have intensified to link it to ethnic studies or other critical-education approaches to ensure that it still serves marginalized students.[130] These calls focus on developing youth's critical consciousness and include developing critical-*racial* consciousness, meaning critical consciousness about race, racism, and racial ideas, and that moves one toward anti-racist actions.[131] The aim is for dual language to center racialized-Othered students, which necessarily connects bilingual education back to an ethnic-studies education, with its focus on teaching about race, power, and justice.[132] If bilingual schooling is not connected to its race-radical roots, it may miss opportunities to enhance students' critical-racial consciousness, becoming a false champion for a future anti-racist, anti-imperialist, anti-colonial Latinidad.[133]

A NOTE ON THE "ENGLISH LANGUAGE LEARNERS" LABEL

The Oakville Urban School District classified certain bilingual students as ELLs. I disagree with this labeling, preferring instead asset-based terms to signal students' strengths and possibilities rather than marking deficits. Consider the reverse: designating and stigmatizing monolingual English speakers as deficient due to their lack of additional languages in an interconnected world.[134] In this book, I employ "ELL" intentionally to underscore that these students are marked and subjected to policies and ideologies associated with this label's effect of Othering. Another reason for using the term is that my study focuses on secondary-level dual-language students who—regardless of racialized identity—self-identified as bilingual. Replacing "ELL" with asset-based terms such as "emergent bilinguals" would be inaccurate, as the students were already bilingual. Furthermore, using the "emergent bilingual" label would include White students who were learning Spanish, which then obscures the intended Otherness of the original ELL label. Ideally, to spotlight different labels' Othering—including racialized and gendered categories—I would use phrases such as "students designated as ELLs," "people labeled as Asian American," but I do not because doing so for some social constructions and not others may make some categories seem more natural (rather than ascribed) than others.

CONCEPTUALIZING TEACHERS' PRACTICES

Teachers' ideas and practices can reflect schools' structures and expectations of teachers. These structures and expectations not only influence but also restrict how teachers think and talk about their students and about racial ideas. I conceptualize teachers as institutional agents whose collective practices effectively form the program's policies.[135] Viewed from this perspective, it becomes clear that teacher practices not only reflect *but also* construct the program's approach to teaching race and addressing racial inequities. The next chapters show how teachers' aggregated practices contribute to determining the program's approach and policy toward teaching about race and anti-racism—and, as a consequence, whether dual-language programs can fulfill their social justice missions and equip youth to enhance their critical-racial consciousness.

A CAVEAT

As with other books, this one may also give the impression of the context's stability, as if Oakville's program is immutable. Since the time I spent at the schools for my study, people have changed and so has the program. Some parts have improved, while other issues persist. So I ask readers to remember that this book offers a timebound snapshot, and only from my perspective. Multiple stories could still be told; this book tells *one* story of how the present-day institution of schooling contributes to racialization processes, and how this then disadvantages racialized Others, focusing on Latinxs. Of course, people were not passive in the racialization process, and some resisted it. This is not a story about bad people and good people or a particular school. This is *a* story, not *the* story, about how schools' institutional decisions impact the learning and teaching of racial categories and thus contribute to how our society perpetuates these ideas. The book details tensions that emerge from teachers, students, and other community members trying to make sense of race, and along the way reinforcing and resisting ideas about race and Latinidad.

One of the people you will meet along the way is Ms. Schloss, an Amlie teacher whose commitment to teaching about race and injustice led her to design an ethnic studies course for the program. Years after she had left the school, this course remained with the goal of assisting students in understanding the concept of race as a category. In the first section, Ms. Schloss and her colleagues endeavored to make sense of the notions of race and Latinx as a racialized category.

PART I

Teaching Racialization

CHAPTER 1

Making Sense of Race

started spending time at Borane Middle School and Amlie High School in
February 2016. By September, I had observed many courses and dual-
language teachers that I wished I could have had in my own secondary-
level schooling. Ms. Schloss's ethnic studies course was one class that I looked
forward to visiting in Amlie High School. Amlie's brick building is unremark-
able for a single-story urban US high school campus. Walking through the
main entrance, a visitor would see a professionally made permanent 5′ × 3′
wall plaque with information about the school's namesake, an early-
twentieth-century progressive politician of the midwestern state I call RedRock.
In the central office, a guest can see displayed, at an easy-to-read height, a lone
framed award from a local progressive organization congratulating the high
school for exceeding the state average and for having the highest graduation
rates of "Hispanic and African American students" in the district. In fact, the
Oakville district had significantly improved the percentage of Latinxs graduating from high school, cutting in more than half the pushout/dropout rate over
the last ten years.

Walking toward the heart of the building, one would see glass cases in
the hallways exhibiting color copies of college acceptance letters received
by seniors. Next to each was a photo of the beaming student next to an
Amlie faculty or staff member the student identified as making a significant
impact on their high school experience. This offset Amlie's public image as
one of Oakville's worst high schools, an opinion probably linked to the
fact that it was one of the city's "less White high schools." Amlie's total
enrollment was about 1,500. Fifty-four percent of students were from low-
income families, 25 percent were labeled ELL, and 20 percent were in special education.[1] Yet despite its image, the school had, like other Oakville
high schools, a robust Advanced Placement (AP) program, which attracted
some high-achieving students, especially those who wanted to remain in
the dual-language program.

Amlie High had over 140 faculty and offered over 230 courses of a highly tracked curriculum, which provided some students with rigorous instruction while limiting other students' opportunities. It provided almost twenty courses that followed the rigorous AP curriculum for college credit, including AP Calculus, AP Statistics, AP Chemistry, and AP European History. Along with a variety of required subjects (history, English, math, science) in special education, regular, or honors tracks, the course offerings also included world-language courses (American Sign Language, French, German, and Spanish) and a large selection of specialized courses in business (e.g., accounting, marketing), vocational areas (e.g., automotive technology, culinary basics), and music and art (e.g., ceramics, jazz ensemble).

Because Amlie ran on a block schedule, most of the courses were half a year (e.g., dual-language Spanish for freshman) instead of the entire academic school year.[2] Some classes met every other day for the entire year (e.g., AP Literature), or every day for the full school year (e.g., remedial math). A few elective courses were only nine weeks; for example, the dual-language electives Ethnic Studies and Latin American Studies, which were both taught in Spanish.

As I headed to the Ethnic Studies course, I recalled past conversations with the teacher, Ms. Schloss. Ms. Schloss, a White woman who had recently graduated from her university teaching program, had been hired as a social studies/history teacher the year that Amlie adopted the dual-language program. In that year, the administration tasked Ms. Schloss with organizing the program's social studies and history course offerings. She dedicated a lot of time and thought to what a bilingual program would need in order to be social-justice oriented. When it came time to decide what would be the third-year course offered to students, she shared:

> The assumption was made that we were going to do "Modern US History" because that was the next course [in the school's course sequence], but I advocated pretty hard instead to replace [it] with an Ethics Studies course. . . . Ethics Studies could lend itself a lot more richly to a bilingual curriculum or an interrogation of what it is to be bilingual and what it means to be bicultural. I felt like it was a better fit for the, I guess, the goal and the model of the [dual-language] program.

Ms. Schloss said that she was committed to advancing "social justice and creating a critical consciousness in students." She also advocated for the Latin American Studies elective:

I wanted to choose courses, and specifically Ethics Studies and Latin American Studies, where there would be a rich array of primary sources in Spanish and that also would allow kids to explore their bilingual and bicultural identities so that they would be bringing in things that they could actually reflect upon. Instead of just learning about X country, Y country, Z country, they're like, "Oh, I've had this experience," or, "This is my experience with such and such a thing." And so that they would be using their, I guess the academic word is like, funds of knowledge, but like, you know, that there is a focus on bringing things in that are connected to them and relevant to them as bilingual and bicultural students.

Ms. Schloss's political clarity led her to design a program that dealt with questions and topics usually ignored in the mainstream curriculum (at least in Amlie's social studies/history courses). She planned her classes with this same commitment to social justice. She reflected, "Race comes up all the time, not only in the curriculum, but just like in things students say day-to-day, and I try to think of that." And one of the topics with which she started her Ethnic Studies course was the difference between race and ethnicity.

In this chapter, we will see how the dual-language teachers' classroom pedagogy, as part of a racial project, offered teachings and ideas about race. We hear from students as they make sense of racial ideas. We'll also see some lessons that were explicit about race, like the one in Ms. Schloss's ethnic studies class. But most of the program's lessons about race and racial ideas were conveyed implicitly, as I highlight in later chapters. In this chapter's last section, I show students making sense of the incoherence about whether Latinx is a racialized category or something else.

THE ETHNIC STUDIES LESSON ON RACE VERSUS ETHNICITY

Ms. Schloss started the discussion that day by asking the seventeen students, mostly juniors, to review the lesson from their previous class. She asked for answers to the question written on the board, "¿Qué es la diferencia entre la raza y la etnicidad?" (What's the difference between race and ethnicity?)[3] Through students' murmuring in English about the day's gossip, one student, Mari, answered, "Características físicas." (Physical characteristics.) I later found out Mari was only one of the two Asian Americans in the dual-language program of the two schools.

No one besides Ms. Schloss expressed agreement or much interest in Mari's response. Ms. Schloss continued, "¿Cómo se usaba la idea de raza en el pasado?" (How was the idea of race used in the past?) As the volume of the chatting increased, a White student answered, "Históricamente para justificar que unas personas son mejores que otras." (Historically, to justify that some persons are better than others.) The chatting and lack of student attention so early in the school year—it was barely the first week—surprised me, but then I remembered that most of the students had known each other since elementary school. Ms. Schloss moved to the other side of the board to write down their answers for ethnicity: "Cultural," "Conexiones históricas" (Historical connections), "Se puede *auto* determinar" (Can be *self*-determined).

The explicitness on the differences between race and ethnicity matched the lesson's objective, which Ms. Schloss had written in the far corner of the board: "Explorar las clasificaciones raciales/étnicas para entender su historia y su poder." (Explore the race/ethnic classifications to understand their history and power.) Although many lessons implicitly taught about race and ethnicity, this was the first one I observed that dealt with this head-on. The discussion presented three main ideas about race: first, that race was about physical characteristics; second, that it could not be self-determined; and third, that it was used in the past. These definitions could imply that race is a biological or innate characteristic, so I was hoping to hear it mentioned that race was *not* biological or innate, but a socially constructed category. From the little I knew of Ms. Schloss, she seemed a socially conscious teacher, so I assumed the reference to the past did not mean to imply that racism was not a contemporary problem. I also figured it was a matter of time before the class would discuss these ideas and how white supremacy fit in.

But soon after defining ethnicity, Ms. Schloss distributed a handout listing twelve identities: gender, age, nationality, social class, legal status, family status, occupation, sexual orientation, (dis)ability status, language, social group, and ethnicity. In groups of two or three, students were to define the terms by selecting from definitions listed in the handout and writing them down. They also had to provide examples of these identities and note whether they were privileged or oppressed (see table 1.1).

TABLE 1.1 Example of student written responses in *italics* to one of the twelve identities from the handout

Palabra	Definición	Ejemplos y Privilegiado/Oprimido
orientación sexual	*diferentes gustos*	*gay, LGBTQ oprimido*

Then students walked around the room asking their classmates which of the identities they most associated with. Once students returned to their seats, Ms. Schloss asked which identities were most common. Two students responded, "género," "etnicidad," "nacionalidad" (gender, ethnicity, nationality). She followed with another question, "¿Por qué es tan importante la nacionalidad?" (Why is nationality so important?) The same two students responded, one answering that nationality was important, "Pero eso no está bien. (But that's not right.) I don't think it's right." Her classmates still seemed uninterested in engaging in conversation. Ms. Schloss pressed, "¿Por qué son tan poderosos las identidades?" (Why are identities so powerful?) After some more silence, Ms. Schloss switched to a PowerPoint slide titled "Construcciones sociales" (Social constructions) with a drawing of a man vacuuming the living room. She noted that identities, like "mexicano" or "bilingüe" are social constructions, that our society give these meaning. She added "Es un sistema social desigual. Ciertos grupos tienen más poder o estatus más alto, o menos poder o un estatus más bajo." (It's an unequal system; certain groups have more power and higher status, or less power and lower status.) She ended by stating, "El hecho es que vivimos en un mundo desigual." (The fact is that we live in an unequal world.) While others were gathering their backpacks anticipating the bell marking the end of Wednesday's last class, a White male student sheepishly asked "¿Cómo la raza?" (Like race?)

I was not the only person who remained puzzled after the lesson, questioning the concept of social construction and its link to race, as well as the implications of identities existing within an unequal system.

Ms. Schloss felt an urgency in having students learn about these concepts, and she had planned for her lessons to cover a lot of ideas, leading to not making explicit connections or addressing students' questions. Having been a former high school teacher myself, I could identify with Ms. Schloss's practices, which resembled my own during my early years as a teacher. For instance, I would often plan multiple activities, which led me to prioritize moving on to the next task rather than delving into students' questions. In our chats after her classes, Ms. Schloss mentioned wanting to better scaffold her lessons and felt that this was barely a "first draft" (she had taught this course only once before).

The newness of the course added to the difficulty of making it a bilingual space that challenged schools' status quo racial hierarchies. For example, I observed mostly White students participating, perhaps a sign that the lessons attended to their development of anti-racism and/or ignored Latinxs' development of understanding racial issues.[4] Still, it was encouraging that the bilingual education program taught students about race outright.

Apart from complicating the idea of what bilingual education looks like, the elective course helped the program live up to bilingual schooling as a progressive project by providing a radical departure from the race-evasive schooling that many teachers offer and youth suffer through. The lesson I had just observed also offered a break from the other dual-language classrooms' more typical lessons, which centered the different grammatical rules and prepositions in English and Spanish or took the form of textbook readings with multiple-choice questions. Although other teachers shared Ms. Schloss's commitment to having students learn about injustice and racial issues, few of their lessons centered on the definition and meaning of race. Having an ethnic-studies course for the dual-language program provided the structural opportunity to explicitly discuss and learn about racial issues.

THE IDENTITY PANEL IN THE ETHNIC STUDIES COURSE

In the fourth week of the nine-week course, Ms. Schloss invited me to be on a panel entitled "Language and Identity" for her Ethnic Studies course. I accepted, feeling grateful that I could help in some way. I had offered to assist teachers in classrooms; for example, by helping answer students' questions on group or individual work (one Spanish-language teacher asked me to give a lecture on written accents in Spanish, which I also accepted). But Ms. Schloss's invitation came early in the school year, which I saw as a welcome sign of the rapport I was developing with teachers, especially Ms. Schloss, whom I admired for her political clarity and commitment.

On the day before the panel, she emailed me and the other panelists a list of questions the students had written for the panel, which included:

1. Tell us about your identity.
2. What parts of your identity do you think are most important?
3. Have you faced any barriers because of your identity?
4. Do you think it is OK that we sometimes separate ourselves by ethnicity or sexual orientation, like for clubs?
5. What is an example of discrimination that you've seen?
6. What do you love to learn about other people?
7. Why do you think people judge others based on identity?
8. How has your identity affected your job as someone who works in a school?

The questions made me reflect on my background and my experience in fostering adolescent Spanish-English biliteracy as a teacher, both of which allowed me to be at times a linguistic insider in the Oakville community. My body also informed people's perceptions of me. I am a small-framed cis woman with dark hair and eyes and an olive skin tone, lighter than my childhood's sunlight bestowed me. Politically, I identify as Xicana, but my curly hair and other features make me racially ambiguous when I am outside of México and Arizona. For example, when I taught in Philadelphia, students would tell me that I could pass as Puerto Rican—that is, until I spoke. Individuals still usually identified me as Latina, even if they were not certain if I was Mexican. These experiences taught me about the importance of nationality, of physical appearance, and of speech in ascribing and making a person's group affiliation. I wondered what from this I would share in the panel.

On the day of the panel, students took turns asking the listed questions to the panel. I was up first. I introduced myself as an immigrant from México, a Xicana, who used to be a high school teacher of Spanish but was currently a university graduate student. I also mentioned that I did not practice a religion and identified as a cisgender heterosexual woman. The other members were school staff: (1) Ms. Houston, a "mixed Black/White woman" who was Amlie's social worker, (2) Mr. Morris, a Black man, the school's multicultural services coordinator, and (3) Mr. Noriega, a Latino man, an immigrant from México who was one of the school's bilingual support specialists.

Although the questions were about identity, most of the answers turned to racial issues. For example, members of the panel shared experiences of being excluded from a group and being stereotyped by others because of physical characteristics. For question 5, about discrimination, I described a news story I had heard that morning about how the US government had refused to grant refugee status to immigrants from Central America. I stated that I saw this as a double standard because people fleeing violence and political instability from countries that were seen as having White populations were labeled refugees, a label that comes with legal protections. But aside from this, most of the panelists' answers relayed firsthand experiences. Nothing really rallied the students or sparked their increased participation.

As the hour passed, students yawned more frequently, more heads came down or were propped up by hands, and texting started to be more visible. I could relate to this response. Hearing four adults talk about experiences such as being stereotyped—which were not that surprising and that the students had heard since elementary school—was, I must say, a bit boring. Throughout the hour, the panelists tried to impart the importance of being proud of who you are and where you come from and being open to and not making assumptions about other folks. The panel illustrated the program's prevalent lesson about racism, which primarily revolved around the idea of causing offense to others and understanding race as a concept centered on excluding because of identity.

Still, I wondered, why would students be so disengaged in a course dealing with racial issues, yet repeatedly express in interviews that they wanted to learn more about social justice and race and racism?

THE SAME HISTORIES, THE SAME LESSONS

In their interviews, I asked each student to think of different lessons that they had learned in the program that related to topics like race, racism, or other social-justice-related topics. Most students shared lessons about not discriminating against others. For example, Jonny, an eighth-grade Mexican Latino, shared that he had learned that "Todas las personas son iguales, y no tienen [pausa], sobre su raza y su color [sic], no juzgar a las personas." (All people are equal, and they don't have [pause], about their race and their color, don't judge people.) It became clearer to me that the lessons about race and racism that the dual-language program taught to eleventh-graders were lessons they had been hearing since elementary school.

When I asked Kiara, a high-achieving Black tenth-grade girl who participated in Amlie's Black Student Union, she briefly answered "We've learned about slavery and the underground railroad." After my probing, she shared,

We learned about the culture of the Aztecs and basically how those different groups . . . and the Incas . . . how they conquered different territories. And we've learned about how the Spaniards came to Latin America and took slaves from Portugal and Bolivia and put them in horrible conditions to work for little to no pay.

She elaborated:

I learned the history of Latin America and Spain and how those things . . . how they interlap [sic] with each other and I have, not experience, but I've . . . in learning, witnessed the pain that some . . . in history that they've had to go through, like through slavery. And I was able to connect that with my history and so I feel like if I wasn't in the program, I would just feel like "Oh, my history is the only one and there's really nothing else, . . . no other history that I need to dive into really.

When I asked Kiara to specify whether she was speaking about slavery in and outside of the United States, she replied, "Slavery in, basically, Latin America and the Indigenous people. Basically, when the British came and the Spaniards came to conquer, I could empathize with their pain because my people went through the same thing, sort of." Kiara credited the program for helping her make connections between the Spanish colonization and the English and American system of slavery. She shared being more "open-minded to different cultures" from seeing how people shared some of the same histories, something she really appreciated.

Still, Kiara felt that the same history lesson was being repeated and she was not learning new information. She complained to me about the program being repetitive after I asked her what aspects of the program were challenging: "I'm a fan of history but when I take it in Spanish, it seems like we learn about the same stuff each year because I feel like . . . they run out of the history to teach in the Spanish language." This repetitiveness suggests one reason why students disengaged.

In a history class where Kiara was not a student, when Ms. Schloss mentioned the California Farm Workers' protest, a student interjected with an exaggerated monotone voice, "Yes, we know about la huelga, huelga, huelga" (the strike, strike, strike). In another class, Ms. Schloss set up the class to watch a documentary on Latinx immigrants by asking the class to think of actions they could take to alleviate social problems. The only Black boy in the class sarcastically suggested, "hacer una tienda de vender mangos" (to make a store to sell mangos). The mockery was met with blank stares from the Latinx students. So although the dual-language program had a social justice lens, the lessons did not engage Kiara and other students, perhaps because the lessons were not scaffolding how to take action or moving past the same topics, thus not expanding students' knowledge.

While a few students shared learning about a few unique topics, such as social class in Cuba, most lessons did not add new knowledge about race. I also observed the repetitiveness throughout the program about other topics. For example, students had a weeks-long unit on Chinese philosophy in two different grade levels; thus they received repeated ideas. They interpreted this repetition to mean that their high school teachers were less skilled than their elementary or middle school teachers. One student shared, "I just felt like our teachers in middle school and elementary school were a lot more knowledgeable on Latino history, like old Latino history and the more modern stuff, than the ones that we had in high school."

Students did not know that high school teachers dealt with structural limitations. Teachers attributed the repetitiveness as stemming from the limited availability of curricular materials in Spanish, and thus adapting the same district-provided materials for different grades. In terms of the repetitiveness of lessons about race and racism, teachers felt limited by the lack of available materials or even their own training and knowledge of topics. Teachers who traveled to Spanish-speaking countries brought back literature and other material for students to read. But not all teachers had the time or resources to find materials.

Mr. Ochoa, an Amlie history teacher who identified as an immigrant teacher from Spain and as White and culturally Hispanic, had lamented to me about the curricular resource limitations in Spanish. He felt he had to incorporate English materials in order to broach racial topics with relevant and stimulating materials and without spending too much time searching for high-quality Spanish-language materials; for example, he showed Chimamanda Ngozi Adichie's "Single Story" TED Talk. He elaborated on his decision:

> Me imagino que si tuviéramos un poquito más de contacto intelectual con el mundo hispano aquí, pues si podríamos saber pues que hay un escritor boliviano que ha hecho este libro, una escritora nicaragüense, que ha hecho aquello; pero no es tan fácil porque hay que dedicarle mucho más tiempo a buscarlo. (If we had a little bit more intellectual contact with the Hispanic world here, then maybe we could know that there's a Bolivian writer who wrote this book, or a Nicaraguan writer who has written that. But it's not that easy because one needs to dedicate a lot more time to search for materials.)

Mr. Ochoa's feeling of being disconnected from critical Spanish materials and current topics may have been exacerbated by the district's relatively recent growth in Latinx population, compared to cities with established Latinx and/or transnational populations. Dual-language teachers like Mr. Ochoa, who tried to teach about social justice issues, had trouble finding relevant materials, and had easier access to many options that deal with social justice in English. The school provided no structural support to make relevant materials available, resulting in repetitiveness that students like Kiara noticed when learning history in Spanish.

Observing this repetitiveness and recognizing that its mere curricular inclusion did not necessarily lead to sophisticated representations of Latinx histories prevented me from idealizing the program.[5] Still, it was an improvement compared with many other options, including my English-only race-evasive schooling in Arizona (which was more than 85 percent Mexican American). There, I never heard of the Chicana/o Movement or Latinx struggles, but I did learn about, for example, the Trail of Tears, broken treaties, and the American civil rights movement. My educational background highlighted for me the importance of culturally relevant, race-conscious teaching. This perspective, coupled with my teaching experience, prompted me to view the missed opportunities in the dual-language program within the broader context of the challenges faced in overcoming race-evasive education. And I also empathized with the program's teachers and the constraints they faced in managing without appropriate curricular materials. As a teacher in Philadelphia, a large underfunded public school system, I had also experienced the limits and pressures inherent in such environments.

Along with the repetitiveness of the lessons about race and racism was the issue of what ideas the program circulated, over and over, about race and racism. Having observed other ethnic studies classes of this eleventh-grade group, I had left the panel with the feeling that the questions and answers helped to reinforce the idea that identity, including race, is something that is innate to the person (even if identities can change). I wondered how teachers and students made sense of race and racism and of these' concepts relation to each other.

RACISM WITHOUT RACE

I asked students what the dual-language program taught them about race and racism. Like Jonny, students responded that they had learned that racism was not acceptable. They shared examples of discrimination; for example, the anti-Latinx and anti-immigrant sentiments that had garnered more national attention and resulted in RedRock almost passing legislation that mimicked that of other states, like Arizona's anti-immigrant law SB 1070, the so-called "Show-me-your-papers" law.[6] Activists and many in the Latinx community mobilized to fight against the legislation. They organized for a Day Without Immigrants, which included a boycott, school/work stoppage, and a protest march attended by many dual-language students.

In one sixth-grade class, the teacher and students talked about the protests, sharing their indignation. One Latina student said the proposed law was unfair because the police would ask only Latinos for their immigration status and not immigrants that "looked White." Heads nodded in agreement. The teacher also agreed, noting that many people saw this as unfair, as racist, and "based on skin being darker." Then a Latino boy opined that the law was "messed up" because if the police looked at him and his skin, they would think he was from México. A White student chimed in that the police would think he was from Europe. Heads silently nodded in agreement.

Although a major and persistent lesson was indeed the idea that racism was unacceptable, the discussion left some questions and tensions unexplored. The discussion left no indication or acknowledgment that the Latinx students in the class represented different skin tones. Yet there was consensus that, regardless of what they looked like, the proposed bill was anti-Latinx and that Latinxs would be discriminated against. So how would they be discriminated against?

The program provided few educative opportunities for students to consider "what race is" apart from skin color and appearance, or how this immigration proposal would discriminate against lighter-skinned Latinxs. Often, teaching about race and racism meant constructing race as something that others could see and use to discriminate against them (or that would provide privileges), and then focusing on and condemning racism. Without further nuance, race was left as something innate that was read only on the body. In this class, this view resulted in students' confusion and contradictory ideas about what this implied for Latinxs.

As the school year progressed, other lessons helped me see how the program taught the definition and meaning of race. It became clearer to me that people described race as skin color and as an identity.

RACE AS IDENTITY (BUT MOSTLY BASED ON YOUR LOOKS)

Andrea, a Latina eighth grader at Borane Middle School, hung out with the other two popular girls in her class and often drew a little heart after writing her full name. Of this trio, Andrea struggled the most to achieve the top grades she wanted. This was not because she was not capable of it; she felt that her classes were boring, and she would "just space out" when she did not understand something. Andrea was not able to drop "boring" dual-language courses because Borane's dual-language students had no option but to enroll in all the program's courses or drop from the program entirely. Borane's program required Spanish-language arts, social studies, and science courses in Spanish, with English language arts and math, along with course electives (such as music and computers) taught in English. Although Andrea liked her social studies, she shared with me wanting to have social studies classes that were "more relevant . . . more up-to-date," or that had "something that's interesting that will really change things."

But one social studies lesson that I heard her keep talking about with her friends was a guest panel of adults whom Ms. Lucas invited to speak about race. Ms. Lucas, a White woman, was one of Borane's dual-language social studies/history teachers. (I further elaborate on the panel in the following chapters.) She organized this panel after overhearing a group of Latino students express anti-Black ideas. Andrea also mentioned the panel when I asked her to share a lesson that she had found interesting. She started by answering

> Race and racism is something we've been focusing on this year, about who we identify with and how we identify other people, and . . . if the way that we identify them is okay. We've been talking about how like race doesn't really mean the color. When we think about race, we think about it like White, or Black, or Latino, but really race, scientifically it means "the human race." That's what it's really talking about, but we use it as this thing to describe us like the color of our skin and where we come from, but that's really not right.

Andrea continued by reflecting that people discriminate against and "pity" Latinxs for who they are. In noting that the concept of race does not really mean the color but "the human race," Andrea got at the idea that we are all humans, one biological species. She perceived the incorrectness in the idea that our phenotypical characteristics indicate something else about ourselves. However, that "something" was more closely associated with ethnicity and perpetuating stereotypes about people rather than recognizing racist practices as a system designed to categorize and oppress specific groups. After I asked Andrea, "Did you like hearing what the panel had to say?" she immediately replied,

> I did. If I just saw them, I would say that they were all Black people, but once we started talking about it, they revealed that they were Dominican, and Peruvian, and Hawai'ian, I think. And that was like, "Oh, they're not just Black people, they're—actually have different backgrounds."

Andrea appreciated that the lesson helped her not be so, as she put it, "uncultured" and "close-minded." The panelists had shared some of their experiences of not being identified as Latinx because of people seeing them as Black, which made an impression on her. "We were talking about race and how you shouldn't assume who they are just because of their skin tone, that you should really just see." Andrea's comments pointed to her viewing "just Black people" as African Americans, contrasting them with the panelists who identified as being of Hawai'ian or Afro-Latinx descent.

District data on the percentage of students in the program who identified as mixed race or specifically Afro-Latinx was not available. However, based on my conversations with teachers and students, it appeared that around ten students in Borane/Amlie's program fit this category, out of a total of almost two hundred. (Borane Middle School's student population was approximately 34 percent Latinx, 31 percent White, 19 percent Black/African American, 10 percent Multiracial, 5 percent Asian American, <1 percent Native American and <1 percent Pacific Islander.)

Andrea's comparison of race with other categories pertaining to ethnicity and nationality shows how people often conflate race with ethnicity. One could make well- or ill-informed assumptions about another person's ethnicity, religion, language, and a myriad of other cultural practices based on that other person's looks. But these assumptions do not have to lead to the pernicious ideas or the structural discriminatory practices of racialization. At times, for teachers and students, making assumptions from a person's appearance (e.g., Black men are good basketball players; Latinxs speak Spanish) was equivalent to engaging in the pernicious aspect of race: the idea that there are different human lineages, the practice of sorting them into categories to distribute resources based on the racial hierarchy, and justifying that discrimination on the group's inherent worth, intelligence, and humanness. By focusing on assumptions, the panel's lesson left the pernicious and structural aspect of racialization unexposed and unchallenged and, importantly, disconnected from the anti-Blackness that prompted Ms. Lucas to create the panel.

Still, the lesson made an impression on the students. It prompted a side conversation I heard between Andrea and her two friends during Ms. Lucas' class, with one of her friends declaring clearly, "I'm White," as an assertion of identity. Yet, even with all this explicit talk about race, Andrea still voiced doubts in her interview about talking about race. "We're talking about whether it's OK to use the word race or not, because of what it's really supposed to mean" (meaning "the human race"). Finding myself a bit unclear about how she understood race based on the program's teachings, I asked her about this, and she replied,

> Race? [I reply "yeah"; she pauses.] I guess it's who you identify with, how you—not maybe how you grew up, but like but how you see yourself.

I was mostly—yeah, I think it's just how you see yourself and [pause] the way you were raised can really impact that. It has to do with your background and your customs and things that you do. The culture that you've adapted, even if it's not your culture.

The program introduced Andrea to the idea that "race" meant "the human race," emphasizing the absence of biological differences between humans. Andrea, an olive-skinned brunette, had expressed that race did not really mean someone's skin color, an answer that referred to what race was not. Yet, she had difficulty answering what race *was*.

In her attempt to answer the question, Andrea mentioned that race was related to a person's appearance, identity, and culture—a common perspective conveyed by the program. Andrea's conflicting ideas also stemmed from the lessons in her other dual-language courses.

For example, Andrea's science teacher, Ms. Íñiguez, a Latina/Mexicana immigrant, recalled sharing a video from Spain with students. In the video, a reporter asked pedestrians and some tourists to answer, "¿Tú que raza eres? ¿100 percent qué?" (What race are you? 100 percent of what?) People answered being 100 percent German, 100 percent English, for example. Then the reporter asked, "¿Tú que piensas de los turcos?" (What do you think about the Turkish people?) Some answered, "Ay, no, los turcos son de lo peor." (Uh, no, the Turks are the worst.) Ms. Íñiguez excitedly shared that the respondents were then asked to volunteer to do a DNA test to confirm their answer about their race. After hearing the volunteers receive their DNA results, Ms. Íñiguez emphasized:

> OK, "Fíjate bien lo que dice aquí. Tú eres 30 percent alemán, eres 40 percent esto, 30 percent . . ." Y les dicen los porcentajes de su raza, "¿No que dicen la raza pura?" Y resulta que muchos se quedan bastante impactados porque dicen "realmente no soy puro." (OK, "Notice what it says here. You are 30 percent German, 40 percent this, 30 percent . . ." And they tell them the percentages of their race, "Didn't you say pure race?" Which results in many being very shocked because they say, "I'm not really pure.")

Ms. Íñiguez then went on to explain that this lesson taught the students that, "Entonces, es tiempo de que la gente debe de ya evitarse ponerse etiquetas de que es o que no es, ¿no?" (So now it's time for people to avoid putting labels on what you are or are not, right?) While trying to trouble the idea of a "pure race" using DNA as a proxy for nationalities, Ms. Íñiguez sought to promote the idea that all labels were irrelevant. Ms. Íñiguez also presented "race" as if the concept has the same meaning in Spain and America. But most disturbing was that Ms. Íñiguez did not repudiate the white supremacist idea of Europeans being better than others. Perhaps she thought this was obviously abhorrent and need not be asserted. (Further conversations with Ms. Íñiguez confirmed that she took a race-evasive perspective about systemic racial injustice, even while noting racial patterns and racialized groups and expressing racist ideas, as later chapters reveal.)

The program's teachers and students clearly espoused antidiscrimination (that is, the idea that people should not be discriminated against because of their skin tone, culture, language, etc.). They also rejected white supremacy— the idea that Whites are better than and should materially benefit at the expense of racialized Others. But they were less clear about what "race" referred to. This was the case even in the classes where teachers like Ms. Schloss and Ms. Lucas wanted to deal head-on with racial issues. For example, Jada, a tenth-grade Black/African American student, shared that in her history course, "We talk a lot about the racial groups, how they were treated and stuff like that." But when I asked Jada how she had learned to define race, she answered that "it has to do with your skin color and your looks." As with Andrea and Jada, when race came up in other interviews and in classes, the attention was also on phenotype.

STAYING AT SESAME STREET

I would characterize the type of ideas that the dual-language program offered as reminiscent of a *Sesame Street* sketch, where Elmo, along with Mr. Elijah and his son, Wes, teaches kids about race.[7] Elmo asks why Wes's skin is brown, and why dad and son have different skin colors. Elmo learns that having more melanin gives people a darker skin tone. Mr. Elijah mentions skin color, eye color, hair texture, and other physical differences as what defines race. Mr. Elijah adds, "But even though we look different, we're all part of the human race." This video serves as a useful tool in helping young children make sense of the physical differences they observe. It also teaches them that recognizing variations in physical appearance is normal.

I mention this sketch because, as I was thinking of what the dual-language program kept teaching about race, it struck me that many of the dual-language program's teachings about race stayed at this *Sesame Street* level of understanding. The program sought to have students view the different racialized groups, in the words of twelfth grader Mia as "all equal and that we should be proud of who we are. We shouldn't try to change our identity to be part of some sort of group. We all have our different cultures, and they should all be celebrated." It is understandable why schools promote a celebration of cultures and respecting others. To be fair, most teachers made getting along and learning an essential goal for students in their classroom community, especially when the program's students did not all act with this sentiment. I recall when Ms. Thomson, a White teacher at Amlie, asked her Spanish language arts class to ask fellow classmates, "¿Qué es lo que más te gusta de Amlie?" (What do you like most about Amlie?) A White ninth-grade boy answered, "What I like most about Amlie is the White people." Then he repeated, "I like all the White people," as a couple of his friends giggled. These statements revealed the need for a *Sesame Street* level of teaching about getting along and celebrating all cultures.

For some teachers, valuing diversity was all there was to know about race and racism. After all, most of them were trained in their subject (science, math, etc.) and then maybe in language acquisition, and not at all to teach about race or racism. Some teachers' own education had not pushed their knowledge beyond the *Sesame Street* level of "we're all part of the human race." And most people (including bilingual education advocates and parents) saw the goal of the program as promoting languages and biliteracy for all. Some considered learning about race as beyond the scope of the program, which would imply viewing teacher training on how to teach about race as unnecessary. This couples with our dominant society not prioritizing—and even attacking—the development of students' critical-racial consciousness.[8] Consider the curricular sequencing of racial ideas that, unlike those in subjects such as math, English, and even history, often lack any planned inclusion. This neglect extends to areas, including teacher training, and further highlights the insufficient attention given to racial learning.

Teachers like Ms. Lucas and Ms. Schloss, who noticed that racial issues mattered in their classrooms and who wanted to address those issues in their students' lives, took it upon themselves to design their own lessons. They proceeded to teach about race and racism without a programmatic sequence to help them and the program guide students' learning about race. They took this approach without much community advocacy; indeed, Oakville's bilingual education proponents did not push for the program to teach about these topics, nor was it raised as a need in community meetings or by parents I interviewed. For example, three Latina mothers (all immigrants) expressed to me in interviews that they were not interested in having the bilingual program teach about racial issues. But a fourth mother, Mrs. Matilda, thought it was a good idea:

> Yo creo que es muy bueno, porque da un conocimiento a los estudiantes desde temprana edad de que no importa el color de la piel, todos somos seres humanos, y es abrir la puerta a tener esa parte humanitaria de respeto también, para mí es muy importante esa parte. (I believe that it's really good, because it gives students knowledge from an early age that skin color doesn't matter, all of us are human beings, and it's opening a door to also have that humanitarian part and to respect others, which is very important to me.)

Mrs. Matilda seemed to interpret my question not as pertaining to lessons about structural racial issues, but to the teaching of multiculturalism as the dominant perspective in the program.

The program offered students the "multicultural type" lessons about race and racism: to be proud of who you are and where you come from, and to be open to and not make assumptions about other folks or treat them differently. Youth, of course, are not passive recipients of lessons, and they learn about race outside of school. Many of the Spanish-speaking Latinx students were immigrants or from immigrant families, and they learned ideas about race from their homelands.[9] However, most students expressed to me that they wanted school to address social justice and racial issues. By middle and high school, some students were ready for lessons that pushed their understanding of race beyond the commonplace definition of appearance à la *Sesame Street*.

The absence of a curriculum and pedagogy in the dual-language program, designed to guide and nurture students' critical-racial consciousness, led to significant repercussions. Students complained about lessons being repetitive and curricula lacking rigor. In Ms. Lucas's class, Andrea's White friend shared that she was tired of "always talking about race and social justice"; Andrea looked on without responding. While students may have been tired of this focus for different reasons, the repetitiveness was unlikely to develop most students' critical-racial consciousness. The continual restatement of multiculturalism also meant that teachers were not scaffolding for diverse racial experiences—something important, considering that the students' racial diversity also brought diversity in their racial experiences.[10] Additionally, the repetitiveness revealed the program's lack of intentionality and coordination between grades about how to progress students' knowledge about race and racism, especially, structural racism and complicating race beyond skin color.

MAKING RACE

As a racial project, the dual-language program had contradictory roles and outcomes, including in what it offered in terms of teaching racial ideas. For example, through the ethnic studies and Latin American studies electives, the program provided structural support for teaching about race. However, this support did not include sequencing the program's curriculum or offering help for scaffolding lessons about race, racism, and racialization. Its structural noncommitment to sequencing racial learning defaulted to pedagogy that focused mainly on bilingualism/multiculturalism, which did not scaffold for advancing critical-racial consciousness and actions. Moreover, not having this structural support and political clarity across the program resulted in most of the program teaching about race by staying at a *Sesame Street* level of explaining race (skin color) and racism (maltreating/excluding others).

As I have noted, people in Oakville's dual-language program (as much of our society) defined race by limiting it to "looks," to phenotypical characteristics—especially skin color. This made students like Andrea and Mia have trouble making sense of society's incoherence about whether Latinx is a racialized group.[11] Limiting race to skin color makes race be seen as if it were biological, inherent, natural, as if what "makes race" *is* looks. This conception results in not seeing Latinxs—with their different hues—as a racialized group. A racialized group *is not* made by skin color, an idea that the program could have offered to enhance students' critical-racial consciousness.

Another idea that probably would intrigue students like Andrea and Mia is that *racism makes racialized groups.* That is, what makes a racialized group is *racism against* the people who are perceived and made an Othered group (rather than the categories/groups first existing and then groups being discriminated against). Racial oppression creates the need for people to racially affiliate with each other to fight against racism, and this further reinforces distinctions between racialized groups.[12] The difficulty in acknowledging this emerges from society defining race as a category formed from a racialized group's appearance (or even culture). The incoherence is compounded by schools and society defining race as about looks but then society *treating* Latinxs as a racialized group. (I elaborate on this idea in the next chapter.)

The emphasis on identity presented some contradictions that lessons did not acknowledge. For example, on the one hand, an individual's Latinx identity is something to be proud of and links the individual to the Latinx community, which is connected by shared cultural practices. On the other hand, there were racialized stereotypes (that is, not all Latinxs share the same cultural practices). Aside from Ms. Íñiguez's lesson offering race-evasive ideas, the program hinted that we cannot escape racial ascription and suggested that society's racial stereotypes are misunderstandings. Lessons rarely pointed out the nefarious aspect of racial identities limiting people's possibilities. That is, the lessons did not flesh out that society has constructed roles, behaviors, and expectations associated with different racialized groups and that these indeed restrict people's actions and ideas.[13] These contradictions were seldom exposed as part and parcel of race in society.

While individuals often associated skin color and physical features with race, their responses also implied that race encompasses broader concepts, such as culture and identity. This observation raised the questions: What did it mean to equate race with skin color, particularly for Latinxs, a group with a wide range of physical appearances, as observed by students like Andrea and Jada? Within the Spanish-English bilingual education program with numerous Latinx students, how was "Latino culture" specifically defined, and what was its relationship with race?

CHAPTER 2

Race vis-à-vis Latinx

I
n February 2017, Latinos Unidos, Oakville's education-focused Latinx community association, organized a public meeting with the school district to discuss the dual-language program's history, triumphs, and challenges, and to hear from the community and the program's students. The Hispanic Community Center of Oakville, the only center of its kind in the city, hosted the meeting. The brightly decorated main room featured wall paintings of portraits labeled "Heroes of the Hispanic World." These included, among others, Celia Cruz, César Chávez, Rigoberta Menchú, Pablo Neruda, Che Guevara, and Óscar Romero, each labeled with their name and country of origin in large text and a lengthy biography in tiny font. Painted on a prominent wall was a framed oval mirror with the phrase painted below it "The Next Hero." A smaller room boasted a brightly colored mural of an idyllic scene. It featured chinampas (floating gardens indigenous to central México) set on a lake framed by nopales and palm trees. México's Popocatépetl and Iztaccíhuatl volcanos towered in the background, presenting a stark contrast to Oakville's grass-green or snowy-white landscapes.

As people started arriving on that brisk Saturday morning, friends greeted each other with a hug and sometimes a side kiss. Community members warmly welcomed unfamiliar faces with coffee and Mexican pan dulce. Smiling kids grabbed chocolate conchas as big as their little faces. After several minutes of people arriving, the chatter in the room made conversation partners get closer together to be able to hear each other. The president of Latinos Unidos went to the microphone and asked us to please take a seat so the meeting could start. We had gathered there to learn about the dual-language program's progress and discuss its challenges, especially now that the program was about to graduate its first seniors, the cohort that had initiated Oakville's program twelve years ago.

Following a fifteen-minute speech by the president about the importance of being bilingual, a panel of community members took the makeshift stage.

These Latinx adults had been among the original advocates and founders of the program. They were invited to recall their experience advocating for the implementation of the dual-language program and to recount the politics behind its establishment. Later, a panel of four twelfth graders who had been in the program since elementary school spoke of their experiences and opinions about the benefits and challenges of being in the program. As they spoke, people listened intently, and cheered when one of the White students said she was going to attend a university and major in elementary education to become a dual-language teacher.

In the next part of the meeting, we divided into groups to discuss the program's challenges, each group focusing on a theme such as the secondary-level program implementation or teacher-related issues. After our breakout meetings, each group reported back on their discussion to the whole group. Parents concurred about the importance of the program teaching their children to be proud of their culture and teaching non-Latinxs "about Latino culture," an idea I had heard in other public and one-on-one discussions about the program. One parent connected this to who should be teaching in the program, "Tiene que ser alguien que es bilingüe pero también *bi*-cultural." (They must be bilingual, but also *bi*cultural.) Repeatedly, parents and students voiced the need for "teachers to know the culture and language," all agreeing that the Spanish language was the "tie to culture and history." However, the concept of "Latino culture" remained vague. The prominent murals could lead some to infer a unified culture shared by the meeting's attendees, Pablo Neruda, César Chávez, Miguel Hidalgo, and the others whose portraits adorned the wall. That almost all the luminaries were Latin American silently reinforced the Latinx category as made up from various nationalities, obscuring the cultural differences and epochs distinguishing their lives.

As the community members emphasized the importance of teaching "Latino culture" and "the culture," two other ideas struck me. First, I noticed that the attendees spoke passionately about culture, seemingly presuming that the audience, especially teachers, needed to be reminded of its importance. Although most of the district's dual-language teachers did not attend the meeting (only two out of the fifteen teachers from my study's schools were present), I knew many teachers shared these beliefs and goals, expressing their aim to promote students' "language and culture, and a sense of pride in these." Teachers had mentioned to me that one of the program's benefits was that the "Latino families . . . get their culture valued." Most teachers conceptualized their equity work as—and engaged in—practices to improve biliteracy achievement and affirm the Spanish language and "Latino culture."

Second, I noticed that no attendee mentioned the need for the program to include or improve its teaching about injustice or racial issues, a stark omission given that racial issues were foremost for many in Oakville schools, especially within the Black/African American community. This absence also struck me because, although people emphasized that empirical evidence supported bilingual education for improving student academic achievement, no one mentioned that teaching anti-racist ideas could have a similar improvement on student achievement.[1] Indeed, no one mentioned race or racism at all. The program seemed to frame Latinx concerns primarily in terms of language while sidelining racial considerations.

In this chapter, we hear from teachers and students about their perceptions of "Latino culture" and Latinx as a category, and how this contributed to them making sense of race. They share how some of the dual-language teachers' classroom practices construct a Latinx category by speaking about its culture, while referring to nationalities to give examples of cultural practices. We learn how students and teachers had trouble making sense of whether Latinx was a race (or something else), and the tensions created by defining race in terms of skin color and appearance.

TEACHING LATINO CULTURE

When I posed an open-ended question to the dual-language teachers about the program's teachings on "Latino," their answers unfolded with a common theme: the program sought to "validate Latino identity." When I asked the teachers to elaborate on the concept of "Latino," they often responded with vague ideas of "culture," "ethnicity," and "community." One answered, "It's about sharing values and culture, like being family oriented." One Borane teacher, Ms. Nader, who self-identified as a person of color and had a Middle Eastern background, also mentioned Latinxs sharing culture, but quickly added, "I know that's totally problematic; there's not a singular Latino culture." Although the other dual-language teachers did not express a qualification like Ms. Nader, their practices generally indicated an understanding of multiple Latinx "cultures." The dual-language program emphasized culture by presenting different cultures of Latin America or other parts of the world. In this way, it did not teach that a singular culture made the Latinx category, even as ambiguity blurred the idea of what the Latino culture was (as we see later).

Some teachers worried that students essentialized cultures, so they tried to counter this. Ms. Lucas shared, "Within our program, there's a lot of lack of understanding about the variety of Latino cultures." She continued that she would tell the students, "You guys, you have a ton of variety amongst you that you don't recognize." She listened to her students' questions; for example, their noticing and curiosity about "different accents, but they didn't understand why [there were those differences in spoken accents]. The students were asking, 'Where does that come from?'" She wanted to instill in students the importance of them continuing "to develop their language and connection to their culture, and to investigate other cultures as well." For instance, Ms. Lucas taught her students that Dominicans have distinct cultural practices from Mexicans; she shared that, for example, Dominicans point to something with their lips instead of their index finger. But once the idea shifted to Latino culture, what that encompassed was unspecified beyond including the different nationalities like Mexicans and Dominicans.

While teachers presented readings and activities that dealt with various parts of Latin America, they focused more on (and perhaps were most knowledgeable about) Mexican customs. (For example, students learned about the Day of the Dead and decorated altars for their deceased relatives—a cultural practice of some Indigenous groups in México.) But teachers did consider representation and diversity. One stated, "I don't want them to exclusively study Mexican American Latino literature." Throughout the program, students learned about different countries through histories of, for example, Simón Bolívar, Eva Perón, and Argentina's Dirty War and read Colombian magic realism. They perceived all of these as teaching them about these diverse cultures that made up "Latino culture."

Many students mentioned they liked learning about other cultures. Nancy, an eleventh grader who emigrated from México as a young child, shared with me, "Cultura es lo que me gusta aprender. . . . Como cultura mexicana. Yo soy mexicana, pero hay cosas que no conozco. . . . Todo lo que es con una cultura diferente es lo que me atrae." (Culture is what I like to learn about. . . . Like the Mexican culture. I'm Mexican, but there are things that I don't know. . . . Everything that has to do with different cultures is what attracts me.) Nancy went on to share that she liked learning about Chinese culture and learning to differentiate between cultures; for example, between where she is from Puebla (a central Mexican city) and northern México.

Like Nancy, many of the program's Latinx students were immigrants or from immigrant families, and most of them felt they hardly knew anything about their family's origin country. As one Borane Middle School teacher generalized about the Mexican students,

Our kids really know nothing about Mexico. Their grandparents lived there, and that's it, that's all they know. We get them to interview a family member in this past year and write a paper about it, and a lot of them interviewed either a parent or a grandparent who either was born in México or currently lives in México. . . . Then they go, like, "Ms., did you know that—'whatever town' is like known for avocados—they are like the number one avocado producer in México?" and I was like, "Cool." They were getting excited.

Through activities like these, Latinx students learned about their family and ancestral homelands. More generally, the program offered all students the idea that "Latino culture" comprises the cultures from Latin America.

CONSTRUCTING LATINX AS INTERNATIONAL

Just as the Hispanic Community Center's portraits of Rigoberta Menchú and Violeta Parra sent an implicit message that "Latinx" encompasses people who lived in Latin America, the dual-language program also propagated the idea that Latinxs are from elsewhere. The program presented "Latino cultures" as from specific Spanish-speaking countries, as something from *outside* the United States. By primarily highlighting cultures outside of the United States, the program positioned Latinx culture as perpetually foreign, despite Latinxs having an established history in the United States that spans generations.[2] While recognizing and celebrating the accomplishments of Latin America does not necessarily negate or undermine the presence and history of Latinx individuals in the United States, it does present the term "Latinx" as if it transcends time and context, and as if it is legible in Latin America in the same ways as it is here in the United States.

One way the program reinforced the perception of the Latinx category as international was through its curriculum. Because of the lack of Spanish-language materials for high school bilingual programs, teachers resorted to using materials from other Spanish-dominant countries. For example, César, a twelfth-grade Latino who wanted to be a scientist, shared learning about magic realism and that it came from Colombia. He mentioned he really appreciated readings that were originally in Spanish (not translated). As we continued to chat, César shared that he liked these texts because it was important to be "perfectly bilingual." He subscribed to the idea of the ideal Spanish speaker as someone without an accent—as someone like the Spanish speakers in Latin America.

But focusing on Spanish meant also including Spain, which many students saw as having the correct, or at least the most prestigious, version of the language. In an activity in Ms. Thomson's Spanish language arts class, she asked her ninth graders to write on a poster board which languages they thought were the most correct ones. Students mostly said the original (from Spain) was the better and more correct one (as compared with varieties from Latin America). Ms. Thomson explained that Spaniards had set up the Royal Spanish Academy (RSA) to police the Spanish language. (She did not mention that Spain was a colonial power and imposed the Spanish language on people, or that elite Spaniards had set up the RSA to prevent the "uncivilized" Indigenous languages from corrupting their Spanish language.[3]) The students' faces expressed dislike of this "language policing"; but Jeff, an outspoken White student, argued that it was proper for Spaniards to keep their language original.

The perception of European Spanish as the correct version was subtly reinforced by district hiring practices. The district recruited teachers from Spain to address the lack of bilingual teachers for the dual-language program.[4] Few teachers or students critiqued this practice of hiring Spaniards to teach (and correct) Latinx students' Spanish. Most did not see a problem with this practice because, like César, they wanted the program to teach "correct Spanish." For example, Nancy, who was taking the AP Spanish Literature course, compared Mexican Spanish to that of Spain. She shared that, "dicen que el español de España es el original," (they say that the Spanish from Spain is the original) and went on to say one of her teachers was from Spain and his Spanish "obvio que está bien" (obviously it's correct).

But Ms. Nader objected:

> They bring people in from Spain, which to me doesn't reflect the cultural background of any of the students in the program. And also was, like, all the way from Spain when you have all of these people here in Oakville who could be doing that.

Ms. Nader ended by adding that the district "should be hiring Latino teachers." Her critique also revealed that she did not see Spaniards as Latinxs.

Other teachers also challenged the idealization of Spain's version of Spanish and were conscientious about including different Spanishes. For example, Ms. Schloss showed the dramatic movie *Walkout*, based on the 1968 Chicano school walkouts. She chose the film to expose students to Chicano Spanish and struggles. But she admitted to feeling torn about showing the film because of the amount of English it contained, which went against the dual-language model of doing all instruction in Spanish. To still commit to immersing students in Spanish, she showed the film with Spanish subtitles. Although Ms. Schloss and other teachers were thoughtful about including different Spanishes from Latin America, this film was the only instance I observed of including Chicano Spanish. And no one described Spanish as an American language.[5] For the most part, the program propagated the idea of internationalizing Latinx by framing Spanish as from Spain and Latin America and focusing more on these regions while giving less attention to Latinx literature and history, such as the Chicana/o Movement and the Puerto Rican Young Lords.

This was especially evident with the AP Spanish Literature and Culture course, which for some culminated the dual-language program's Spanish courses. The materials that students had to review in preparation for the AP exam mostly included works by writers from Spain and Latin America. The teacher, Ms. Cander, a White woman, described the reading list like this: "There's a lot of countries represented, Spain a little bit more heavily than the others but probably only because there's a longer history of written literature from Spain." The list reinforced the idea that Spain has a more extensive Spanish-language written history than Latin America, disregarding which is more extensive in the modern era or more relevant/meaningful to students today. Additionally, the course included only three texts out of forty that originated from Latinxs—Tomás Rivera, a Chicano from Texas; Julia de Burgos, a Puerto Rican independence advocate; and Sabine Ulibarrí, a New Mexican poet. The implied message was that the Latinx literature and culture worth studying, worth sharing, is from elsewhere, specifically Latin America and Spain. Propagating an international image of Latinx, constructing its culture and language as from outside of the United States, framed Latinxs as perpetual foreigners or at least immigrants.[6]

PORTRAYING "LATINX" AS IMMIGRANT . . .

While the dual-language program affirmed Latinx culture, it did so by conveying an idea of Latinxs as immigrants, even though most of Oakville's Latinxs were born in the United States (>65 percent). One way the program transmitted the idea was how it filled the English-dominant spots in the elementary schools. Oakville's non-Latinx families (that is, the White students who comprised 43 percent of the district) also vied with English-dominant Latinx students for the English-dominant spots. The program's practices did not give preference to English-dominant Latinxs, even though about two-thirds of the district's Latinxs spoke English "only" or "very well."[7] Consequently, White students, being the majority in the district, received most of those spots.

For the program's Spanish-dominant spots, the program targeted Latinx students labeled as English language learners, who mostly were immigrants or from immigrant families. I noticed this overrepresentation of immigrants in the program's Latinx population in my informal classroom conversations with students. For example, whenever I did not get a chance to introduce myself to a new class I was observing, a student would ask me "¿De dónde eres?" (Where are you from?) After answering, I would return the question. The majority of the program's Latinx students identified as Mexican immigrants (or Mexican American). I also met a couple of students in each class who identified with a combination of heritages. For example, a student told me, "Mi papá es cubano y mi mamá dominicana y ecuatoriana." (My dad is Cuban, and my mom is Dominican and Ecuadorian.) I met students with a parent from Colombia, El Salvador, Venezuela, Honduras, or a combination, and a student who was born in Guatemala and adopted as a baby by White parents.

Along with the program's composition implicitly constructing Latinx as an immigrant category, RedRock politics also conveyed that one of the defining issues for the Latinx community was immigration. Latinx activists organized rallies calling attention to RedRock's anti-immigrant proposal, which was very similar to Arizona's "Show-me-your-papers" law.[8] In my interview with Andrea, she mentioned feeling that the program really made kids socially aware of and care about society's injustices. She noted as an example the protest for the Day Without Immigrants and added that the program's teachers and students were sensitive to the proposed policies and choose to rally against them. Thus, the program emphasized and cultivated social awareness about issues of immigration and the Spanish language.

. . . AND WHAT THIS IMPLIED ABOUT LATINXS AND RACE

The idea of "Latinx as immigrant" influenced how people viewed Latinxs in relation to race and racism. For starters, whenever I asked students to recall any lessons on race and racism, I noticed a peculiar pattern. Several students associated my question with Black/African Americans (similarly to Kiara's observations in the last chapter that they learned about "slavery and the underground railroad"). Susana, a program graduate who identified as "mixed race" Asian American/Latina), replied, "I feel like we talked about

these kinds of issues more in elementary school than middle and high school."
When I asked her why she thought this was the case, she explained:

> I remember in elementary school, we learned about Martin Luther King's
> Day and learned about the civil rights, and continuously through elemen-
> tary school to high school, we would learn about different cultures, differ-
> ent components of culture, but I don't think we ever really specifically
> talked about racism or microaggressions or anything like that. At least
> I don't remember.

César also mentioned learning "about Rosa Parks, and everyone learns
about the civil rights movement." When I followed up by asking whether he
had learned about race and racism regarding Latinxs—or example, Chicanx
history—he replied, "The only thing we did was the immigrants that were
protesting in California" (referring to the United Farm Workers movement
and strike in the 1960s). Other students also mentioned learning about the
immigration protests. For example, Jada shared learning, "about different
movements, people trying to get into the US."

These exchanges implied that students associated race and racial issues
with Black/African Americans. The program's lessons about social justice and
Latinxs frequently portrayed Latinxs as immigrants or the perpetual foreigner
group who dealt with immigration and language issues. The emphasis was
largely limited to these two concerns, even though the Latinx community also
faces other social issues, including discrimination in unequal school financing, lack of housing access, and incarceration, which also play a significant
role in determining the type of educational opportunities available to Latinxs.

REJECTING THE INTERNATIONAL FOCUS

Some students noticed this idealized international or immigrant image, an
image which contributed to some students feeling alienated. I noticed this
with David, a Latino/White ninth grader, who described himself in his interview as "probably really weird, maybe a little annoying" and who "didn't
really have any friends, [pause] like, one friend." David's mom, a Latina
(David's father is White), shared with me that she had enrolled David in dual
language because she wanted him to know Spanish, unlike her.

In his interview, David was one of the few students who shared that the
program did not teach about race or racism at all. His answer puzzled me
because I had been visiting the program's courses for almost a year and a half
and had witnessed such lessons. To better understand his ideas, I asked about

social justice issues more generally. David expressed not really seeing the Latin American issues and culture as connected to or affecting him. He recalled learning in ninth-grade dual-language Spanish about social classes in Cuba, but quickly added that the teacher "didn't trace it back to 'This happens in the US' . . . She didn't really connect it to, 'Oh yeah, we have that in the US, and it might affect us this way and this way.'" He then shared he would have liked learning about political issues in the United States: "We talk about an issue going on in Nicaragua. It's not like I live there, so it's not like it affects me." He then explained that contemporary US culture issues were something he "definitely" would have liked to learn more about "'cuz it's something that's going on right now in our society, and I think it's important to learn more about it."

In addition to the program constructing Latinxs as foreigners/immigrants, which David seemed to reject, imagining Latinx as international raised other problems. First, people from Latin America do not refer to themselves as "Latino/Hispanic." Usually, they refer to themselves by their country of origin, and/or perhaps to their region, city, and/or Indigenous group. So unless they come to the United States (and Miguel Hidalgo, Pablo Neruda, Violeta Parra, etc. never immigrated to the United States), they are not socialized into the US category of Latinx/Hispanic.

This first point is the case because of the second point: racialization is a context-dependent process. The idea that race is historically, legally, and socially constructed in a particular context means that Americans' understandings of race and the various racialized groups are not always shared by people in Latin America. The countries of Latin America have their own histories, legacies, and social constructions of racialization. This difference is exemplified by Guatemala's Ladino (non-Indigenous) category, a racial category that is not used in the United States. Of course, the movement of people and media leads to changing ideas that influence both their new and original locations. However, this does not mean that these ideas are adopted in the same manner or carry identical meanings.[9] Therefore, using "Latinx" to describe the people in Latin America *imposes* the racial category Latinx onto them without the category being an organizing label in that context. Moreover, even if individuals in Latin America were to use the term "Latinx," it would carry different meanings there.

IS LATINX AN ETHNICITY OR A RACE?

Other lessons also illustrated how individuals tried to make sense of race vis-à-vis Latinxs. Ms. Lucas conducted one of these lessons. She wanted to address the lack of understanding of the diversity in the Latinx community and an anti-Black comment in her classroom. Ms. Lucas organized a panel of speakers to talk about Afro-Latinxs. After the panel, she talked with her students about Afro-Latinxs and asked them, "*Is* race actually a real thing? Or is it ethnicity?" Ms. Lucas wanted students to understand that Latinxs have a vast variety of cultural practices and that this was what was real and that race was not biologically real. She later mentioned to me that she aimed to talk about race from a scientific perspective and the social perspective as a construct. She was pleased that "the kids were like 'okay'—they got the idea."

When I asked Andrea about what the panel's lesson taught her about race and Latinxs, she replied, "I think it would be more specific to use 'ethnic identity' or something along those lines." Like Ms. Schloss's ethnic-studies lesson on the differences between race and ethnicity, Ms. Lucas's panel to address anti-Black ideas conveyed the notion that Latinx is an ethnicity. But doing a panel with Afro-Latinxs and talking about race made it seem as if, once "Afro-" was prefixed to "Latinx," it became a racial term. In other words, the "Afro-/Black" pertained to race and "Latinx" to ethnicity. Ms. Lucas and Ms. Schloss taught that race was a social construct and that Latinx was an ethnicity, but it was unclear whether Latinx was also a racial category and whether ethnicity was also socially constructed. Like its teachers and the US discourse, the program offered inconsistent teachings about whether Latinx is a race.

When I mentioned learning about "race and racism" in interviews, people usually shifted to talking about Black/African Americans, sometimes mentioning Afro-Latinxs. Estefania, a seventh-grade Latina, shared learning from Ms. Lucas' panel:

> That there's different races, like African American, Afro-Latino, and if you're Afro-Latino, then you can't just be identified as one—that you're Afro-Latino, you're not just Latino or African American. And that if you don't like how people are treating you, that you have to speak up, and you have to tell them that if they offend you by your race, that that's called racism and you can call someone on it, because that's not really being respectful to the person.

She continued sharing that they learned "not [to] judge people just by their race." While Estefania listed "Afro-Latino" and "African American" as races, her answer was less clear about whether Latinx was a race.

Others in the program shared Estefania's noncommitment, but this uncertainty did not deter people from listing White, Black, and Latinx within the same category system. For example, when talking about the advantages of the dual-language model, Mrs. Teresa, a mother and school volunteer who identified as Mexican/Latina and said her race was "raza humana" (human race), shared:

> Me gusta la idea de unir a los muchachos para que ellos aprendan a convivir con otras razas, y que no sea una cuestión separada porque tenemos suficiente de eso en nuestra sociedad. . . . Había en el salón de mi hijo, muchachos afroamericanos, blancos y latinos; afroamericanos muy pocos, muy pocos, la mayoría son blancos. (I like the idea of integrating the kids so that they learn to live with other races, and that it's not a separate thing, because we already have a lot of that in our society. . . . In my son's classroom, there were African American, White, and Latino kids; very few African Americans, very few, the majority were White.)

Praising the program's racial diversity was a repeated narrative that included Latinxs (compare this to the graduation speeches, described in the preface, that mentioned the school's diversity as a strength).

While some of the program's teachings painted Latinx as an ethnicity, teachers and students also categorized Latinxs along with the racial categories Black, White, and Asian. For example, when Ms. Íñiguez told me that she did not think the program should teach about race, she explained that when she forms class groups, "Yo nunca me fijo si está un blanco, un morenito, un latino y un asiático." (I never check whether there's a White, Black, Latino, or Asian.) For example, when talking about student discipline, Britney, a White student, shared:

> There was a group of Black students that I distinctly remember in high school social studies class, who they seemed to be in trouble a lot. . . . And our classroom layout was that like that group and they were in the corner, and then students who paid attention generally White students with like a few Latino students.

This example listing Latinx along with other racialized groups shows how people discursively implied they understood Latinx as a racialized group, despite lessons teaching that Latinx was an ethnicity. Yet when I asked people explicitly whether Latinx was a race, some people hesitated, at times because of the idea that race was indicated by skin color.

RACE AS SKIN COLOR

One of the most telling interviews about how the program helped students make sense (or not) about race and Latinxs was in my second interview with Mia. Mia identified as "half Black and half Serbian," a gifted writer who loved learning about politics. I reached out to Mia and other participants who were still in the program to ask about their experiences six years after my initial study. Mia, who was now a dual-language twelfth grader, enthusiastically agreed to participate. In our video chat, I quickly recognized her, always smiling and now wearing her hair in a short Afro. She happily told me that upon graduating high school in a few months, she would attend a very elite private university in a coastal state.

I asked Mia, "Can you tell me about a time in the program when you think that the program was teaching you how to be socially conscious or to be aware of injustices?" Mia mentioned learning in her ethnic-studies course about "different ethnic groups and how they fought against racism." She then added that the course "definitely focused on the social construct." This struck me because "the social construct" did not seem connected, so I followed up by asking what that meant. She answered, "I would say gender, race, etc. Those things about how race was invented, and it's not really a thing, if that makes sense. It's not ethnicity."

Intrigued, I asked her, "So if it's not scientific and it's like invented, did you get into what it was? What is race?" She answered, "Yeah, more so what ethnicity is, more so, is what we focused on, that race is just the color of your skin, although it's not really a scientific thing, because, I mean, I don't know." Even though Mia added, "I don't know," she exuded confidence. She later continued, "It's the color of your skin versus your ethnicity. Like, it's 'Oh, I'm Latino,' or something like that, versus, 'Oh, I'm the color of my skin.'" Mia went on to detail that ethnicity had to do with the regions, family tree, and cultures, and she mentioned different Latinx cultures and that "it's super diverse." Her answers seemed to indicate that Mia saw Latinxs as an ethnicity.

Later in the interview, when I asked Mia, without mentioning Latinxs, if the differences between race and ethnicity made sense to her, she asserted, "Yes, it does, because there's no way someone can tell me that someone Latino is White. I don't believe in that. Yeah, it's literally just the color of your skin and it's not even, I don't know. But yeah." This time, Mia's hesitation and expression showed she was not so confident now. I knew she had Latinx classmates of different complexions, some who could pass as White. Yet Mia would not label these Latinxs as White, even though she saw race as about skin tone and that some Latinxs are as fair-skinned as some White folks.

When I verified whether I understood correctly that she did not see Latinxs as White, she quickly affirmed,

> No, I don't. I mean, if you're very White passing, I guess if you want to consider yourself as that, go ahead, but if you're, someone's my skin tone, no, I don't think, I don't see that person as a White person at all.

Thinking about her answers, considering how adamantly she repeated "race is literally just the color of your skin," I kept wondering, if race is indeed about skin tone, then how did she make sense of some fair-skinned Latinxs not being White? But I thought of taking an indirect tack.

Mia identified as "half Black and half Serbian," the latter she preferred to White because, as she explained, her mom was more European than American and no one was technically the color white. In sixth grade, for instance, she referred to a "peach friend" instead of a "White friend." I decided to ask Mia whether Black and Serbian were races or ethnicities or both or something else, her tone became contemplative:

> I would say Black is more so, [pause] I probably wouldn't say Serbian's a race because that's not considered a race in papers at all. More so Black. But then also Black is African American, and Serbian are my ethnicities as well. But usually whenever someone sees me, they think that I'm just Black, or sometimes when I speak Spanish, think I'm like Puerto Rican or Cuban or something like that.

The more Mia tried to make sense of race and ethnicity and the categories, the more puzzled she seemed to become. Perhaps feeling uncomfortable with the questions or from not feeling her usual confident self, she then changed the topic by returning to a previous question, sharing with me that she learned about Argentina's Dirty War in ninth grade.

AN AMALGAMATION FROM ALL CULTURES

In the end of the interview, I asked, "What does the dual-language program teach about what it is to be Latino?" She replied:

> That you don't have to confine to one box. It teaches that to be Latino is very diverse. You have your own experiences. You are a person that has gone through a lot and is very strong. You have a lot of culture. There's a lot of different parts of you, and that it's a community. It's really a community, is what I would say.

Mia's description could describe other ethnicities or racialized groups— Black, Asian American, and so on. So then, what does the program offer as specifically Latinx?

Many participants in my study equated Latinx with ethnicity, an amalgamation from all cultures from Latin America, without specifying Latinx cultural practices. While individuals expressed that Latinx was an ethnicity because of some common cultural practices, they were vague about what those practices were. This confluence of broad, undefined cultural references paradoxically points to why Latinx is more aptly understood as a racialized category, rather than just an ethnic one.[10]

People like Ms. Lucas and Ms. Nader recognized that it did not make sense that Latinxs would all share the same cultural practices. It is simply not the case that people from a region so vast would immigrate here and then adopt the same cultural practices.[11] In other words, Latinxs, like other racialized groups, also have diversity in cultural and linguistic differences. Although ethnic categories could serve the purpose of determining in- and out-groups, they do not have to be used in such a way. Racialization was invented to oppress, which racialized Others can then resist.

COMPLICATING INCONGRUENCIES

Apart from her own identity and perspective, Mia had a dissimilar curricular-program experience compared to some of her dual-language classmates. First, because the Ethnic Studies course was an elective, dual-language students had the option to take it *or* Latin American Studies (the courses alternated years). Unlike Mia, students rarely took both, meaning that about half of the program's juniors and seniors took the Ethnic Studies elective. Second, almost half of the dual-language students dropped the program before even taking any of these elective courses.[12] Thus many students who participated in the program would not have ever had a course dedicated to discussing race and ethnicity in the way Mia had. From the rest of my study (and verified by my second interview with Mia), that course, thanks to Ms. Schloss, was the program's structural attempt at providing its students with curricular opportunities for challenging dominant ideas about race.

Despite the dissimilar experiences, Mia's ideas provide insight into what the dual-language program taught about race through its attempts to challenge dominant racial ideas. These insights extend to showing how race is connected to the Latinx category and reveal some incongruencies stemming from these teachings. For example, while scholars understand race as unstable and contextual, the program did not emphasize that people made sense of the race concept itself differently throughout time and place. That is not to say that non-US-based racial categories were not brought up. The ethnic studies course touched on colonial Latin American mestizaje and mestizo as a category, yet none of my participants mentioned mestizo as a category in our society. Still, the program imparted the idea that race was a constant category based on looks.[13] For instance, when Mia talked about some of the lessons on race in her Latin American studies elective, she reflected:

> There's a lot of diversity in Latin America. Not everybody looks the same, not everybody's the same race. There's Indigenous people inside of Latin America. They have their own languages compared to just Spanish or Portuguese. . . . We learned, "Hey, it's really diverse" and stuff like that. But I say that was a more implicit approach of race and stuff like that.

Mia's observation again shows that the program reinforced the notion that race is about "looks," an idea shared by the other participants. Additionally, race was more of a constant category based on physical characteristics than a context-based unstable category that is not interpreted everywhere through skin color, as social scientists have shown.[14] Teachers and students did not discuss the concept of race and the racial categories as different and changing depending on the context's histories and discourses.[15] What was constant was the idea of defining "race as skin color," which repeatedly circulated in the program.

Still, this stability created incoherence in how Mia then understood Latinx vis-à-vis race. Based on lessons she took from the program, she adamantly viewed Latinxs as not White because Latinxs faced discrimination. Mia described Latinx more like an ethnicity and saw race as about skin color. But she did not sort Latinxs under another racialized category, such as White, based on skin color. Thus making sense of race as skin color left her unclear about how to make sense of the Latinx category. So settled was the idea that race was skin color that it was not possible to consider it as something more than just skin color. Indeed, the incongruities Mia experienced manifested from reducing race to skin color and might be alleviated by concluding that race is not about skin color and thinking of Latinx as a racialized group.

"IQ AND INTELLIGENCE . . . A GENETIC FACTOR"

While most participants generally shared that Latinx was an ethnicity, some did suggest the dominant narrative of having different biological groups—

races. For example, in a conversation about why not all the Latinx students were doing well in the program despite the program being *for* Latinxs, Mr. Clarke, a White man and a Borane science teacher, opined that parents' lack of intelligence caused differences in achievement. He explained, "I don't know if IQ and intelligence and that sort of thing is got a genetic factor where maybe the parents themselves, and I'm not saying it's all IQ or not, but maybe they themselves." I stayed silent, so Mr. Clarke continued by comparing Latinx and White families. He elaborated that Latinx parents come from

> a pretty low educational background. Are [youth] getting a message at home like . . . "You can work for me, you don't need [school]." It's kind of a complacent attitude. . . . I don't think the parents themselves really even have parenting theory . . . We need to do more parent outreach and kind of teaching of the parents about how to be parents. This is a contrast between some of the really overachieving type of White families.

Most dual-language teachers did not voice this type of racist, deficit opinion so explicitly. Mr. Clarke did not hesitate in racializing Latinxs by implying a shared "genetic factor" that affects IQ, invoking the biological idea of race. Given that his Latinx students had different complexions, his comments exhibit ideas about race and Latinxs that contradict the simplistic idea of race being about skin tone and appearance. They indicate how his conception of race derives from not only a false biological basis but is also being linked to culture as a proxy for race. In the end, the program did not escape the racist idea of racialized intelligence (more on this in chapter 5).

TEACHING LATINX AS ETHNICITY, DISCRIMINATING LATINX AS A RACE

A few teachers (three out of the thirteen participating in the study) regularly included lessons that challenged dominant ideas of race and racism and that went beyond "racism exists, racism is wrong." While I have described mostly explicit lessons about race from Ms. Lucas and Ms. Schloss, most of the dual-language-program teachers' lessons taught about race implicitly (as I share in other chapters). What was an explicit and regular topic for most teachers was anti-Latinx discrimination.

When students mentioned learning about Latinx culture, their examples were often embedded in a lesson on the discrimination Latinxs faced here in the United States. For example, in an English language arts dual-language course, the students watched the film *Precious Knowledge*, about the struggle to save Tucson's Mexican American Studies (MAS) program. Mia, then a sixth-grade student, shared in an interview that she felt annoyed that the MAS program was attacked because it was "just teaching more of their culture they might not know."

While discrimination could be based on ethnic prejudice, linguicism, nationalism, classism, sexism, and other -isms, people in the United States usually make sense of discrimination through a race lens.[16] The dual-language program also espoused the idea that Latinxs experienced being targets of racism. This is what Mia meant by saying, "There's no way someone can tell me that someone Latino is White. I don't believe in that." Mia did not have to reach far for examples of Latinxs suffering from discrimination or of people framing Latinxs as inferior to Whites, another racialized group. For example, the anti-Latinx, anti-immigrant bill proposed by some right-wing politicians in RedRock was a clear example to teachers and students that Latinxs suffered racism.

Although the program's participants described Latinx as an ethnicity and a community sharing history, culture, and values, the existence of and the program's focus on anti-Latinx discrimination led participants like Mia to perceive Latinx as a race, even amid the differences in skin color and appearance among Latinx individuals. That is, in the program focusing on anti-Latinx racism, the program (although inadvertently) gestured toward the idea that racism is what forms a racialized group. More specifically, the racism directed toward Latinxs, and its subsequent anti-racism, creates the Latinx racialized group. But by the program leaving this unsaid, by not teaching about the racialization process, people's dissonance defaulted Latinx into being labeled an ethnicity and the program missed an opportunity to denaturalize racial groups. Additionally, the program's emphasis on Latinx as an ethnicity and on culture and Spanish as points of pride mirrored the approach multiculturalism takes in teaching about race. This hindered the program advancing critical-racial consciousness about the nefarious aspects of race.

RACISM CREATES THE LATINX RACIALIZED GROUP

Students like Andrea and Mia learned that biological race did not exist or, as Andrea put it, "scientifically it means 'the human race.'" Instead, the program mostly taught race as an identity and about skin color and phenotype. With this focus on race as an identity, the program mostly supported seeing the racialized groups as a given, not emphasizing race as an imposed category. And with the program's focus on Latinx culture, it taught the Latinx group as an ethnicity. Despite this, participants were clear about putting the group in relation to those understood to be racialized groups. But even though people discursively placed the Latinx group along with other racialized groups, the program's reinforcement of race as skin color led to the impossibility of seeing "Latinx" as a racialized category.[17] Making sense of race vis-à-vis the Latinx category would have meant expanding beyond constructing race as skin color or an inherent characteristic.

The program focused heavily on anti-Latinx racism, a focus that is justified and needed. Indeed, it squares with historical and social science scholarship, which demonstrates that *racism*—not skin color and appearance, not biological lineage—*creates racialized groups*.[18] (I purposefully did not write "racism created race" because, as I explained in the introduction, I find it helpful to use "racialized groups," which has the added benefit of highlighting that this is a *process* done to a *group*.) Rather, by imposing discriminatory and oppressive practices on a group that is thought to be a human lineage, racism makes the racialized group. Racialized Others can also fight this oppression with others in their group, thus reinforcing the group's affinity.[19]

The program needed to expose students to learning that race does not originate from phenotype in order to recognize Latinx as a racialized group. Instead, the program's discussions and practices ambivalently framed "Latinx" as a racialized group. I deliberately describe it as "ambivalently" because the program presented both concurrent and conflicting notions when it came to conceiving Latinx as a racialized category in comparison to more traditionally recognized races like "White" or "Black." This ambiguity stems from the program's failure to adequately introduce the idea that society constructs racialized groups through racist practices—racism. The program taught "race" as if there are human groups that were naturally formed or invented due to certain markers, such as features indicating Asian heritage.

What would that marker be for Latinxs? In other words, since Latinx is a racialized group, what delineates Latinx as apart from other racialized groups? How did the program contribute to delineating the Latinx racialized category apart from other racialized categories?

In the next section, we turn to how the program contributed to the *relational* aspect of the process of racialization, the construction and positioning of racialized groups in relation to others.

PART II

Making Latinidad

CHAPTER 3

Our Relations

Ms. West, a White teacher at Borane, was warm and caring toward students, and she worked to provide them with a culturally relevant curriculum with rigorous activities. The dual-language program, as a strand program within both schools, mostly followed the rest of the school's curriculum, which promoted multiculturalism. But Ms. West and a few dual-language teachers strove to go against the grain and sought out materials that would enhance students' critical consciousness. Ms. West put in this extra effort even though she recognized that as an English language arts teacher, the district already provided more curricular materials than it did to her dual-language colleagues who taught other subjects. It was Ms. West's mastery in designing units that both addressed the standards and interested her students that made me, like many of her students, enjoy going to her class.

One of the days that I visited Ms. West's English-language-arts class, her sixth graders were studying a unit on Greek myths. The students animatedly talked and took notes on a graphic organizer about Zeus and Cronos and on a synopsis of the story of Prometheus (who gave humans fire). They were preparing to read the story of Pandora.

While the students read, Ms. West approached me and said that she was really impressed by their interest in these stories. I replied that I shared the students' interest, origin stories having always intrigued me. She added that she wished the curriculum included stories from Native American cultures so they could compare the various cultures' perspectives on fire. Her comment gave me the sense that she noted the curriculum's Eurocentricity and felt she had not put her usual extra effort of curricular supplementing for this unit. Ms. West's regret suggested she was conscious of the curriculum's explicit exclusion but lacked the structural support—for example, time to find materials and develop activities—to challenge mainstream schooling that implicitly lifts some knowledges over others.

Absences in the curriculum convey ideas about race and racialized groups and also hinder the envisioning of alternative pedagogies. One such alternative could involve inviting students to explore different stories of fire from RedRock's contemporary Indigenous nations. This would teach students about the original caretakers of the land where their school, home, and city were settled. Learning about Indigenous knowledges of fire could also prompt discussions about humans' responsibility toward our planet, especially in the context of climate change. The unit could also have asked students for their family's stories about the creation of or humans' relationship to fire. Such an exercise could broaden their understanding of these stories or expand their ideas of what "Native" means, for some Latinx students (the majority group in the class) were from Indigenous groups. (While the schools did not collect information to determine the number of Latinxs with Indigenous ancestry, the program's students where mostly from México and Central America, which have more immigrants from Indigenous backgrounds compared with, for example, Cuba.[1])

Ms. West did not mention to me that some of her Latinx students were Indigenous. But had she considered them as Indigenous, perhaps the curricular absence of a Native American perspective about fire's origin could have been addressed by exploring Latinxs' Indigeneity. Not seeing Latinxs' Indigeneity, I add, is exactly one of the functions of racialization: to group people into a category without regard to how they associate themselves in terms of cultural practices, furthering the colonialist project of erasing Indigeneity. Thus—without intending to do so—schools make race: they perpetuate our society's racialization. Of course, disconnecting Latinxs from Indigeneity is not exclusive to the way teachers are teaching; rather, it speaks to US schools being a racial project meant to erase Indigeneity.

Disconnecting people from their Indigeneity is part and parcel of three projects—colonialism, imperialism, and racism—that share in ignoring people's cultural practices, severing their connection and responsibility to nature and others, and making their knowledge less known and valued by themselves and others.[2] Simply put, these three projects attempt to break people's healthy relations with the natural and human world. In restricting how people relate to the land and to others, they also restrain who people can be and how they can act in a future world.[3] As racist projects disconnect people from the natural and human world, they construct racialized groups in relation to other groups.

This chapter shows how the dual-language program offered teachings and ideas to make Latinidad, and how it made Latinidad in relation to other racialized categories. We begin by learning about the curriculum's teachings about Indigenous peoples and how the program relates Latinidad to Indigeneity and to Asianness. I point out curricular absences, inferring how these demonstrate how teachers discursively (and through their pedagogy) made and positioned Latinxs in relation to other groups. I then move to how the Spanish language was used to relate to other Latinxs, that is to bind the Latinx group, and we begin to see how the program reinforced the Spanish language as the signature boundary that delineates the Latinx racialized group.

"LEARNING ABOUT THE AZTECS AND INCAS SINCE SIXTH GRADE"

As Ms. West's classroom scene suggests, the dual-language program did not explicitly guide students in thinking about or connecting to their Indigeneity. I did not observe the program calling attention to the schools being on Indigenous land occupied by settler descendants of English and other European colonizers. I rarely heard mention of the Indigenous peoples who were displaced and racialized.[4] These absences helped to construct Latinidad as mutually exclusive from Indigeneity and as separate from the natural world. They also reminded me of my own education, having to learn as an adult that I grew up in the traditional homelands and unceded territories of the Tohon' O'odham Nation and of the Chiricahua Apache Nation, and having to learn as an adult how to learn about my relations and responsibility to the natural world.

One approach through which the program's curriculum and instruction addressed Indigenous peoples was by exploring Latin America and providing lessons about Indigenous civilizations, particularly focusing on the Aztec and Inca empires.

Students like Kiara, a Black tenth grader, recalled learning about the Aztec and Inca civilizations repeatedly throughout the program (see chapter 1). She shared:

> I like learning about it, but I just dislike how it's redundant. Like I said before, we've been learning about the Aztecs and Incas since sixth grade. Not that—it doesn't bore me. It's just, "Oh, class, we're going to learn about this." And it's again, "Oh. Going through what I already know." . . . It gets a little irritating at times.

From my informal conversations with two dual-language history teachers, I gathered that teachers chose to teach about these two groups because of the availability of materials for lessons and that these civilizations were important in Latin American history. As a teacher who had taught similar history lessons, I recognized their answers as ones I would also give. I now imagine, although the teachers did not phrase it this way, that these empires are well known, perhaps considered more important than others, because they are associated with being conquered by Spanish conquistadores. Unfortunately, one implicit message the lessons conveyed was that the Indigenous groups worth studying (that we know more about) were those who were consequential to European invaders. Another implied message was that Latinxs' connection to Indigenous people was of the distant past and through colonization.

Along with teachers, students connected this past when talking about present-day Latinxs. For example, when I asked twelfth grader Mia, "What are some of the things that you think the program teaches about what Latinos have in common?" She responded,

> I would have to say the history of things that happened with the colonization, how that happened. Then also the Indigenous cultures. . . . I think that [the program] teaches how connected Latin America is; although it's super diverse, there's so many connections and how many things you guys have been through together.

The program's Latin American Studies elective did help students like Mia appreciate the connections of other Indigenous cultures, even though less time was spent on studying Indigenous cultures relative to other history and culture. Mia described learning about Indigenous people through a group project:

> We had to talk in our groups to make posters and stuff like that. We made posters about Indigenous tribes back in Latin America.

She continued describing the project:

> My group was Las Olmecas. So we learned about how they were the mother culture of the Mayans, how many technological advances they had. They're a pretty big agricultural Indigenous group.

These lessons expanded students' image of Indigenous peoples beyond just the rest of the program's repeated focus on the Aztecs and Incas. Including them earlier in the program might have allowed more time to bring up diverse groups and connect to the present.

These types of lessons, especially coupled with the curriculum emphasizing the Aztecs and Incas, had students associate Latinxs with an Indigenous past that hardly featured present-day Indigenous peoples. Compared to the school's regular curriculum, the program's curriculum was attentive to the diversity within the Latinx group. Yet it was still inadequate in acknowledging thriving contemporary Indigenous communities in the US, such as the Maya, P'urhépecha, and Zapotec. Only one teacher ever mentioned in passing to me that a couple of her Latinx students in the program were speakers of Indigenous languages (and of course, some Latinx students may identify as Indigenous regardless of whether they speak an Indigenous language).[5] Apart from this one comment, my observations suggest the program overlooked present-day Latinx Indigenous peoples.

Instead, the dual-language program's curriculum, discourses, and enrollment practices, as discussed in the previous chapter, framed Latinxs as an immigrant group. Even though Indigenous and immigrant are not mutually exclusive categories, this dominant framing of Latinxs as immigrants thus contributed to making the program's Indigenous Latinx students invisible.[6] Even though the program had many immigrant students, it did not help them engage deeply with their own displacement and settlement. For example, the program did not teach about racialized diasporas being created through ignoring those displaced people's Indigeneity.[7] It did not expose students to issues related to Indigenous sovereignty, for example, or the problems with nation-states imposing borders and migration restrictions on Indigenous Nations.

The repetitive lessons "since sixth grade" about the Aztecs and Incas showed that teachers lacked structural support. This support could include a sequenced curriculum that scaffolds Latinx and Black students' critical consciousness, rather than repeating a multicultural celebration.[8] For example, a structured curriculum for high school could guide teachers to traverse more advanced topics such as settler colonialism or the myth of mestizaje.[9] It could lead students to learn that many people come in relation to each other via colonial ways of thinking and identifying others.[10] Lessons could engage students in learning about their (or other people's) Indigenous ways of knowing and being in the world.

Overall, the program's practices and discourses tended to separate Latinidad from Indigeneity, given that the program failed to teach or even acknowledge Indigenous ways of relating to the natural and human world. Furthermore, when certain teachers and students addressed the subject of

Indigenous peoples of Latin America, their portrayals were not always favorable, as illustrated in the following section.

PROBLEMS WITH WATER

From the first week of classes, Mr. Ochoa prepared activities to foster a friendly and respectful community. His dedication and amiability created a caring classroom climate that encouraged productive relationships among students and between students and himself.

At the beginning of Mr. Ochoa's tenth-grade World History period, he announced that the class had a visitor, Rachel, a White dual-language eleventh grader whom most students seemed to recognize. Mr. Ochoa shared that she had requested to share a PowerPoint presentation with the class, and he asked them to welcome her and listen to her presentation. Rachel projected the website of a US-based nonprofit organization. She explained this organization sponsored a competition for funding projects that help women and children in "regions ravaged by war and famine." She had submitted a proposal to travel with a group to educate Guatemalans about the environment and clean water. She explained that her project's goal was to educate about the environment because the Guatemalan people have problems with water. With a slide showing small photos, including Maya women smiling in the background, Rachel finished the presentation by appealing to the class to vote online for her project.

Once the applause quieted, Ochoa praised her for going out and using the Spanish she had learned from the dual-language program to help Latin American countries in need. He shared with the class that he would have loved to have had her social consciousness when he was young. The other students also nodded and seemed impressed with Rachel's plans.

This student presentation was the only example I observed of the dual-language program featuring a contemporary Indigenous group. And it focused on them as needing help. Seeing this lesson about the Maya's water problems along with lessons of the great Olmecas ("the mother culture of the Mayans") makes for a stark contrast. It paints past Indigenous groups as great civilizations while present-day Indigenous peoples need help with procuring their necessities. By presenting some people as useful (Rachel's US organization) compared to others as destitute, the lesson could also hinder some Latinxs from wanting to relate to present-day Indigenous peoples.

Neither the students nor Mr. Ochoa questioned Rachel's plan to engage in this work. The acceptance of the plan and the praise it garnered revealed a gap in the program: students had not been exposed to the well-documented United States' imperialist role in Guatemala's history.[11] Because of this omission, the class failed to link the polluted water issue with European/American imperialism and the corporate exploitation suffered by the Guatemalan people. Mr. Ochoa knew of US interference in Latin America—something he brought up in informal conversations with me—yet I did not see him ever teach about it. No one commented on the problem of Americans' "voluntourism" or the fact that the presentation perpetuated ideas about Indigenous peoples not being able to self-govern. The presentation and the absence of questioning by both the teacher and the class revealed one way the program taught about Indigenous peoples. It also signaled other absences in the curriculum, particularly that the program did not offer lessons for advancing students' critical consciousness about issues related to Indigenous peoples' struggle for sovereignty and their land. All of this contributed to making Latinidad separate in relation to Indigeneity.

While teachers did not acknowledge Indigenous students (Latinx or not), this was not the only group that received scant attention.

"THERE'S NO WAY THERE ARE CHINESE PEOPLE IN TIJUANA!"

Ms. Lucas marveled at what would astonish her eighth graders. She told me how they did not believe some of the new information she would share with them: "They're, like, 'There's no way there are Chinese people in Tijuana [city in northwestern México]!' I was like, 'There *are* Chinese people in Tijuana! There's a whole population of Chinese people!' and they didn't believe me all these things!" (I could relate to the students' surprise; at about their age, I was shocked when I learned from my father that his grandfather—my great-grandfather—was a Chinese immigrant to México. Later as an adult, I learned that northern México, where I grew up, has a long history of immigration from China.) What may be unsurprising to most people was that, besides Ms. Lucas mentioning Asians in Latin America, the program gave little attention to Asian Latinxs.

Susana was the only student in my study who identified as Asian American and Latinx, elaborating, "My mom is Mexican/Mexican American, and my dad is Laotian." Susana described herself as biracial, having a flat nose, long black straight hair, and brown skin darker than people's "idea that Asian people are more fair-skinned." Other program participants assumed she was just Mexican, even though some would comment "that I have Asian-looking eyes." In her dual-language cohort, which was the district's first cohort, there were no other Asian-identifying students. Susana also recalled that people not in the program would ask about who took part in it: "A lot of times when I do say that I'm in dual language, people will also ask about the dynamics between students, 'Is it mostly just Latinos, or are there White students and Black students?'" Individuals did not even ask Susana about Asian Americans; instead, they mostly imagined the dual-language program as having Latinxs, White, and Black students. This image also informed the program's lack of attention to Asian Americans and Asian Latinxs. For example, Susana did not remember any lessons about these groups throughout her whole time in the program.

Teachers spoke about Asian American students differently (and with less frequency—perhaps because the program had only a small number of Asian American students) than they spoke about other racialized groups. First, only three participants mentioned them in our conversations about recruitment/enrollment (it turned out the district did not recruit Asian Americans for the program). While people overlooked the absence of Asian American students, people regularly remarked on the small number of Black students (the next chapter shows there were even comparisons of the "good" Black students in the program versus the non-dual-language Black students).

Second, even though the district had a growing number of students from immigrant families of Southeast Asian descent—such as Hmong students, whose group's lower achievement was a concern—they were not mentioned as missing from or underrepresented in the Spanish-English dual-language program. The community had plans for a Hmong-English dual-language program, which people perhaps saw as a more suitable option for improving that group's achievement. However, the silence also could suggest that educators perceived the *non*-Hmong Asian American students as doing well academically and/or already speaking another language.[12] This makes sense, considering that the problematic assumptions about Asian Americans as model minorities makes them invisible and thus disregards their academic needs and struggles.[13]

Third, and related to the other points, no participants mentioned Asian American students as model minorities in the dual-language program, even though in many contexts, they are viewed as such compared with other racialized Others.[14] Perhaps them not being seen as model minorities was due to their very low representation in the program (most classrooms had none at all).

One similarity in how participants talked about Asian Americans and Black Americans was the exclusion of Latinx from these categories. RedRock's context—the geographic and demographic particularities—contributed to the program's making the racialized categories discrete, providing little room for imagining Asian Latinxs.[15] I never observed teachers talk about Asian Latinxs (or White Latinxs), perhaps because they had even lower numbers than Afro-Latinxs in this school community. The closest approach to the issue was from Ms. Lucas, who, as her interview quote above shows, mentioned teaching students about Asian Mexicans (that is, Asian descendants in México). Thus, even Ms. Lucas's example was not about Asian Latinxs in the United States.

By distinguishing Latinx from Asian and Black (categories that are more commonly perceived as racial), the program gestured toward positioning Latinx as a racial category. As we see next, the program reflected and advanced the idea of binding the Latinx racialized group with the Spanish language.

SPANISH BINDING THE LATINX RACIALIZED GROUP

I often asked participants why they believed the Spanish language mattered for Latinxs. Latinx and non-Latinx participants often mentioned the connection to family and culture; for example, Andrea, who said, "It's our culture." In his reply to the question, César explained,

> It should matter to them because that's where their roots are. That's a big part of their culture if they choose to remain in that part of, if they choose to remain with that identity.

César spoke of language as part of what *makes* the Latinx group, what connects Latinxs to their relations ("roots") and to other Latinxs. Like César, people's coupling of culture and language connected these to identity and relations.

Other participants linked language to individual and group identity. For example, when I asked Mr. Estrada, a Mexican/Chicano Borane teacher, what led him to become a dual-language teacher, he answered, "I've always wanted to work in the Latino community." He added that his parents instilled in him that "Spanish is our language, this is us," and "Language was a big part of identity." Teachers like Mr. Estrada assigned work that helped students think about their connection with the Spanish language.

When I asked Susana why Spanish mattered for Latinxs, she smiled and replied, "I wrote a small essay on this question" for a class assignment. She recalled writing, "For me, the Spanish language has been important, because it has bridged a relationship, a stronger than it would've been relationship with my heritage, where I come from." Susana shared:

I am studying the culture and the language, and I'm immersing myself. And learning about these things has been really important for me, because it's connected me to—it's been important for me because it's a part of who I am, even if it's not directly.

Susana explained that, unlike her cousins who did not know Spanish and had not studied the culture, she had a "different relationship" with her mother's side of the family, "I'm really close to my grandparents." Susana's knowledge of Spanish helped her form close relationships with her Mexican/ Mexican American grandparents. Susana shared that the program helped Latinxs "just stay in contact with your culture and have an understanding of where you come from." Susana, like others, mentioned that her mom had enrolled her in the program because her mom did not learn Spanish, explaining "there weren't a whole lot of Latinos here" when her mom moved to RedRock. Susana and her mom understandably associated knowing their family's language with the ability to connect with their relations, to live in right relations. The dual-language program helped make the Spanish language bind Latinxs to their relations and culture, thus associating the Spanish language with the Latinx group and even with being Latinx.

For students, parents, and teachers, Spanish provided a connection to their family, their family's culture, and "who I am" and "where I come from," which they associated with their Latinx identity. And identity, as we read in chapter 1, was also how people understood race. Participants recognized that Latinxs were racially discriminated against through using language as a tool. For example, Susana noted, "In the past, the traditional way to go about ESL students would be to separate them from White students and to have their own class." Participants saw the dual-language program, which provided students with culturally representative schooling opportunities to develop biliteracy while accessing the regular school's curriculum, as a counter to ESL. But practices like ESL were still widely common, making participants sensitive to Latinxs suffering from language discrimination in schools, which prevented them from benefiting from education and valuing their community, among other challenges.

I certainly relate to the participants' ideas about why the Spanish language matters for Latinxs. As an undergraduate student, I debated between becoming a teacher of Spanish or history, but Arizona's Proposition 203 banning bilingual education focused me on language. Proposition 203 made me view anti-bilingual-education policies as anti-immigrant and as attacks on Latinxs. It emphasized for me that the Spanish language and bilingualism were key sites of political struggles for Latinxs. Choosing to become a teacher of Spanish also made sense to me because I had already believed that for Mexican American and Latinx students like me, maintaining Spanish helped us connect with family and the community.

Linking language to our relations and identity makes sense when we think of how we transmit cultural practices and ideas, through our interactions—through languages—with others in community. It also makes sense that a bilingual education program, with the goal of developing biliteracy and biculturalism, would further tie Latinidad to the Spanish language and a shared culture/biculturalism. Hence, Latinxs (and others) use the Spanish language to define the group, and language discrimination, both in its negative forms (ESL or Proposition 203) and affirmative forms (dual-language education), contributes to forming and binding the Latinx racialized group, marking its boundaries.

While people did not explicitly state that the Spanish language identified (or delineated the boundaries of) the Latinx group, when they spoke of Latinxs, most immediately and directly tied the language to the group. For example, when I asked Nancy what "Latino" was, she replied:

> Hay diferentes latinos, que de Honduras que de El Salvador, que de México, que de [sic], cada uno habla diferente su español, y como ahora que los de Centroamérica también hablan su español pero tienen sus palabras, ellos mismo, que tal vez se las inventan o tal vez sean reales. (There are different Latinos, from Honduras, El Salvador, México; each one speaks their Spanish differently, and now that those from Central America also speak their Spanish but they have words, they themselves, that perhaps they invent or perhaps they are real.)

The program helped students like Nancy expand their idea of what "Spanish" was and relate to different customs. And for students like Susana, it connected them to their relations.

Yet, there was another side to the program's inherent work of marking Latinxs based on Spanish. It essentialized people. By the program reinforcing the Spanish language to delineate "Latinx," the program disregarded Latinxs' Indigenous languages and reinforced contrasts between Latinxs and other racialized groups.

"JUST A BUNCH OF MEXICANS"

Nancy's response also reveals how the program reinforced the Latinx racialized group by lumping its students (Boricuas, Guatemalan Mayans,

Venezuelans) into a category along with others whom they may not have associated with otherwise. The program noted differences in the Latinx category—for example, preferences of food or music—but it still unified the groups based on language and a vague culture in order to offer them a bilingual education. In its work, the dual-language program functioned as a racial project—both to connect Latinxs to their relations *and* to essentialize them into the Latinx racialized group.

Students and teachers outside the program also essentialized (albeit more crudely) Latinxs. For example, some called the Latinxs in the program "Mexican" as the racialized-group epithet instead of "Latino."[16] When David talked about stereotypes of dual-language students, he stated that non-dual-language students presumed the program's students were Mexican: "just that they're Mexicans." He recalled that people would ask him, "'Isn't that more Mexican? Like, Mexicans doing Spanish?' And, 'Oh, you have to be Mexican.'" Non-dual-language students did not know that the program had students from many Latin American heritages (although Mexicans were the majority of Latinxs) and included students who did not identify as Latinx.

Sometime this essentializing descended to racial slurs. Susana recalled a "rivalry" between the elementary non-dual-language school (mostly Black and White) and her dual-language cohort.

> I remember one time at recess, some of the kids got in fights . . . one of the kids from [non-dual language] ended up calling us a bunch of illegal aliens and just a bunch of Mexicans, when that's not true. We're a pretty diverse student body group. So yeah, I think a lot of people were hurt by that.

Susana's story demonstrates how all Latinxs (and even non-Latinxs) were cast as and called "Mexican" as a racial slur. Ms. Lucas shared a similar story, "There's a lot of [non-dual-language] students calling all the [dual-language] kids 'Mexicans.' So, we get a lot of that." People outside the dual-language program saw the program as for "Mexicans" (a stand-in for Latinxs sometimes used pejoratively). By mere association, students in the "Spanish classes" (including White or Black students) were cast as "Mexicans" (that is, Latinxs). At the same time, some non-Latinx students, as we learn from Jada in the next chapter, were differentiated with "Mexican wannabe."

NEEDING PERFECT SPANISH

In classrooms, community meetings, and interviews, people voiced the importance of the Spanish language for the Latinx community, culture, history, and identity, so they rallied around the language. One consequence of constructing the Spanish language as something so defining of the Latinx category was that several students and parents repeatedly raised the need for teachers who spoke "perfect Spanish." For example, the participants in the Hispanic Community Center meeting (described in chapter 2) agreed on the need to have teachers who were "native speakers" or "100 percent bilingual." Perhaps this call came from wanting to prevent the exclusion felt by Latinx students who did not feel fully proficient in Spanish; for example, Susana shared having "experienced certain, I guess, situations where I don't necessarily feel like fully included with other Latinos. Because they, they do speak primarily Spanish." It may have also been the case that the demand for "perfect Spanish" came from participants sensing that Latinxs were judged based on their Spanish and English language practices.[17] For example, César shared that one of the reasons he dropped the dual-language program in high school was that he did not want one of his teachers whom he perceived as not having proper Spanish to "contaminate my Spanish."

One consequence of using Spanish to delineate the Latinx group and calling for perfect Spanish was dramatized in a conversation I had with Ms. Schloss. She and I had agreed to chat after one of my observations of her ethnic-studies course. Once all the students had left the room, Ms. Schloss sat down, took out a pen and notebook, ready to take notes. She requested that I give her feedback, which I had not expected. I told her that I was genuinely impressed with the content she offered, that even though I saw some areas for how to improve the delivery and scaffolding, these seemed minimal to me and part of the normal course of learning to teach. But what really caught me by surprise was the type of feedback she wanted. She asked me to point out errors I noticed in her Spanish language. This took me aback because I had not described my study as examining teachers' languaging patterns. I also had had conversations with Ms. Schloss that showed she saw language education as not about correctness. But I also knew she had attended community meetings where parents expressed dissatisfaction with teachers' Spanish proficiency. I interpreted her question to me as wanting to address the community's concerns and become a better teacher for her students.

As a former high school teacher of Spanish, I pushed back against the expectations of my colleagues and students that I correct all the students' Spanish-language errors and that my own Spanish be error-free. My approach was informed by the belief that as long as students communicated their message, grammar was secondary, and correcting all mistakes could discourage language use—an outcome contrary to my goal of encouraging students to practice their Spanish as much as possible. Additionally, I have been influenced by the ideas that the context matters in determining correctness and that groups with power often dictate standards in schooling and other institutions.[18] So I am suspicious of the call for a "perfect Spanish," and I agree with critiques that call out the language education field's propensity to correct language usage.

Hesitant to play into the idea that there is a "perfect" Spanish speaker, I replied that students need to hear all sorts of Spanish. Ms. Schloss's face reddened. She looked wide-eyed at me, covered her mouth and swallowed, eyes glistening. Gathering her composure, she said that that was the worst answer I could have given her, looking at me as if I had insulted her. I was not sure why—perhaps she sought affirmation that her Spanish was "good," or she might have been looking for feedback to help identify and eliminate her errors. But I was so taken aback—I had not imagined my answer would devastate her—that tears welled in my eyes. To stem them, I did not speak. Thoughts raced in my mind. But I could not make sense of them, let alone share them. For one, I believed the program was fortunate to have her. But would she have understood that as condescending rather than sincere? I sensed that whatever I might say, she would interpret it ungenerously. I wanted to elaborate but words fell short in assuaging her distress.

This focus on a narrow understanding of "correct" language, and the program's lack of teaching against these harmful ideals, served to discourage, perhaps even push out, some of the dual-language teachers who were the most committed to incorporating critical racial lessons in their courses.[19] Ms. Schloss, Ms. West, and Ms. Lucas, all White women, sought to create a culturally and linguistically relevant education that addressed racism and other injustices. Yet because they were not seen as having proficient enough Spanish, some parents and students did not see them as a good language example for the students, and they voiced their displeasure in school and community meetings. Although I am unsure why two of these three teachers eventually left the dual-language program (one transferred to teach in a non-dual-language school), the harmful expectation that they needed perfect Spanish could not have made them feel accomplished and valued. For teachers, as with other professionals, feeling ineffective or sensing that their practice is not improving could potentially be demoralizing enough to jeopardize their continued commitment to teaching.

The community's and bilingual program's emphasis on the Spanish language above other concerns perpetuated the notion that Latinx issues are primarily language-based, which connected with making the Spanish language as the signature boundary that delineates the Latinx group. More-over, the focus on Spanish accompanied several issues in the program. For instance, individuals tended to police language. The idea that Spanish needed to be perfect excluded some White teachers and potentially other bilingual teachers, including Latinxs, who did not see their Spanish as good enough.[20] But the repercussions extended beyond excluding teachers. The overwhelming focus on language proficiency tied to the strong association of Spanish with Latinidad led the community to overlook the importance of teachers advancing critical-racial consciousness, something these three teachers actively sought to cultivate in their students.

DUAL LANGUAGE'S DUELING ROLES

The dual-language program functioned as a racial project with dueling, contradictory roles. On the one hand, it provided students with culturally representative schooling opportunities to develop biliteracy. This helped students stay connected with their relations—family and community. In this role, bilingual education functions as a racial project that helps Latinxs use public schooling for their benefit. But for public schools to offer bilingual education, schools need a critical mass of students for a classroom/program.

Herein lies the conflicting role: the program's gathering of the "Spanish-speaking" students reinforces the notion that the Spanish language is the signature boundary that delineates the Latinx racialized group. So on the other hand, the program functions as a racial project, participating in the process of sorting individuals who may not share much in common into categories—a process that involves excluding, essentializing, and separating them into groups and providing different resources. For example, the program simultaneously taught that Latinxs have differences in language and cultural practices while essentializing these same differences to lump the various groups into the Latinx category.

While the program's participants did not intend to essentialize Latinxs, the program operates within a society where racialized categories and groups are used to create hierarchies and facilitate oppression. Additionally, it was institutionalized in schooling that does not mean to develop critical-racial consciousness. It did not cohesively promote critical-racial consciousness, even though it was said to be for Latinx students. (Consider the problem of the program not structurally acknowledging that it was teaching two colonial languages.) By reinforcing the Spanish language as the signature boundary of the Latinx group, instead of enhancing critical-racial consciousness and forming a collective critical consciousness, the program hindered its ability to provide educational justice to Latinxs.

For example, the emphasis on Spanish disregarded Latinxs' Indigenous languages and disassociated Latinxs from Indigeneity. When the program did expand Latinidad to consider Indigeneity, it did so in problematic ways; for example, by idealizing Latinxs' link to the Aztecs/Incas and constructing Latinidad as disconnected from living in right relations with the natural world. This prevented the program from guiding students to have critical conversations about, for example, relating as recently arrived Latinx Indigenous peoples to a new land and to other Indigenous groups; that is, northern Native communities.[21]

We have seen how the program positioned some groups in relation to each other and how the program advanced Spanish as the marker to delineate the Latinx racialized group. Next, we see how the program reinforced the Spanish language as the marker of the Latinx racialized group in relation to other arbitrary boundaries.

CHAPTER 4

Arbitrary Boundaries

I n one of my morning visits to Ms. West's English language arts dual-language class, her sixth graders were learning about informational text through a reading on Muhammad Ali. Ms. West explained to me:

> Because it's really great to read about him from different people's perspectives because that's one of our standards. A sportswriter would say this about him, but a political writer might say this about him. So, we're viewing him from a lot of different lenses.

Ms. West noted that this lesson helped reinforce previous lessons about a writer's point of view. But her lesson went further than the English language arts standards.

Being conscious that her dual-language classrooms had so many Latinxs, she connected African Americans' struggles to Latinxs' struggles. She masterfully set up her lessons, always thinking of what would interest students to then follow their interests and questions. For example, through learning about Muhammad Ali, students learned "a lot about protest and the rise of African Americans and the struggle for desegregation." During that lesson, she planted seeds to spark students' curiosity; she shared with her students that "Hispanics in California" brought "the court cases that set the precedents for the movement of African Americans." Students exclaimed, "What?" Ms. West then shared:

> Yeah, and did you know, . . . I think it was the first suit to allow Mexican Americans to use public pools; [it] was filed in California. The judge said that they were citizens and they had to be allowed to use the pools, and then they cite all these Mexican American suits, [which] are in the Supreme Court decision for all African American civil rights cases.

Ms. West reflected on how the lesson went: "The kids were totally interested." Ms. West guided her students to learn about *Méndez et al v.*

Westminster School District of Orange County, a 1940s desegregation case with "Hispanic" plaintiffs. Sylvia Méndez, one of the child plaintiffs, had a Mexican American father and a Puerto Rican mother, Felícitas. The plaintiffs won, with the Ninth Circuit Court of Appeals determining four school districts' Mexican remedial schools as unconstitutional. Two months after this ruling, the state of California passed a bill ending school segregation, six years before *Brown v. Board of Education of Topeka*.[1]

Ms. West's students had already learned about *Brown*, the US Supreme Court case credited with desegregating public schools, but they had not heard about *Méndez*. *Méndez* presented a case about *Latinx* school desegregation, and students were intrigued by the idea that Latinxs had, along with African Americans, played a role in desegregating schools.[2]

This lesson did more than teach kids about the *Méndez* case. It also implicitly offered and reinforced societal ideas about the (artificially constructed) distinctness of racial categories through what was not said aloud, since the focus of the case was on Hispanics as a distinct category. Students did not learn about Felícitas being nicknamed "la prieta" (the dark woman) or her parents and siblings being racially identified "as 'mulattos' in Puerto Rico, as 'black' in Arizona, and as 'Mexican' in California."[3] Perhaps this information would have led the students to notice the arbitrariness of racial categories and talk about what makes "Hispanic" and "African American" different groups. This might have included learning about the differences in how these two groups were subjected to racism; for example, Hispanics were segregated based on skin color, last names, and *language*—specifically, a presumed lack of English proficiency.[4] By exploring these nuances, students might have questioned the "neatness" of the categories and broadened their understanding of racism's varied manifestations across different groups. Instead, the lesson reinforced the perception of the two groups as distinct yet omitted the consideration of language in the narrative of how racism specifically manifests for Hispanics.

Despite the lessons about racism and justice, this lesson shows schooling indirectly perpetuated the distinctness of the categories "Black" and "Hispanic." Felícitas's family experience of being racially identified differently based on context hinted that the delineations of the groups are not only about skin color and looks. Different people who have similar skin colors and looks can identify and/or be identified in distinct racial categories, even in geographically close places (like California and Arizona).

As we saw in part 1, many program participants thought of race as skin color and thought about Latinx as having a shared culture, despite participants perceiving Latinx as a racialized group and being unable to specify common Latinx cultural practices. As we learned in chapter 3, the dual-language program positioned Latinxs in relation to other racialized groups and advanced Spanish as what delineates the Latinx racial category. In this chapter, I continue to show how the dual-language program makes Spanish delineate the Latinx racialized group by differentiating the boundaries of the Latinx racialized group from and in relation to the Black racialized group.[5]

"DIVERSITY" MEANS BLACK STUDENTS

One of the ways people in the program differentiated the various racialized groups, especially Latinx students and Black students, was by the way they spoke about the lack of diversity and who counted as adding "diversity" to the program. When people talked of the program's diversity and/or other racial issues, they often inferred or explicitly referred to the participating Black students, which often led to mentioning their underrepresentation there.

Most dual-language classrooms had only one or two Black students, and these students, along with mostly White students, made up the English-speaking half of the classrooms. This meant Borane's dual-language English-speaking half had about 9 percent Black/African American population. Compare this to Borane's Black/African American student population of 19 percent (and 23 percent of Amlie's students). The program's English-speaking population would need two to three Black students in each classroom to have representation parity. Consequently, concerns over representation of the Black students predominated.

Only two teachers mentioned that the program would have a disproportionate number of Black students because half of the program would consist of Spanish-speaking Latinxs who, like the population of the district, consisted of very few people who identified as Afro-Latinx.[6] Thus, people in Oakville saw the Latinx community (with more than 66 percent being immigrants) and the Black/African American community as distinct from each other. Separating the two categories contributed to people seeing a need for more Black youth in the dual-language program.

There were also other reasons for calling for the program to have more Black students. Because some advocates promoted the program as being a research-based model that "guaranteed success" for improving students' achievement and framed knowing Spanish as a commodity for all, participants reasoned that the program would benefit all students. Educators and advocates such as Ms. Schloss mentioned research suggesting that the program benefits underserved students: "I've read research that [dual-language education] can also uplift in a positive way other groups that are traditionally underserved in education—so Black students, poor students." Several other teachers also thought that the program would benefit Black students.

People saw Black youth as needing the achievement boost the program promised, especially because these students had the lowest academic performance in the Oakville district. Additionally, not having a proportionate number of Black students in the bilingual program troubled many people who saw it as an enrichment opportunity that Black students were denied access to, as happens with other opportunities.[7] One teacher reasoned, "We don't want kids to not have that opportunity because of racial disparities."

But at times, the logic behind *how* the program would benefit the students was based on racist ideas, revealing that Black youth's Black American English bilingualism was devalued or simply overlooked.[8] For example, some people reasoned that the program benefited all students because brain research shows that bilingualism develops an individual's cognitive functions. Teachers and advocates mentioned that because the program gave that opportunity and advantage to Latinxs and White children, Black children should also have the chance to be bilingual and benefit cognitively. For example, when I asked Ms. West why people saw Black student underrepresentation as a problem, she replied slowly and nonjudgmentally. Her deliberate pacing seemed to indicate that the answer was self-evident:

> I think you don't want to tell an African American student that they're not capable of learning two languages. You might be shutting doors for opportunity in the future, all the brain research that shows they're better problem solvers, so I don't want them not to be exposed to the chance to develop into that way.

According to this logic, which many participants shared, the dual-language program should have racial proportionality because Black students should also become bilingual to access the benefits afforded other students, such as job skills and enhanced cognitive development. While I do not ignore the historical and contemporary inequities of providing educational opportunities to youth from subjugated groups, this logic betrays that although Spanish was seen as a language that would enhance the cognitive development of Black students, people did not mention Black American English as providing comparable advantages to its speakers.[9]

Although teachers mentioned they were linguistically sensitive and framed Black students as English speakers, I did not witness teachers recognizing Black students' bilingualism in Dominant American English and Black American English (BAE).[10] For example, in none of my observations did teachers incorporate BAE into their lessons. Nor did teachers mention it as an asset in our conversations, suggesting that Black students' linguistic repertoires were undervalued in the program.[11] Teachers did not claim that Black youths' bilingualism would provide cognitive benefits to these students, as they asserted of Spanish/English bilingualism for students. This exposes an anti-Black idea of disregarding some Black youths' existing bilingual knowledge of BAE or devaluing Black language variations.[12] These anti-Black ideas frame Black youth as linguistically deficient by not seeing their bilingualism in BAE as beneficial for their cognition whereas others' languages were considered advantageous.

These contrasts delineated the categories *and* positioned the different racialized groups in relation to each other. Teachers appreciated Black youth bringing diversity but did not consider their language(s) beneficial as they did Latinxs' Spanish. Additionally, the fact that people made discrete the language practices of Latinx and Black people shows again that they viewed the groups as separate. Besides not valuing Black students' language practices, other racist ideas further delineated and relationally racialized the groups. The next sections show how the different racialized groups were described and expose how comparing Black students with each other served to maintain ideas which worked against Black youth *and* Latinxs.

"GREAT LATINO STUDENTS"

Ms. Thomson had just been hired to teach Amlie High's Spanish language arts for the dual-language freshman. Like most of the other participating teachers, she was from the Midwest but, unlike the others, she had been teaching in Asian and European private schools for several years. She had transferred to Amlie after one year as a teacher in Oakville's Oakleaf Elementary, where she felt "totally unqualified" to teach. She found it "really, really tough" especially as she had taught abroad where "all our kids were really, really high, really motivated. With Asian culture in general, education is so valued, and also the respect for teachers is so different."

Like her comparisons of students in and outside the United States, Ms. Thomson also compared the students within her school. She shared that Oakleaf Elementary's dual-language program had "most of the Latino kids and . . . most of the kids that have more educated parents that wanted them to really do this [dual-language] program." She compared this with the non-dual-language classrooms that "ended up being kids that were much more transient, that were also often economically disadvantaged, or academically lower, and more of a behavior problem." Ms. Thomson later specified: "It ends up being like, the Latinos and the Whites are in the dual-language program, and then the African American students are in the non-dual-language program." Although Ms. Thomson had not been in Amlie for long when I first interviewed her, and so perhaps she mostly related her elementary-school experience, I already had been hearing similar comparisons from others.

Ms. Cander, another Amlie teacher of Spanish assigned to dual language, expressed a preference for not teaching in the dual-language program. Instead, she preferred to teach the higher-level courses such as Spanish 5, AP Language, and AP Literature. These courses were perceived as having more college-tracked students and typically had a higher enrollment of White students. Amlie's tracking system did not give dual-language courses the grade-scale weight of honors/AP courses, and more White students took the latter course options. Consequently, some Amlie teachers judged the dual-language program as not having the top students compared with the honors/AP tracks, even though they perceived the program as having better students than the "regular" track.

This was a common sentiment at Borane too. Ms. Nadia was a White middle-class mother of a Borane dual-language Latina student and a former dual-language staff member. When I asked her about some of the challenges of dual language being a strand program within non-bilingual schools, she openly described these comparisons. This extended quote also hints at some of the structural conditions that contributed to the comparisons:

> There's a lot of resentments in schools. This half of the hallway is dual language, and this half isn't. And what happens is that the Latino kids often have such better behavior, right? They're supported, and less mental illness, less homelessness—all of those issues are less. So they're just easier students. The dual-language classrooms are made up of families who had White kids who are already kinda advantaged for several reasons [and] these great Latino students, right? So those are like [smiles and lets out sigh of relief] awesome easy classrooms. And then there is the other side of the

hall where they have the hard-behavior kids, the homeless kids, whose families didn't want their kids in dual language. The lowest-scoring students. And that's incredible pressure. I felt resentment by [non-dual-language] teachers that looked at the dual-language students. The dual-language classrooms are so much calmer and easier. Special ed students are in their [non-dual-language] classroom, high-behavior needs are in their classroom. [That's] just resentment, I think—we're talking about having a school that isn't all dual language. It's really a challenge, I think, and doesn't look good for, I think, families looking in: "What the heck is going on? Why is it so calm over here and horrible over here?" It's tricky and stressful. It's never anything specific about a certain teacher or a certain school, or even, like, all those African American kids. You know, it's not what I mean. I'm just trying to say it in a politically correct way.

Ms. Nadia, like Ms. Thomson, did not distinguish the groups only along racial lines; for example, she delineated groups by housing insecurity and mental illness. However, she eventually insinuated that the kids with the difficult characteristics were Black. She also acknowledged certain structural conditions, such as mental health issues, that contributed to these challenges (I discuss structural conditions later). Ms. Nadia was not alone in perceiving the anti-Black stereotypes and comparisons of Black youth and Latinx youth.

Ms. West was another teacher who noted that the non-dual-language teachers described the dual-language students as behaviorally better than the general school population. Ms. West worked against being race-evasive (colorblind) in her teaching as well as her conversations with me, which I conjecture contributed to her feeling she should not "politically correct" some of her colleagues' problematic ideas. She shared:

It's very racist, but I heard it said several times that African Americans are harder to deal with behaviorally, and so they think that's why we [the dual-language program] have this reputation that "It's easier to teach Hispanic kids. They're all well-behaved."

Teachers saw the program as having a "better" student population, and the comparisons exposed racist assumptions not only about students' academic abilities but also about behavior. Ms. West relayed that non-dual-language teachers complained about this difference: "They definitely see dual-language as teaching the easier kids behaviorally. We get that all the time."

Another Borane dual-language teacher, Mr. Estrada, commented in the same vein. He remarked:

> I don't think [non-dual-language teachers] feel that we're skimming the academically high achievers. I think it's more in terms of behavior. They feel like we don't have the behavior problems that they do, because Latinos tend to not have as many high [*sic*] of the behavior concern and because other parents choose to be here.

Mr. Estrada and some dual-language teachers pointed out that their Latinx population also had "behavior problems," including students who had suffered trauma and acted out in class, but then they noted that the Latinx students did behave well. Ms. West shared, "They're the sweetest kids, and they do whatever it is we tell them to do." Educators repeatedly mentioned that the program had "well-behaved Latinos," middle-class Whites, and significantly fewer Black students than the rest of the school.

These repeated comparisons (even when done through coded words) reinforced a racist stereotype that described Whites *and* Latinxs as more desirable than Black students. Additionally, because how one racialized group is described influences how other groups are perceived, the discourse reinforced racialized differences. Simply, the comparisons relationally racialized the groups. These ideas naturalized the comparisons of race and the distinctions of the racialized groups from each other.[13] Indeed, the discourse of "great Latino students" positioned Black students as undesirable racialized Others, even portraying Latinxs as "model minorities" in terms of their behavior.[14] This positioned Latinxs more favorably in the racial hierarchy than Black students.[15]

However, Latinxs' position relative to Black folks in the racial hierarchy had inconsistencies within the program. For example, Latinxs were the "model minority" in terms of behavior, but not when it came to academic achievement. Most teachers would name as the high achievers the program's White students *and* Black students. Accordingly, if the label "model minority" in terms of *academic achievement* were to apply in this dual-language context, it would describe the program's Black students, especially those who came from immigrant families (which I explicate in an upcoming section).[16]

The repeated ideas relationally racializing Latinxs versus Black students, describing Latinxs as better-behaved students, almost painted the behavior as if it were intrinsic to the groups. The easily available anti-Black tropes created a common sense implying the behavior was inherent, making it challenging for teachers to articulate a different explanation, especially considering that people often did not fully acknowledge the impact of structural racism.

Comparisons of students were often created by reading race patterns instead of recognizing our society's structural racism. RedRock had a racialized, disproportionate distribution of services that underfunded some schools and communities, especially those servicing the Black community. Eliding structural factors that affected people's lives resulted in making as common sense the descriptions of the groups, naturalizing this as "race," and then placing the racialized groups in various positions in the racial hierarchy. While most teachers believed racism existed, how they relayed the comparative discourse shows the difficulty of making sense of the behavior in a different (structural) way once race is naturalized as the accepted explanation.

Several educators did mention that public school conditions—feeling overworked, managing large classes, lacking appropriate training and support for special education, and working with students whose families lacked resources for mental health services and housing—affected their teaching. However, they did not connect these conditions to their ability to work with Black students. Nor did they link the issues to structural racism or link the group comparisons to implicit bias resulting in overdisciplining Black youth.[17]

In conversations where teachers compared student groups, they usually did not mention that Oakville's Black community, being more established than its Latinx community, had been subjected to long-standing, persistent structural racism in, for example, housing, health care, and incarceration. Oakville's county disproportionately incarcerated Black men, who comprised about 5 percent of its population but over 50 percent of those incarcerated. This structural racism factor usually went unacknowledged as contributing to or as a sign of Oakville's racism, racism that Black children and their families had to navigate. Yet it connected to the district's disproportionate rate of school suspensions, with Black students making up about 10 percent of the district student population but about 50 percent of students suspended.[18] Disregarding these systemic factors and others' perceptions resulted in the anti-Black discourse that cast Black kids as being naturally undesirable students.

As a racial project, schools perpetuated these ideas, which, along with the schools' geographical and racial composition, affected Latinxs living in this community. Individuals' focus on the groups rather than the structural, systemic racism influenced how people thought of race. This affected how some teachers, like Ms. Íñiguez, viewed and treated Black students and consequently the material outcomes of students, which also relationally influences the construction of Latinidad.

A LATINA TEACHER'S ANTI-BLACKNESS

Ms. Íñiguez warmly welcomed me to her classroom. I noticed that she, being an immigrant herself, related to me and to her Latinx students. She saw her Latinx students as English language learners who needed help because of their lack of fluency in English and thus worthy of attention and cariño (care/ caring). But she did not extend a similar cariño to everyone.

In several of my informal conversations with Ms. Íñiguez, she described the few Black students who were in the dual-language program as usually different than the rest of the school's Black students (who were less likely to be middle class than their dual-language counterparts) and that teaching the latter was particularly challenging. Within the first ten minutes of our first meeting, she went off topic about the program's attributes to express her anti-Black feelings outright. When speaking about the program's benefits, she exclaimed, "¡Es mejor ser maestra bilingüe que tener que batallar con los alumnos del resto de la escuela!" (It's better to be a dual-language teacher than to deal with the rest of the school's students!) She then went on to explain at length that the Black students in the school disrespected teachers, were uncontrollable, and that many were delinquents. She asserted that their parents did not care to discipline their children, did not support teachers, and wanted to have the school solve all their problems. "Los papás no se involucran en la educación. No importa que currículo avanzado tengas, si los papás no se involucran, no funciona nada." (The parents don't get involved in their education. It doesn't matter how advanced the curriculum is, if the parents don't get involved, then nothing works.)[19]

Ms. Íñiguez was the only teacher to describe Black parents so negatively. More common were educators and community members casting Latinx students as easier to teach than other students, including White students, because of their parents. Some teachers saw White parents as demanding and felt that Latinx parents deferred to teachers more than Black or White parents. But whether explicit or implicit, the non-dual-language Black students were categorized as undesirable students compared with the dual-language Latinx student population.

Ms. Íñiguez also expressed other anti-Black ideas, such as believing that because Black parents were not bilingual, their children took longer to learn Spanish:

No a todos [los estudiantes afroamericanos], pero en general, les cuesta un poquito más. No sé por qué, cuál es la situación, pero les cuesta un poquito más. Obviamente, puede tener razón porque cuando llegan a casa no vuelven a hablar español, entonces, y como sus padres no hablan español, pues obviamente tienen menos posibilidad de repasar, o de estar, o sea en el idioma. (Not all [of the Black students], but in general, it takes them a little bit more. I'm not sure why, what's the issue, but it takes them a bit more. Obviously, it can be the case that when they arrive home, they don't speak Spanish, and because the parents don't speak Spanish, well, obviously they have less possibilities of reviewing, or of being in the language.)

Ms. Íñiguez's comment belies the fact that most of the White students in dual language (and even some of the Latinx students who were from English-speaking homes) also would not have that exposure to Spanish outside school. What Ms. Íñiguez's statements do show is an example of teachers' anti-Black ideas positioning Latinxs as more desirable students than Black students and painting the former as "model minorities" in terms of behavior, parent involvement, and disposition. Ms. Íñiguez's ideas not only exemplify Latinxs engaging in anti-Black discourses; they also contribute to positioning Latinxs as superior to Black students in a racial hierarchy.

As my study progressed, Ms. Íñiguez's comments about Black students became more restrained and "politically correct," maybe because she noticed that I did not validate her opinions. But even toward the end of my time at the school, she repeated explicitly—though with less intensity–that teaching the school's Black students was particularly challenging. She added that the few Black students who were in the dual-language program were usually different than the rest of the school's Black population.

These anti-Black ideas affected Ms. Íñiguez's actions in her classes and consequently the students' material outcomes. For example, she was strict and warm with most students, calling them "mijito" or "mijita" (a term used in Mexican Spanish to express cariño for a younger person). She shared that she felt her cultural connection to the Mexican families helped her interactions with youth and parents. Ms. Íñiguez said "mijito" to the Latino boys, even when she was correcting their behavior, making the discipline feel motherly. However, I observed that she did not demonstrate cariño to Deidre, the only Black student in her classroom, as she did with the other students (White or Latinx). Ms. Íñiguez did not use "mijita" with Deidre, instead calling her by her first name, making Ms. Íñiguez sound a bit harsher toward Deidre than the other students. Additionally, although she was strict with all her students, she paid particular attention to Deidre, ever watchful of Deidre getting out of line, and was especially stern with her. In one science class, after Deidre prematurely filled her group's beaker (which another White male student had also done), Ms. Íñiguez gave her a verbal warning (the precursor to a formal disciplining like detention).[20] Deidre's example shows how Black students, even though they were desired in the program, were not always in classrooms that promoted their academic achievement.

Teachers disproportionately disciplining Black students is a widespread issue that extends beyond dual-language classrooms.[21] However, I focus on it in the context of the dual-language program for specific reasons. First, the program was generally perceived as embracing diversity among most participants. Second, administrators wanted to recruit more Black students, touting the program's teachers as culturally sensitive. Spotlighting these points reveals the contrast between the program's inclusive image and the reality of its disciplinary practices. Additionally, it highlights that just as racist disciplining manifests in other schooling spaces, Black students also suffer from overdisciplining in dual-language education. This challenges the assumption that bilingual teachers' care for one group of color (Latinx youth) extends to others (Black youth).[22]

Actions like Ms. Íñiguez's unequal vigilance surely made her class unenjoyable to Deidre, and they also potentially furthered Oakville's school suspensions, which connect to the disproportionate incarceration of Black folks. As institutional agents, teachers' anti-Black actions contribute to continuing an anti-Black common sense in society's social and institutional structures, policies, and practices. Importantly, the anti-Black actions of Latina teachers contribute to constructing a Latinidad that positions itself in contrast to—and higher on the racial hierarchy than—Blackness.[23]

"GOOD BLACK STUDENTS"

Even as Ms. Íñiguez shared her anti-Black ideas, she added how excited she felt when she heard her Black dual-language students speaking in Spanish: "Yo bien emocionada [sic] ver a mis niños afroamericanos hablando español." (I get very excited seeing the African American children speaking Spanish.) In her view, their ability to speak in Spanish elevated Black students in dual language over non-dual-language Black students.

Her comments also show that although teachers negatively compared Black students to Latinxs, teachers also made distinctions between Black students. In the words of another teacher, the Black youth in the dual-language program were considered "good Black students" while Black youth not in dual language were "not school motivated."[24] Teachers and other adults knew that the Black parents (and White parents) of dual-language students, who were mostly middle class, had "gone through the hoops" to place their children in the program. This spoke to the program's recruitment and enrollment practices tending to select students who were perceived as easier to teach (something I discuss in the next section). Still this discourse of the "good Black student" insinuated that other Black students—the non-dual-language students who were most of the Black student population—were not so good.

Like Ms. Íñiguez, some educators expressed anti-Black sentiments by negatively comparing Black non-dual-language students to Black dual-language students. For example, Mr. Clarke, a White teacher whom we met in chapter 2, blamed the disproportionately small number of Black students in dual language on non-dual-language Black parents. When I spoke with him about the program's lack of racial diversity (which mostly referred to Black students, even though the program also had few Asian American students and Indigenous students), he faulted the parents of non-dual-language students: "Their parents are kind of complacent. They don't really understand the benefits of being bilingual." Mr Clarke assumed they misunderstood dual-language and/or devalued education.

Mr. Clarke also thought that the small number of Black students reinforced the problem of low Black enrollment, saying:

> [It] can be hard for the kids that are in the program, sometimes their friends are in a different part of the school, so they don't like the dual-language program, or for whatever reason they really are resistant to doing it. . . . African American kids that want to leave the program because I feel that they feel that they don't fit in.

Black students feeling like they did not "fit in" could also have been a sign that the program was not culturally relevant for them or did not benefit them. However, Mr. Clarke did not entertain these possibilities. The discourses these participants used when discussing Black dual-language students framed them as those whose families took education seriously and recognized the value of the dual-language program; accordingly, this positioned Black families who did not pursue dual-language for their children as less school motivated, playing on a racist idea that Black families did not care about education. The racial comparisons allowed and reinforced a certain perspective on what was identified as "the problem." Notably, this perspective did not include questioning the program's cultural relevance for

Black students. Additionally, these comparisons narrowed the range of possible solutions envisioned for the program's addressing the needs of Black students. For instance, they forestalled efforts to make the program more culturally relevant for them.

Because some people like Mr. Clarke viewed Black families as not understanding the dual-language program or the benefits of bilingualism, the proposed solutions for increasing the number of Black students included informing parents about the program's advantages and better recruitment. (Because the dual-language program started in elementary school, these solutions implied a need for the dual-language elementaries to recruit more Black students for the secondary level to have better representation.) Ms. Aguirre, a dual-language Latina advocate with a long history in the community, stated that White parents did not need to be recruited, but it was difficult "trying to attract diversity":

> That's been one of the criticisms, not being able to have more African Americans, Asians students in the program. In fact, I think they just held a meeting to explain charter schools and dual language to the African American community. In the hopes of—so people would understand those kinds of things.

The assumption was that Black parents had to be educated about the benefits of the program, a negative expectation compared with the assumptions about Asian American parents. Even if their parents did not enroll their children in the program, Asian American students were still seen as valuing education, excelling academically, and/or already bilingual. Thus, no one spoke of a need to educate Asian American parents about the benefits of bilingualism; accordingly, they were not targeted for recruitment through informational meetings. This shows the specific anti-Black idea of needing to educate Black parents about the value of education.[25] The anti-Black comparison of Black students and their parents' choices versus those other groups and assuming they did not value bilingualism elides how the dual-language program shaped its recruitment in its early implementation.

"SELECTIVELY RECRUITED AFRICAN AMERICANS"

I first met Mr. Figueroa in one of the Latinos Unidos community meetings. Mr. Figueroa identified as Chicano, one of the few in leadership positions in the district. More than twelve years ago, he had worked in the early advocacy and implementation of Somos Bilingüe Elementary School, Oakville's first dual-language school. He related to me how difficult it was to get the district to approve of dual language.

When discussing the early recruitment efforts of the then-new dual-language school, I asked him about the disproportionate numbers of Black students. After a pause, Mr. Figueroa got up, walked to look out the window, then turned toward me to share that not all Black families were recruited for the new school. He reflected on the early recruitment efforts to have more Black youth:

> We should have done a better job at recruiting more Black kids. . . . I think we selectively recruited people. We selectively recruited African Americans that didn't have behavioral problems or didn't have learning disabilities or didn't have all these other negative things.

Mr. Figueroa went on to share that the Black families who were recruited, and thus were more likely to enroll their child in dual language, were those who were likely to do well in school: "When they were there in the classroom, those kids were going to do well regardless of what [classroom] it was."

Because implementing a dual-language elementary school encountered much opposition and needed the approval of Whites (who held the majority votes), advocates strategically decided on how to make the school succeed. One of these decisions was to informally recruit students from Black middle-class families who, as Mr. Figueroa described, would "do well regardless." Their reasoning was that if the dual-language school did not improve Black achievement, then it was likely to face opposition from the Black community, which Latinx community leaders felt had more political power than they did. The dual-language elementary school's practice of recruiting Black middle-class students supported the outcome of having Black students who would do well academically (just as with middle-class White students). This strategy and outcome led to Black dual-language students being seen more favorably in terms of academics compared to the Latinx youth who were mostly from working-class immigrant families.

Since the dual-language program included Black families who had the tools needed for their child to succeed in school, the program helped those Black youth who were already set up to be high-achieving students. As Mr. Ochoa put it:

> El programa dual-language en término de los afroamericanos, les ayuda a los que de todas maneras ya tienen muchas ventajas. Porque es self-selecting. Si tú tienes la conciencia, por lo tanto, el capital social, cultural para entender las ventajas del programa, entonces, eso quiere decir que ya están

en la segunda base. (The dual-language program in terms of African American students, helps those who already have many advantages. Because it is self-selecting. If you have the consciousness, hence, the social and cultural capital to understand the advantages of the program, then that means they're already on second base.)

However, the success of the few Black students in the dual-language program, who likely would have thrived even outside of it, challenges the prevalent notion that the program significantly benefits the Black community—a contradiction Mr. Ochoa also recognized.

Mr. Ochoa went on to dispute the commonly shared idea that the dual-language program was helping the Black community. He explained that because the Black students in the program would have been successful anyway, the program does not benefit the Black community (he considers African Americans culturally Anglo instead of, for example, culturally Hispanic[26]):

> Entonces, en realidad, se podría decir, de que el programa no está ayudando a la comunidad afroamericana. No, el programa beneficia sobre todo a las familias anglo que tienen mayor capital cultural." (Then, in reality, we could say that the program is not helping the African American community. No, the program benefits above all the Anglo families with more cultural capital.)

However, Mr. Ochoa was alone in sharing with me that the dual-language program was not specifically benefiting the African American community. Rather he believed that it benefited Anglos with cultural capital, which might include some African American students in the program.

Most people considered the dual-language program better at providing good instruction to all students, thus benefiting the (few) Black students in the program and consequently, the Black community. Because the program had high-achieving Black students, even if these students were just a few compared to the rest of the school's population, it was easy to state that dual-language helped improve Black student achievement and helped supporters of dual-language claim that the program benefited all students.

Additionally, this again framed how people understood Black underrepresentation in dual language as a problem. Accordingly, people pointed to the need to recruit more Black students and educate their parents about the benefits of dual language, rather than examining whether the program met Black students' needs. In other words, how people explained the problem of Black student underrepresentation limited what solutions they imagined for the district's larger problem of meeting the needs of Black youth. And how people saw the problem of Black student underrepresentation was colored by anti-Black ideas that compared the racialized groups and negatively framed Black people.

BLACK IMMIGRANT STUDENTS AS MODEL MINORITIES

Other nuances existed in teachers' differentiations of Black students, differentiations that were then employed against Latinx and other Black students. Apart from describing the Black students in dual language as "high achievers," teachers also mentioned that a disproportionate number of the Black students in the program were from African immigrant families. Some teachers elevated the Black students with African and European immigrant parents who spoke a language other than English above Black Americans by stating that the former already valued bilingualism. For example, one teacher shared: "My dual-language students that are African American, most of them were actually from immigrant families that spoke a different language at home. So, they already came here with a family that valued language or has had to learn English as a second language."

Mr. Clarke shared the same sentiment about the valuing of bilingualism, and used as an example a biracial student, Mia (one parent Black; the other parent Serbian immigrant):

> She is really kind of the prototypical dual-language student because she really tries to learn Spanish. Her mom's European and she already has another language, and she has traveled to Europe. I think she has a sense of how big the world is and how many different languages are spoken in the world and the advantages. So, she really, really tries to speak Spanish.

It is interesting that Mr. Clarke described Mia as a "prototypical dual-language student"—this despite Mia's middle-class status and racial underrepresentation in the program. Importantly, teachers saw European and African non-English languages as a benefit to bilingualism but rarely mentioned Black American English in the same way or even saw it as an additional language.[27] Teachers' comparisons elevated some Black students as model minorities over Latinxs *and* other Black students, again resulting in anti-Black racism.

When I discussed with Ms. West the general concern of the program not benefiting the Black American community because of the lack of Black students, she mentioned: "I've had several students of parents of African descent—like, their parents are from Africa, so a different country. So, [Spanish] is their third language. I don't think that's the same situation either." Ms. West noted that it was not "the same situation" because when people said the program served Black youth, they did not imagine that, in fact, many of these youth had parents who were African immigrants and might already be bilingual. Additionally, African immigrants were sometimes held up as a Black model minority compared with other Black Americans.[28] However, her description of Spanish as the third language of Black immigrant students suggests elevating an official language of foreign nation-states and/or Black African immigrants above Black Americans and their language/bilingualism.[29]

Ms. West's "not-the-same-situation" comment makes sense when one considers that Black immigrants have a different connection to American racism and a different relationship to educational equity than do Black Americans. This fact makes it difficult to argue that the program benefits the larger Black community, when Black (non-immigrant) Americans—with a history of racial discrimination—are largely excluded from the benefits the dual-language program grants Black youth from immigrant families and other youth from marginalized backgrounds.

However, teachers' framing of Black students from immigrant families as Black model minorities did not prevent these youth from being subjected to racial discrimination, as Jada described. Jada was a Black/African American tenth grader with African immigrant parents. She wore her black hair in long micro braids and had a dark mocha complexion. She frequently participated in class, giving thoughtful and soft-spoken answers. She excelled in the program and was one of the popular students and leaders in her classes. Jada started our interview by sharing, "I consider myself trilingual in school. I speak Spanish, English, and French at school, but then at my house, my parents speak another language from Africa. I also speak and comprehend that language too, so I consider myself multilingual." Yet, her answer to my second question, "Could you tell me how your experience has been being in the dual-language program?" was much different from other students I had interviewed. She replied, "Yeah. It's been bumps in the road."

Jada suffered through what she characterized as "bullying" in her elementary school and later through racist assumptions about her ability to understand Spanish. Jada shared that she had one middle-school teacher who

would repeat things more than once to me like I wasn't [pauses] that I didn't understand. She'd go, "Wait, wait, wait"—go to my face and be like, "¿Comprendes?" [Do you understand?] It was really annoying."

Jada recalled going to talk to the principal because she felt the teacher

was babying me in a way. . . . I was getting an A in her class, and I don't know why she thought that I wasn't understanding. She was that one teacher that did that to me because of the color of my skin.

When the principal and Jada confronted the teacher with this idea, the teacher replied:

"Oh no, Jada, it wasn't because of the color of your skin. It was just, I don't know. There was a lot of native Spanish speakers and you're the only one in the class." I was like, "But I wasn't, though. There's White people here too and their first language isn't Spanish too."

Jada's experience illustrates that neither the model minority stereotype nor her immigrant-family background shielded her from being perceived as inferior compared with other students. She still faced racist assumptions about her intelligence, highlighting the pervasive nature of such biases.

Jada shared that the bullying from other students and the racism eased up as the years passed. Students and teachers began to praise her for knowing so many languages: "'Whoa, wow, you speak more than all.' They're very impressed." People eventually appreciated Jada's multilingualism, a value many bilingual-education advocates hope dual language fosters in participants.

Jada's experience also improved through teachers' attention to students with an African immigrant family background. Jada mentioned that one of her teachers taught about Africa, which she appreciated.

I like how my history teacher, Mr. Ochoa, he had a whole presentation about it. He showed pictures, stereotypical pictures of what people think Africa looks like, but how it really looks like. . . . He gave a presentation about that, just saying how "African" isn't a language. Like, "Yes, I speak African," that's not something you say. So, I liked how he gave points like that.

Mr. Ochoa's challenge to students' anti-Black assumptions about Africa not only improved Jada's experience in the program, it also acknowledged the discourses circulating about and affecting Black immigrant students.

I highlight the differentiations that teachers considered significant, such as those based on immigration and language, as teachers' differentiations reflect *and* help construct society's boundaries of the racialized groups and their position in racial hierarchies. These differentiations help explain outcomes, such as Black students doing well, that do not neatly align along anti-Black ideas. These differentiations show competing racial projects simultaneously operating and affecting different groups in this context. The examples also allow for comparisons to other contexts and time, which can then contribute to more readily seeing racial categories as a social construct.

THE PANEL TO ADDRESS ANTI-BLACKNESS

The program's eighth-grade cohort was atypical because it had four Black Latinx students, compared with other dual-language cohorts that had none. Ms. Lucas imparted to me, "We have a Dominican boy, a few Puerto Rican boys, a Honduran boy, who all consider themselves Black."[30] Even though the other Borane teachers also had taught Ms. Lucas' same eighth graders, she was one of only a couple of teachers to mention Afro-Latinx students to me in interviews.

In one of our conversations about diversity in the program, Ms. Lucas recalled an interaction in this classroom where one Latino student called a dark-skinned Latino "Negro" (Spanish for "Black"):

> In Spanish, a lot of the kids will just be like "Oh yeah, Negro," they'll call them negros. But those boys amongst themselves call one another Negro. Because for them, it's, like, culturally appropriate. Well, the other boys who were calling them "negros" were using it in a negative way. Plus, so not only are they using it in a negative way from their cultural perspective, and they're all Mexican, but they're also adding on our perspective in this country of what it is—so they're thinking of the n-word in English and then calling them that with "negro" in Spanish.

From this interaction, Ms. Lucas shared that she thought to herself, "Oh, this is not going to happen with this group." The interaction prompted Ms. Lucas to quickly alter her plans for the next lessons, which included showing a PBS series called "Black in Latin America." Drawing from her social relations, she also organized a panel of adults who identified as Latina/Latino *and* Black, the latter identification being a surprise to some students. The panel spoke about being both Black and Latina/Latino. The conversation sparked students' intense interest in racial identity. Even weeks after the panel, youth mentioned it in interviews I conducted (recall Andrea's experience/interview described in chapter 1) and talked about it among themselves in class.

This example shows Ms. Lucas' lesson offering students a broader understanding of the Latinx group and who are considered Spanish speakers to include people who also identify as Black. She shared with me, "I was trying to explain how African languages have influenced Spanish, and they didn't believe me that there was like Black Mexicans in México." She explained:

> I had so many kids not knowing Black people can speak Spanish as their native language. They hadn't been exposed. Some kids had, but a lot hadn't. . . . They didn't believe me that there are Black Mexicans. I was like you can do a whole PhD study on just what it means to be Black in México. They're like "no way." I'm like, "yes."

Ms. Lucas expressed surprise at her middle-school students not believing that some Black people spoke Spanish and not having their previous schooling ever address the issue of Afro-Latinx identity. However, she also knew that her lessons were atypical—outliers in constructing expansive ideas about Latinx, Black, and Afro-Latinx folks.

Ms. Lucas felt dismay that her efforts in directly addressing anti-Black racism were alone in Borane's program. Through the panel she organized, she challenged the anti-Black stereotype of a static Black identity that paints people who identify as Black as not being native Spanish speakers. Ms. Lucas's disappointment at the lack of teaching by her colleagues matched my own observations that Ms. Lucas alone addressed this racial issue in her classroom.

Apart from Ms. Lucas' efforts, more often the program constructed Latinx people, however unintentionally, to be separate from—and at times in antagonistic relation to—Black people. Consequently, students who identified as both Latinx and Black were marginalized. The formation of the racialized categories also affected how the people perceived the two groups' interests and needs.

Years after my classroom visits, I learned from twelfth grader Mia that the new teacher of the Latin American studies elective showed videos featuring Afro-Latinxs speaking about their experiences, and that the students then did a biographical research project on an Afro-Latinx personality (Mia chose Celia Cruz). This suggests more (or other) teachers increasing the program's attention to teaching that people can identify as Black *and* Latinx, or Afro-Latinx.

To imagine an alternative, dual-language programs could expose students to the existence of Black Mexicans and Asian Mexicans by teaching students the history of slavery and human migration in Latin America. This history, along with teaching about and comparing the Latin American colonial racial caste system with the US racial categories, could encourage discussions about the arbitrary nature of racial categories. Students could then explore stereotypes of how Mexicans are supposed to look by comparing the use and designation of various racial descriptors. These conversations could move students toward seeing that these boundaries do not exist naturally. They could also tie to students' own experience in different contexts to help show that how individuals experience their identities is not static or absolute. Using these changing conceptions could illustrate to students how the social process of racialization creates group boundaries to delineate the groups and create racial hierarchies.

POSITIONING BLACK SEGREGATION VERSUS LATINX ACHIEVEMENT

Along with the district staff and educators regularly mentioning their concern about the program's lack of diversity, people also stated that the program segregated student groups, which exposed how the groups' interests and needs were positioned as different. For example, during one of her interviews, Ms. Thomson shared, "Even though [the program] is supposed to create more connections and make a level playing field, in a way, at the same time, it's almost segregating [within the schools] more." Almost all the adult participants shared this concern, frequently mentioning the underrepresentation of Black students as creating racial segregation.

So, it surprised me to hear a critique of the focus on the small number of Black students. Two teachers complicated the segregation concerns by questioning the attention devoted to it at the expense of other issues. These teachers, although they agreed it was important to have more Black students in the program, expressed in interviews that the concern of having more Black students in dual language outweighed attention to improving the outcomes of Spanish-dominant Latinx students—a group that was underachieving compared with all other groups in the program. Indeed, the lowest-scoring dual-language students were not the Black students, but the Latinx students.

Ms. Nader was one of the teachers critical about the level of attention on Black student representation leading to the disregard of Latinx outcomes. In discussing Black student achievement and representation, Ms. Nader, whom we met in chapter 2, shared that because the Black students in the program were high achievers,

> I'm much more concerned looking at the numbers of Latino achievement in the program. It appeared to me as the native English speakers as a whole, including Black students, including Asian students, their achievement is where you would want to see them. The Latino students' is not.

Ms. Nader felt that the district and school were not paying enough attention to Latinx underachievement, especially the Spanish-dominant Latinxs, leaving them behind.

When I asked Mr. Ochoa about the repeated calls to have more Black students in dual language, he mentioned not questioning it much before; but upon reflection, he contrasted the education of Latinxs and Black students:

> Si lo que más te preocupa es la falta de afroamericanos, tu prioridad no es este grupo de hispanos porque tú concibes el programa dual-language como una ventaja para él que no habla español, sobre todo cuando esa es la máxima prioridad. (If what most worries you are the lack of African Americans, your priority is not this group of Hispanics because you perceive the dual-language program as an advantage for non-Spanish speakers, above all when that is the highest priority.)

He critiqued the district's focus on the program benefiting non-Spanish dominant students, which he saw as overshadowing another important question:

> La óptica es, hay blancos beneficiándose de esto, ¿por qué no se están beneficiando los negros? Y es una pregunta justa, pero hay otra pregunta muy importante que es ¿cómo conseguimos que este programa cumpla su potencial para los estudiantes hispanos que para eso lo empezamos? (The optics are, Whites are benefiting from this, why aren't Blacks benefiting? And it's a fair question, but there's another very important question: How can we get this program to meet its potential for Hispanic students? Which is why we started this.)

As I moved to ask my next question, Mr. Ochoa interrupted by critiquing the district's sole focus on the disproportionate number of Black students in dual language and not addressing the poor achievement of some Latinx students in the program:

> [El distrito] está muy preocupado por la participación de los afroamericanos. En vez de hacerse las preguntas [de la participación y el logro académico] a la vez. Pero a mí nadie me ha preguntado esto. A mí lo único que me han preguntado mis administradores es como conseguimos los afroamericanos, y es la única reflexión que ha habido desde los administradores. ([The district] is very worried about the enrollment of African Americans. Instead of asking itself the questions [of enrollment and achievement] at the same time. But no one has asked me this. The only thing my

administrators have asked me is how do we get African Americans, and that's the only thought that's come from the administrators.)

In discussing the problem of the program excluding Black students, both Mr. Ochoa and Ms. Nader observed Black interests, perceived as segregation from the program, to be oppositional to Latinx interests, which seemed to center on low academic achievement. Although Mr. Ochoa and Ms. Nader were thoughtful teachers, wanted the program to be diverse, and worked to address Black youths' needs, the districts' dominant discourse delimited the problem and limited the imagined solutions of what could be possible.

When speaking with me and reflecting on the critiques of the program being segregationist, Mr. Ochoa, who also taught the ELL courses, said that for many students schooling already was segregated. He shared that the dual-language program, although it might segregate to some extent, was at least benefiting the students—especially those considered ELLs—through the exposure to the Spanish language and other benefits:

> Si podemos cambiar a una experiencia educativa, que sea segregadora en algunos aspectos, pero que potencie la identidad, la cultura y las capacidades, no puede ser peor. . . . La experiencia ya es segregadora para esa parte de nuestros estudiantes que más lo necesitan, sin ofrecerles nada positivo. (If we could change to an educational experience that is segregated in some respects but that lifts up identity, culture, and capacities, it can't be worse than what we have now. The experience is already segregationist for some of our most vulnerable students without offering them anything positive.)

Mr. Ochoa's observation that bilingual education, even if still segregated, provides a better schooling experience to ELLs than the more typical non-rigorous, segregated ESL schooling, is backed up by research.[31]

Although the communities recognized that the district underserved both Black and Latinx students, Mr. Ochoa's comment reflects a discourse that positioned Black segregation against Latinx achievement, at times creating antagonisms over the scant resources available to them. This was also a tension at the district level, as shown by one example previously mentioned of an elementary school deciding not to offer a dual-language program for fear that it would create more internal segregation. Opponents of dual language disparaged the program by pointing to it aggravating within-school segregation, but others saw this as arguing against Latinxs' right to Spanish-English bilingual education.

Apart from positioning Latinx and Black students as different in terms of behavior and achievement, teachers perceived racial tensions in the school culture that did not help to unite Black students and Latinx students. Mr. Ochoa observed, "Culturalmente aquí hemos tenido un Black versus Brown, ese es un problema real, y también un cierto desconocimiento y desprecio al güero." (Culturally here, we have had a Black versus Brown, and it's a real problem, and also a type of unknowing and a contempt toward Whites.) I had heard reflected a larger tension in the school community positioning Black segregation versus Latinx achievement.[32] This tension reflected a microcosm of Oakville's discourse of polarizing contests between Black and Latinx groups, a narrative that hinders formation of coalitions, and thus ultimately disadvantages racialized Others.[33] But Mr. Ochoa's ideas of contempt toward Whites surprised me and were not expressed by other participants.

Still, these logics of conflict and tension overlooked other possibilities, such as increasing the number of Black students and decreasing White participation. Instead, they fomented friction between Black and Latinx interests in bilingual education.[34] Ultimately, even though there was anxiety over "Black segregation," White material interests in the program were left unchallenged, leaving White students to continue accruing the "bilingual advantage."[35] Indeed, how people understood these issues seemed to place whiteness's advantages under the radar or even place Whites as victims of multiculturalism, as Mr. Ochoa's comment signaled.

Instead, Latinx (under)achievement in dual language was positioned against Black access to dual-language, while most Black students remained in schooling (either dual-language or non-dual-language) that was unresponsive to examining specific needs Black students might have. This divisive and racist positioning of the two groups obstructed efforts to extend educational opportunities to more Latinx and Black students.

MR. COLÓN DIFFERENTIATING RACIALIZED GROUPS

It was only their fourth class meeting, and Mr. Ochoa wanted to get to know the sophomores in his winter-semester World History course. The dual-language tenth graders, having been in the program since elementary school, knew all the other students, except for some of the school's newest English-language learners. After telling the students about how his week went, Mr. Ochoa asked them to fill out a handout with an "Identity Wheel" (a pie chart with different identities). Ten minutes passed, and Mr. Ochoa asked the students to share with a classmate, "Which of your identities is targeted by society?" Once the chatter seemed solidly about weekend plans, Mr. Ochoa asked them to share their answers with the whole class. Students replied,

"Latina." "Mixed." And "I'm not targeted," said a White male student. Then, the same activity was repeated with the question, "Which of your identities is given advantages by society?" And after another round of chatting and sharing, Mr. Ochoa asked "What was challenging about this act?" Someone lazily replied, "Nothing." The class's ninety-five minutes were slowly dragging on with the next question, "What do you need for this classroom to be a safe space?" Around the room's walls hung five posters for the students to write their answers to this question and for others to comment on the responses.

After the students were back at their desks, Mr. Ochoa transitioned to playing an English audio recording and distributed handouts of the Spanish-translation transcript. The audio featured Mr. Jesús Colón reflecting on a train ride in 1955 New York City, where his Puerto Rican and Black identities seemed to come into opposition.[36] Students were to annotate the transcript with questions or reactions while listening. Mr. Colón recounted getting out of work after midnight and taking the train back home. Then "a nice-looking white lady in her early twenties" got on the subway. "Somehow, she managed to push herself in with a baby in her right arm and a big suitcase in her left hand. Two children, a boy and a girl about three and five years old, trailed after her." She was getting ready to get off at the same stop as him. He knew she would have to manage going down some steep stairs and up again to the street. He thought of offering to help her, "Courtesy is important to us Puerto Ricans. . . . I remember thinking, I'm a Negro and a Puerto Rican." But he confessed that a string of questions passed through his mind, "What do I do if she screamed when I went to offer my help?"

The students and I listened, compelled by the story, hearing his hesitation, wondering what he decided, when Mr. Ochoa paused the audio to ask the class for their predictions. Curiosity got the better of several of the students; some did not heed Mr. Ochoa's instructions and went on to peek at the end of the Spanish-translation handout, which he feigned not to notice. He repeated his question. Some students replied, "He didn't help her," making some of us wonder if they had read the ending. Mr. Ochoa did not acknowledge the guesses, instead shifting and asking us to consider Mr. Colón's identities and the tension he felt "having to choose between his identity and his safety."

The students centered on his Black identity, in chorus responding that Mr. Colón felt conflicted and considered his own safety "because he was Black." The class understood Mr. Colón's choice between one identity (Puerto Rican; should offer help) versus another one (Black; woman will be scared, so better not offer help). Students developed a consensus: because society targets his Black identity, he felt worried about helping a White woman. They did not mention his maleness or the intersection of being Black and male. But even though there was consensus, the students' chatter indicated their interest in this activity much more than in the series of questions with the Identity Wheel. I hoped they would express more interpretations of Mr. Colón's comments; for example, perhaps he was commenting on how sexism/racism (their intersection) dehumanized him, forcing that choice on him.

Being mindful that the period only had a minute left, Mr. Ochoa called for attention and turned the audio back on to play the ending of the story. Through the noises of backpacks zipping up, which were quieter than usual, we finished hearing Mr. Colón's regret: "I pushed by her like I saw nothing, as if I were insensitive to her need. I was like a rude animal walking on two legs." The dismissal bell rang, and it being the last period on a Friday, students hurried out of the room. Yet the fact that they had hushed the usual noises of getting their stuff together to leave signaled their interest to me. And I too was captivated, even feeling the discussion ended too abruptly.

The lesson focused students on thinking about society targeting identities in personal ways, and on thinking about racism as about people's bigotry and stereotypes of others. It did not delve into the institutional practices (policing of Black people) that structure society to have a double standard that disadvantages racialized Others (assuming a Black man's guilt in an encounter with a White woman). But maybe the students would have gotten to those points had we continued our discussion.

But even more poignant for me was something that the audio implied: Mr. Colón described Puerto Ricans as having cultural practices (that the class assumed were shared by other Latinxs) that emphasize helping and being courteous to others; and by saying this, it placed Puerto Rican (read Latinx) courtesy as a counter to Black culture (unless they thought of Puerto Rican as possibly Black, which I did not find as a common idea in the program). The students did not talk about Mr. Colón framing his Puerto Ricanness (Latinidad) as the reason he would want to help, and what that implied about his Blackness. And imagining the class discussing this point seems very unlikely compared with their talking about unjust police practices.

The dual-language program, just as other schooling, had lessons that signaled to students what it meant to be Latinx or Black or Afro-Latinx. But sometimes it overlooked the definition of or blurred the differences between concepts like ethnic/national group (Puerto Rican) and racialized group (Black). While a few lessons explicitly focused on ethnicity and on racial issues, such as the one on Mr. Colón's oral history, many implicitly conveyed ideas about race and racialization. And often the latter lessons laid out ideas about the relational positioning of different racialized groups and Latinidad.

The lesson around Mr. Colón's oral history was implicitly relational: the narrative that Puerto Ricans (an ethnic category that people understood as standing for Latino culture) are courteous implies that the contrasted racialized group—in this case, Black folks—do not value courtesy or that they place it secondary to safety considerations. Another relational aspect, which perhaps the lack of time prevented from being addressed, was the way Mr. Colón dehumanized the choice associated with his Black identity into a "rude animal walking on two legs," as if it is less than human to want to avoid the possible danger a scared White woman can cause.[37] The relational aspects of narratives like these matter because how one group is racialized influences, even implicitly, our understanding of the racialization of other groups.[38] When schooling teaches about the delineations of the groups, it then contributes to the social function of racialization, that of constructing and sustaining racial hierarchies.

Humans sort, group, and categorize to differentiate things from other things. This is how categories work: "This is this, because it is not that." The same type of logic and practice happens with people: "You are in this group, because you are not in that group;" and "This group does that, while this other group does this." The pernicious aspect of race comes from sorting, organizing, categorizing people into groups *to dehumanize*. Racialized groups are constructed by positioning them in relation to other racialized groups. To construct groups, then, is to make them have boundaries that delineate them against the other groups. While individual identities are neither fixed nor absolute, and people can face various forms of racial discrimination, the racialization process refers not to discrimination or individual racial identity, such as Afro-Latina, but to society's racialized groups.

POLICING BOUNDARIES

As this and the previous chapters show, since phenotype does not always bind the Latinx racialized group, then that boundary was the Spanish language. Many people understood that a person's language influences which racialized group they are understood to belong to. For example, Nancy's definition of Latinxs (see chapter 3) was based on the Spanish language. This idea also showed up in Mia's comment in chapter 2, "When I speak Spanish, [people outside of school] think I'm like Puerto Rican or Cuban." People used the Spanish language as the signature boundary that delineates the Latinx racialized group. At times and for some, knowing Spanish caused their Latinidad to supersede the racial categorization of White or Black, for example, like happens in other contexts.[39]

For boundaries to be meaningful, they must be policed. People in the dual-language program at times policed the boundaries of the racialized groups through bullying. For example, Jada shared being bullied during her elementary dual-language schooling.

> I was bullied because I was [pauses]. They would call me a "Mexican wannabe" and that was never the case. I just wanted to learn a language other than English, and I just got treated differently because I was different from everybody else. [My friends], we were the only Black girls there. But I was the only African [immigrant], so I was treated very differently.

Jada could not recall being bullied about this during her middle or high school, but she was not the only one to note that people bullied by lumping the program's students into calling them "Mexican" (recall chapter 3). So tied were Spanish and "Latinx," that even students like Jada who did not self-identify (nor did she ever report being identified as Latinx) who wanted to learn Spanish would be labeled as "Latinx" through being insulted as a "Mexican wannabe."

Jada's and other examples show that Oakville's dual-language program, even if implicitly, contributed to making the Spanish language as the signature boundary for the Latinx racialized group.

RELATIONAL RACIALIZATION IN DUAL LANGUAGE

The program's discourses show how the Latinx group and Black group were relationally racialized between and among each other based on factors such as immigration, class, and language, and then positioned into a racial hierarchy. Ideas allowed racist comparisons between and among racialized groups, showing the interconnectedness of racial categories and how racist ideas against one group can be used against another group. For example, some dual-language teachers described Latinxs as model minorities in terms of behavior but not academics. This positioned Latinxs as different—and better and worse in some ways—than their dual-language Black classmates. At the same time, because the program only had the "cream of the crop" Black students, teachers described the dual-language Black students, especially immigrants, as model minorities when compared with non-dual-language Black students.

Describing a minority of Black students as model minorities while the majority as undesirable furthered anti-Black ideas. Overall, this rationalized Black American students' placement below Latinxs in the racial hierarchy, consistent with other research findings.[40] This hindered the program from providing equity for both Latinx students and Black students, and for students who identified as both Latinx and Black, Afro-Latinx.

Considering the relational racialization described in part 2, the dual-language program's discourses and practices circulated ideas that made "Latinx" as separate from society's other racialized groups. Because how racialized groups are discriminated against *and* positioned against each other contributes to defining the boundaries of these groups, the bilingual program, in turn, mirrored and perpetuated the societal notion that the Spanish language was the defining characteristic demarcating the Latinx racial category. The program also reinforced ideas distinguishing the Latinx group from other racialized groups, leaving little room for considering Asian Latinxs, Afro-Latinxs, and Indigenous Latinxs. Additionally, the Latinx/Black duality made invisible Afro-Latinxs, Asian Americans, and Indigenous students in the program, and this duality obscured whiteness's role in fomenting racial tensions over limited resources and political power.

I observed few pedagogical instances where teachers explored or highlighted the existence of Afro-Latinx, Asian Latinx, and Indigenous Latinx. However, that there was a trend toward increasing the view of that possibility shows that the program would further reinforce the Spanish language as the signature boundary for the Latinx racialized group. That is because knowing Spanish (or being seen as "you-ought-to-know Spanish" through, for example, having a Spanish surname) provides a legitimate claim to being in the "Latinx" group for people who identify as Asian Latinx, Afro-Latinx, and Indigenous Latinx.[41]

In the next two chapters, I continue to see how the dual-language program made race in more implicit ways. We see what ideas and effects the program advances by how it relationally racializes.

PART III

Racialization's Consequences

CHAPTER 5

Racial Structures, Racial Patterns

In a January 2015 meeting of Latinos Unidos, Oakville's education-focused Latinx community organization, some members shared that the district marginalized and ignored the concerns of Latinx residents. The district's large racial disparities had pushed some activists to call for action. Two leaders even floated the possibility of filing an official complaint to the federal Department of Education's Office of Civil Rights for violations of the educational opportunities provided to English language learners. To demand that their concerns be heard but before committing to such action, Latinos Unidos invited the Oakville Urban School District superintendent, Dr. Nancy Lewis, to a public meeting. They asked Dr. Lewis to report on the district's progress and plans for improving the schooling of Latinxs and ELLs.

The meeting was held October 2015 in the Hispanic Community Center of Oakville and was one of several events with district personnel meant to inform the community. Members sat down in the twenty folding chairs set in a circle, and the jovial chatter faded out. As I waited for the meeting to start, I wondered whether and how the members would mention these specific complaints. I knew the community leaders and members were eager to listen to Dr. Lewis but also to voice their concerns about Latinx's educational opportunities and outcomes.

Previously, Latinos Unidos had called for the district to diversify the teacher workforce, so in this meeting, the superintendent started by celebrating that the district had hired twenty new Latinx teachers (out of sixty new hires). No one asked whether these twenty teachers included teachers from Spain, given the district's hiring program of recruiting teachers from Spain. She then noted that the highest rate of teacher turnover was among Latinx teachers. (It was unclear whether the turnover rates for "Latinx" teachers included the program for recruiting/hiring immigrant teachers from Spain.) The attendees asked some questions about what the district was doing to retain Latinx teachers. Dr. Lewis answered that the district hoped that the programs to recruit and prepare teachers from the community would help them with this challenge. Soon after mentioning the "grow-your-own teacher" programs, she emphasized that the district did not want merely tolerance. She and other district administrators wanted the district to show support and care to its students by creating safe schools, while also developing students' critical awareness to challenge assumptions.

Most of the ensuing discussion centered on Latinx students and their achievement. Dr. Lewis shared that the district calculated that ELLs were the group with the lowest high school graduation attainment, with around 50 percent graduating. This percentage had gone up from the previous years, so she remarked on the district making progress for its ELLs. However, Latinx students' high school graduation rate remained stagnant at around 60 percent. The superintendent also reported that Latinx early literacy scores had increased by 10 points in standardized tests, and Black students' scores increased by 12 points. She attributed the improvements in Latinx achievement to, among other things, the district's dual-language program and mentioned the possibility of offering dual language in more schools. She recognized the need to collaborate with principals to form community within schools and to not make the dual-language programs stand separately from the school. Around the circle, people nodded their approval.

While the district responded to concerns to address disparities in the education of Latinx or ELLs by offering various policy reforms, it placed much of its hope on the plan to expand its small-scale dual-language program into more schools. The district's dual-language program was portrayed as mostly for the educational attainment and benefit of all students, but especially Latinxs. Most people saw the program as a way to disrupt the racial patterns observed widely in our society. People especially imagined that it would improve Latinx educational achievement. Yet, the program still delivered disparities.

This chapter demonstrates how the bilingual program made race through structural policies and practices such as tracking, testing, and award systems alongside prevailing meritocracy narratives and constructions of success. These policies, practices, and discourses produced outcomes with racial patterns, which allude to the idea that human lineages exist. They also reflect and reinforce the accompanying societal "common sense" of some racialized groups' natural inferiority, as we will hear Mrs. Blair express. The chapter also shows the tensions from the district wanting the program to advance Latinxs' outcomes, yet the program being unable to circumvent its structural racist practices.

RACIALIZING BRAINS

To promote the dual-language program, the Oakville school district emphasized that it would improve Latinxs' academic achievement and individual students' potential for increased earnings capability from bilingualism. The district also touted the popular narrative of bilingualism as brain-enhancing.[1] It distributed a promotional brochure for dual language with the heading "Learning another language is good for growing brains!" Several teachers, parents, and community members shared that White parents wanted their kids to obtain bilingualism's cognitive edge. Ms. West, a Spanish-English bilingual White teacher/mother in an English-speaking household, shared with me that a bilingual program without White students would "be shutting doors for opportunity in the future" because "all the brain research shows they're better problem solvers" as bilinguals.

Another White mother, Mrs. Blair—a parent of a biracial (Latino/White) student—observed that the district "talked a lot about the impact on the brain of being bilingual," suggesting that the program's cognitive benefits might help alleviate Latinxs' achievement disparity. She expressed confusion about how the program would address Latinxs' disparities in education given that the brain enhancement from bilingualism would advantage *both* Whites and Latinxs:

> What I never quite understood is how they sell, like—okay ideally, we're fixing a disparity for one group, but then what are we doing for the other group? Well, we're giving them some benefit to the brain. But that extends to both groups. So, I'm not totally sure how it's supposed to help the lower group catch up then.

Of course, the achievement disparity between Whites and Latinx is relative; if both White and Latinx students' performance goes up by the same percentage, the difference would remain the same. But the district's discourse—that the bilingual brain is better cognitively than the monolingual brain—mapped onto already problematic ideas about standardized tests showing intellectual aptitude. That Mrs. Blair wondered whether Latinxs' achievement would be improved by the cognitive promise of bilingualism betrayed an understanding of Latinxs' poor outcomes as stemming from low cognitive development. This was a troubling idea that the district transmitted in its explanation of how the program was supposed to achieve equity—and, specifically, improve Latinxs' education.

As Mrs. Blair's doubts show, the "improving brains" discourse, when layered on the goal that the dual-language program would improve Latinx's academic achievement, fomented ill-placed worries about White students also getting smarter, thus canceling out Latinxs' cognitive gains and jeopardizing their academic advancement in relation to others. (Indeed, research suggests Whites receive socioeconomic advantages through bilingualism but is less clear about racialized Others also gaining similar advantages.[2])

Additionally, her comment speaks to the idea that these racialized groups have different cognitive capabilities—unintentionally insinuating the idea that race is biological and that this has consequences for learning.[3] I am sure Mrs. Blair would be aghast that her comments could be interpreted this way. Surely, she did not think that her son was cognitively inferior because of his Latino father, for instance. My point in sharing her idea is not to single her out. Rather her comment and her confusion show just how strong our society's ideas are about biological races existing (which includes the Latinx group), and that some are intellectually inferior.

Ultimately, the district's problematic focus on cerebral and economic rewards for individuals conflicted with the program's equity goals. It also shows the importance of districts considering and challenging society's common sense idea that biological races exist.

But even if the district had not used the popular messages about dual language's cognitive effects, schooling's discourses about smartness and its rewards still perpetuated ideas that biological race existed and positioned Latinxs with other racialized groups.

BORANE'S HONORS ASSEMBLY

Borane's award assembly took place first thing one November morning. I recognized several classes of dual-language sixth graders as they were filing into the auditorium along with groups of other, non-dual-language students. To curb bad behavior, staff asked students to sit every other seat in the auditorium rows, but the considerable number of students and the small size of the auditorium eventually made students share armrests. The school building was not designed to accommodate the large number of students enrolled in Borane. This overcrowding problem made the school have three honors assemblies that morning, one for each grade.

I sat with Mr. Mayer's sixth-grade dual-language social-studies class, a high-energy group. On the stage, Borane's principal, Mr. Jackson, a Black man, stood looking at the audience. As the noise level went down, he announced through the microphone that there should not be any voices when he was talking. Once the chatter settled down, Mr. Jackson gave an introduction and shared that for him it was especially important to honor their names by saying them right, and to please help him.

After some other instructions, Mr. Jackson started calling dual-language students who had earned High Honors. Students, wearing dresses or button-down shirts, walked up to the stage and stayed there with their certificates until a counselor took a group photo. I noticed that out of the three dual-language classes (totaling about ninety students), only seven students had earned the award: there were three White girls, two White boys, one Latina girl, and one Black girl. Then Honor Roll recipients were called up to join the High Honor group; at one point, I wondered if the whole auditorium would be called up, as about thirty more students squeezed into the stage for the photo. At that point, noticing who remained from Mr. Mayer's class was easier: most Latinos and two Black boys.[4] Next came the attendance award: one Latina and most of the remaining Latinos from the audience joined the stage.

Both Borane and Amlie had a flamboyant culture of awards. They awarded students for several types of achievements, and they made these quite public—announcing them over the school intercom, on bulletin boards, and in the school newspaper. As my first time learning of the High Honors award, I wondered whether this was "award inflation" because, in my youth, we called the equivalent just "Honor Roll." Borane's overcrowded stage was trying to show that its students excelled. Celebrating students' accomplishments is a staple of American school culture. But so is providing the inequitable schooling that leads to many of these different achievement outcomes.[5] Indeed, inequitable schooling (evident in aspects such as school funding, teacher quality, access to culturally relevant curriculum) increases the likelihood of attaining awards and achievements for those who already have advantages. When schools and society consistently advantage a particular racialized group and then recognize them with awards, it reveals a pattern that alludes to the idea that this group is inherently "school focused," smarter, better, and superior.

Borane's award assemblies were gendered and racialized indicators of who were the "smart kids." As those dual-language students lined up on the auditorium stage, I saw the overrepresentation of White students. And others also noticed. In my interviews, students often mentioned that White students were smarter. For example, after I asked Larissa, a sixth-grade Latina, if she noticed certain groups doing better than others, she shared,

> Pienso que son más, como, . . . pueden ser más inteligentes que los otros, para hacer muchas cosas, los blancos que los latinos, . . . veo que tienen como muy buenas calificaciones y el resto no tenemos muy buenas. (I think that they are more, like . . . they can be more intelligent than the rest, to do lots of things, Whites than Latinos, . . . I see that they have like very good grades and the rest we don't have very good [grades].)

Thus, Larissa observed that White students in the program did not lose their status as the "smarter" kids.

Andrea, an eighth-grade Latina, also noted these patterns: "I feel like the smart kids in my school are the English-speaking kids who learned Spanish, and the Mexican kids who speak Spanish as their first language are not the smart kids." She referred to the program's smart kids with a linguistic descriptor—the "English-speaking kids who learned Spanish." The students who comprised this group were most likely White and less likely Latinx. But maybe she did not mention racial composition because there were some exceptions; for example, the Black model-minority immigrant students I described in chapter 4. Interestingly, Andrea (dad Peruvian; mom "half" Mexican/White) mentioned the "not smart kids" as the "Mexican kids who speak Spanish." Perhaps Isabel perceived a difference within ethnic groups and that "Mexican kids" were the worst-off Latinxs.

Formal school practices that provided racialized patterns like the one displayed on the auditorium stage served to reinforce to students like Larissa and Andrea that there are linguistic, racialized groups, and which groups are smart and would come out ahead. The honors assembly was but one indicator in dual language showing White students achieving better than even the Latinx students. This did not square with the widespread narrative that the dual-language program provided educational equity to Latinxs and other students.

TRACKING DUAL-LANGUAGE STUDENTS

Why was it that even though the "research-based" dual-language program was supposed to improve the achievement of Latinxs, the program did not live up to this expectation?

The program continued school practices that disproportionately and negatively affected Latinxs, such as tracking by testing and policing English-language acquisition. Perhaps these practices were not known to parents, or parents overlooked them because of the dominant narratives that rationalize tracking as based on merit. Regardless, these practices disadvantaged dual-language Latinx students by tracking them into lower-status and lower-rigor classes.

Amlie High, for example, offered a remedial math course for students labeled as ELLs and who had low math scores or grades. Half of the course's students were dual-language students, and all of these were Latinxs. Indeed, most Latinxs in the program were still classified as ELLs and so took the associated standardized tests (that is, English language proficiency examinations for evaluating ELLs' English acquisition). By following the schools' tracking and testing practices, the program was unable to protect some Latinx dual-language students from being placed in remedial courses and/or summer school (students used the latter to recover credits from failed courses).

Borane also used tracking and testing practices, and these also negatively and disproportionately affected Latinxs. For example, Borane students were tracked by their math courses; everyone took sixth-grade math, and then, depending on test scores, the highest achievers were put into seventh-grade algebra and then progressed to eighth-grade geometry. Students with low test scores would move on to seventh-grade math and then eighth-grade math, courses that had disproportionately high numbers of Latinxs. The English-dominant dual-language students, who were almost all White, selected two electives such as computers, art, gym, music, or college-readiness. However, dual-language students with lower English test scores or grades, who were disproportionately Latinx, took only one elective; instead of a second elective, the school enrolled these students in a "reading course" where they went over English and Spanish phonics and completed a computerized multiple-choice literacy program in English (electives could mix dual-language and non-dual-language students).

Teachers and staff explained that the reading course was the school's response to pressure for higher English language and literacy test scores among its Latinx students. Ms. West shared that dual-language teachers were "very concerned about our lower readers getting put into an extra reading class that is not designed for bilingual students." She added, "They're back breaking down words by sounds . . . And they can't take art because they're in the reading classes. And they don't have parents to advocate for them, either; they just do what the school tells them to do."

Using the evaluation of Latinxs' English language as a way to provide inferior schooling is commonplace in the United States. The dual-language program was unable to escape from also engaging in this practice because of pressures from testing policies and the deficit idea that Latinxs' English language remains deficient. So even when Latinxs were in dual language, the privileging of English attainment based on standardized tests meant that Latinxs were tracked into less rigorous instruction and inferior bilingual schooling. Tracking itself, along with the inferior education that resulted in disparate outcomes, created racial patterns for all to notice, which included positioning Latinx as a racialized group.

BORANE'S BILITERACY COURSE

All Borane dual-language students took a thirty-minute biliteracy course at the school day's end, and each dual-language teacher was free to choose the lesson and language. Students were tracked into low-, average-, and high-ability classrooms.

In one of my visits to the low-tracked group taught by Ms. Íñiguez—a class with all Latinx students, except for one Black student—students sat quietly, eyes fixed on their laptop. (Borane boasted that it was a one-to-one technology school, meaning the school provided each student with their own laptop, which they carried throughout the day along with their binders and other school supplies). Each student individually read a story from an online curriculum, answered multiple-choice questions, and upon finishing, got up and showed Ms. Íñiguez their score from the testing module. This activity happened often for the low-tracked group. Other activities for this class included, for example, selecting the word that does not belong in a group (for instance, *arcaico, viejo, antiguo, joven*).

The high-tracked biliteracy course was taught by Ms. Lucas and had most of the White students. That course demonstrated the program's ability to offer students experiences that educational research would describe as enriching for all. For instance, students could select a book to read by themselves or with friends. However, the program's tracking practices placed Latinxs in the low-tracked biliteracy course thus excluded many Latinxs from the superior learning experiences their White counterparts received. Even though some described the dual-language program as an equity strategy for Latinxs, the program struggled to achieve outcomes that disrupted typical racial patterns for its students, as shown by Latinx dual-language students being over-represented in remedial biliteracy/math.

EXCLUDING LATINXS FROM BILINGUAL SCHOOLING

But Latinxs outside the program were affected as well—the dual-language program also reinforced outcomes with racial patterns by excluding certain Latinxs. This exclusion happened because the district allocated its scarce bilingual resources to offer biliterate schooling to all, thus serving fewer Latinxs.

Another reason Latinx students were excluded from dual language had to do with their being seen as deficient in Spanish or English. To start, Latinx students who had not been in the elementary-level dual-language program were not enrolled in the secondary-level program; thus they were denied bilingual education. There were a few exceptions to this exclusion. Immigrant newcomers who were deemed literate in Spanish were placed in Spanish-based dual-language courses. Other Latinx youth wanting to improve their Spanish could be evaluated on their grade-level proficiency of academic Spanish language, as described in Amlie High's curriculum guide:

> [The] Dual Language (Spanish/English) program aims for student bilingualism and biliteracy. The classes in the program teach core subject curriculum (social studies, language arts) and the language of instruction is Spanish. The program is open to any student who can demonstrate grade-level proficiency in academic Spanish language.

Thus, Latinx youth who were not in dual language but wanted to improve their Spanish literacy had to demonstrate "grade-level proficiency in academic Spanish language" as determined by a dual-language teacher.[6] Requiring youth to prove they had enough Spanish literacy to be successful in the program resulted in non-dual-language students being excluded from a biliterate education unless they *already* possessed the advanced bilingual-language skills needed to pass the evaluation. This testing option was not publicized, and when I asked teachers, none could verify that a student had taken this test.

Secondary-level Latinxs also could be excluded from the dual-language program if their English was deemed inadequate. Because the primary concern regarding Latinx students in dual language was for them to learn English, Spanish-dominant dual-language Latinxs who were not making adequate gains in English tests could be withdrawn from the program by the school or their parents and put in ESL courses focused on learning English. That is, a student could be in the dual-language program *only as long as* they were attaining English as measured by standardized exams. The option of withdrawing students based on the policing of English acquisition determined who had access to the program. This meant that excluded Latinx students might have missed the opportunity to benefit from the program and improve their biliteracy. (Although several Latinx students could have been withdrawn based on their English-acquisition test scores, I found during my study that this practice was applied to only one student. More commonly, students chose to leave the program of their own accord for various reasons, including not feeling competent in Spanish, believing that the instruction was not effectively improving their Spanish skills, and encountering course scheduling conflicts.)

Consequently, the program excluded some Latinxs through its standardized exams and teacher evaluations of Latinxs' "academic" literacy, both of which, research suggests, can be influenced by ideas that devalue Latinxs' literacy.[7] This exclusion prevented many Latinxs from receiving rigorous biliteracy schooling on par with their White and Black model-minority peers. As a group, Latinxs experienced an inferior education, which led to inadequate achievement.

BORANE'S SPELLING BEE

On a Tuesday morning, Ms. West, who had been battling a cold the day before, announced at the start of her class that she was still feeling unwell and had now also lost her voice. The exertions of the previous day had taken their toll on her. With only two days left before the winter break, the students were abuzz with energy—not for schoolwork, but for the upcoming vacation.

Ms. West pressed on and told us that each English language arts classroom would be able to send one student to compete against the rest of the school in the school's Spelling Bee Final. They would start the qualifier today in class for those interested in competing. The winner would represent their sixth-grade dual-language group.

Ms. West informed us that competing was voluntary. Those who wanted to participate should take out a piece of paper and write their name on top. About half the class, which included several Latinx students, took out paper. Ms. West asked me to announce the words for the spelling bee qualifier— *ladybug, sesame, tantrum, gemstone, mower, owed, anxiously, growl, ultimatum, haphazard, aquarium.* As I did so, I noticed Theo, one of the White students, hovered over his paper to prevent others from copying his answers.

I then scored the results (everyone misspelled *ultimatum*). Looking over the Latinx contestants' misspellings of the various words, I noticed that the Latinx students used Spanish pronunciation and spelling to write the phonetic sounds of the English words.

After we arrived at the results, Ms. West announced to the class that the winner, with only one misspelled word, was Theo. The two runner-ups were a White and a Black female student. I found out later from Mr. Estrada, who volunteered as a moderator, that the other sixth-grade dual-language class also was represented by a White male student and the two runner-ups were a Latina and a White female student. Mr. Estrada shared that hardly any of the eighth-grade Latinx students had volunteered for the spelling bee. It seemed that after two years of Borane's spelling bee, most of the Latinx eighth graders had decided it was not even worth competing from the start.

The outcome of the English spelling bee—that White students would represent dual-language classes to the whole school—reinforced who were the "school-motivated" and "smart kids." These competitions and awards disproportionately benefited White students. Even though most of the Latinx students came from families with low income and low education attainment, which determines achievement outcomes, people still judged these competitions as objectively displaying something about the students.[8] That is, they further reinforced Latinx as a racialized group and the common sense of racial inferiority.

PRESERVING DEFICIT NARRATIVES

Several participants rationalized dual-language student outcomes with meritocratic justifications, which reinforced deficit views of Latinxs. For example, Mr. Pérez, an Afro-Latino bilingual resource teacher, found dual-language Latinxs' achievement "frustrating" and "demoralizing." However, he attributed the outcomes to the White students' dedication, saying, "Some of our best kids are the Anglo kids, because they put a certain application, a certain work ethic into it."

Mr. Estrada also said White students "actually [do] the work" (that is, class assignments), leading them to be the "smart students" even in the Spanish courses. Few questioned whether the program elevated certain kinds of school performance over others and constructed high performance based on white-normative practices (e.g., language practices). Instead, explanations for the achievement gap between White and Latinx students reflected deficit narratives that blame Latinxs when they do not achieve as expected.

Research suggests that teachers, even bilingual teachers, perceive White students as smarter and more determined than racialized-Othered students.[9] From the many reasons that this trend exists, it is worth mentioning the popular idea that Whites have the "academic language" needed to succeed. Recent scholarship has unsettled this idea and now points to the racialized status of the speaker as what determines evaluations of their speech.[10] For teachers, who are constantly assessing their students' language, this evaluation is of utmost importance, given that the evaluation of students is based on racialized ways of hearing.

THE SEAL OF BILITERACY

One award that was practically reserved for dual-language students, and that people expected would benefit Latinxs, was the "Seal of Biliteracy." This is a nationally recognized award that confers the title of biliterate. A school district decides how to bestow the award and affixes the Seal to students' high school graduation diplomas. Once the Oakville district began offering dual language in high schools, it also started promoting the coveted Seal. To obtain it, youth were required to demonstrate proficiency in English and an additional language, and to exhibit "high levels of sociocultural competence." Participants spoke of the dual-language program as making students "fully bilingual" and of the Seal as official proof of biliteracy and of "possessing multicultural sensibilities." Moreover, they felt that it increased the marketability of the Seal holders. Educators and parents anticipated the award would be a step toward recognizing ELLs and other language-minoritized students for their biliteracy.

Controversy ensued at Amlie when the district announced the prerequisites for obtaining the Seal. Students labeled as ELLs, which in dual language comprised Latinxs, were required to take an additional exam to prove their English literacy; thus demonstrating how the label and its accompanying assessments (which rely on problematic understandings of what language is, how it is assessed, and what it means to be bilingual) disadvantage these youth.[11]

Teachers expressed that the biliteracy tests favored the English-dominant students, since English proficiency was demonstrated by a college-entry national standardized exam considered more difficult than the Spanish exam. For example, Ms. Schloss noted that the Seal requirements needed changes: "I think it's something that we need to revisit, and if the only people who are getting the Seal of Biliteracy are Anglo kids with college-educated parents, then it doesn't do anything that it's supposed to do." Ms. Schloss's and the teachers' intuition was correct: the district's standards for the award resulted in the majority of those who qualified for the Seal to be White students, while many Latinxs and ELLs did not meet the prerequisites.

The results sparked outrage. Youth and their parents were upset that dual-language students were not automatically awarded the Seal for having participated in the program since elementary school. After all, these seniors were the district's first graduating class of dual-language students.

Ms. Schloss, along with other teachers, youth, and parents, recognized the injustice and some advocated for a change in the policy. They argued that the district had announced the policy too late in the school year. This pressure caused the district to waive its requirements for the first graduating dual-language cohort, awarding all of them the Seal. However, this win was only for that first cohort. In the following dual-language cohort of about 30 students—out of approximately 380 total seniors at Amlie—only seven students obtained the Seal (their racial/linguistic information was unavailable).

Regardless of the number of dual-language students awarded the Seal, the policy perpetuated racial inequities by recognizing biliteracy in a way that favored a disproportionate number of White students at the expense of youth who were racialized Others.[12] This institutional exclusion from dual language (and other biliterate schooling, as we soon learn) placed Latinxs in an educational catch-22: where the program practices (and formal recognition of bilingualism) did not commend their bilingualism if not through the dual-language program and the Seal of Biliteracy. This practice reinforced the common sense of racialized distinctions existing, delineated the Latinx group by the Spanish language, and positioned Latinxs in an inferior position to their English-dominant White peers.

WHOSE BILITERACY GETS RECOGNIZED

César started the dual-language program in elementary school. He spoke to his parents, working-class immigrants from México, mostly in Spanish. A high-achieving Latino high schooler, he sought to challenge himself academically and planned to major in physics in college. In ninth grade, he dropped the dual-language program to take honors courses. He had decided that the dual-language program was not rigorous enough for him and that his Spanish was being "contaminated" by hearing others who were less proficient than him.

Despite coming from a Spanish-speaking home and being biliterate, César lamented, "I probably won't get [the Seal on my diploma] to prove I'm bilingual." César saw the Seal as an official recognition of biliteracy, a recognition denied to him. His statement shows that the district policies about qualifications for the Seal defined who is considered legitimately bilingual. The district's decisions (along with other award recognitions) disadvantaged bilingual Latinx youth who were not in dual language, even though the Seal was technically available to youth who met the requirements regardless of program enrollment. But when I asked a teacher how non-dual-language youth like César would learn about the Seal and its requirements, she replied that it would be difficult to get the information because it was imparted during dual-language classes. In effect, Amlie limited this award to students with the official designation of "dual-language student."

Students like César recognized that the Seal made biliteracy into an exclusive award with requirements designated by the district and dual-language educators. The program conferred the title of bilingual/biliterate onto some students, which established a norm of distinguishing oneself for material rewards to the exclusion of others. By conferring biliteracy as a title, the policy of awarding the Seal disregarded the bilingual repertoires of non-dual-language Latinx youth.[13] The power differences between White and Latinx communities that subvert equity are shown in how the advantages afforded to Latinx youth had to be "made available" to non-Latinxs but still limited through constructing bilingualism based on program participation. Thus, the awarding of the Seal advantaged select students, and in doing so, because the resources were not equitable, created outcomes that showed racial patterns. The patterns in turn perpetuated the common sense of racialized distinctions existing and that some groups are innately smarter, better. This racist idea maintained and promoted hierarchies that positioned Latinx students as inferior to White peers.

RACIALIZATION: WHAT'S SEEN AND UNSAID

Some participants were frustrated that the Latinx students were still not doing as well as they expected, as the district had promised. When they saw the overrepresentation of White students winning awards like the High Honors, or the spelling bee, or the Seal of Biliteracy, they expressed dismay that the program did not level the playing field. For example, Ms. Nader shared,

> We had this idea that the program was really supposed to raise literacy of native Spanish speakers; [it's] supposed to benefit native Spanish speakers. It doesn't seem like literacy of the Latino students is reaching that level of the Latino native English speakers.

It was the case that the dual-language program was unable to level the playing field enough for students for varied reasons. These reasons are rooted in the improbability that underfunded schools can counteract social injustices that affect schooling but originate outside the educational realm; for example, disparate access to health care and housing. There was also the fact that the dual-language program policies and practices did not work in the interest of Latinxs and created patterns showing Latinx underachievement. The unrecognized (or at least unspoken) reality that may have led to dissatisfaction was that the program did not do enough to unsettle racial hierarchies.

In education, we often hear that policies and practices should support culturally relevant education to have students succeed. Since a culturally relevant education includes a linguistically relevant education, that means providing a bilingual education—especially for Latinxs, since language-education discrimination works to racialize Latinxs. We can see how overt discriminatory language policies like English-only schooling and subtractive English as a Second Language programs are tools that work to racialize Latinxs: these subtractive policies mark Latinxs as a group in need of remediation and provide them with a substandard education, unsurprisingly resulting in Latinxs' lower achievement, which works to further the idea that (biological) races exist.

As we see in the next chapter, participants were dismayed that dual language—as a policy and program that should provide a culturally/linguistically relevant education thus improve students' educational outcomes, particularly for Latinxs—still disproportionately benefited White students. Simply, the program functioned as a racial project that distributed resources along racial lines, disadvantaging Latinxs. I pointed out to people when appropriate that Borane and Amlie are not alone in struggling to deliver educational equity to its racialized students.[14] Other schools may share some of the same policy and program decisions that result in unsatisfactory outcomes.

At Borane and Amlie, some of the policy and program decisions did work to advantage a few Latinxs, but this was mostly at the expense of many other racialized-Othered students, including Latinxs. Some of these decisions dealt with how the district allocated bilingual resources and how (or to whom) it promoted the dual-language program. Some decisions deprioritized Latinx students' needs, making them subordinate to those of Whites. Other decisions provided Latinx youth with a less rigorous dual-language program. Still other decisions excluded Latinxs from biliteracy schooling altogether or limited bilingual/biliterate recognition to certain students by formalizing and bestowing a biliteracy award. The community saw how these decisions negatively affected most Latinx students and did not provide them with the same educational opportunities as other students. These structural decisions caused racial patterns in achievement, outcomes that people noted.

What was left unrecognized—or at least unsaid—both at the schools and in some educational scholarship is that the aggregate effect of all these policies and practices means dual language of course contributes to the process of racialization: Latinx students are provided an education that creates disparate and noticeable outcomes in educational achievement, which reinforced the idea of racialized Others' inferiority. These outcomes serve to preserve and uphold a white supremacist racial hierarchy, consequently thwarting the potential of providing youth an equitable schooling.

Structural restraints made the dual-language program unable to change the racialized patterns that contribute to race-making. That is, the structural program practices and policies provided Latinxs with inferior schooling compared with White students. Latinx students were thus not offered the same opportunities, benefits, or attention their White peers received; and most were even excluded from dual language. These practices and outcomes make race and the racial hierarchy into "common sense": some groups are smarter, better, superior to others. In turn, they also make racist practices seem justified and reasonable instead of framing the racial patterns as resulting from racist structural practices, further creating Latinx as a racialized group. The program did not upset the troubling construction of Latinxs' lack of work ethic and achievement in the program. Thus, racial ideas of who is considered smart and who achieves in school perpetuated positioning Latinx students below White students in the white supremacist racial hierarchy, as we see in the next chapter.

Racial Hierarchy, Racial Inequities

L ike any other school day morning, as I walked down Borane Middle School's hallways, I turned to glimpse the displayed student work and posters of politicians like President Barack Obama. Outside each classroom's door was a poster with the teacher's picture and the title of the book the teacher was currently reading.

But unlike other mornings, I had arrived at Borane having learned earlier that morning that Donald Trump had won the presidential election. Many Americans had voted for someone who openly disparaged Latinxs and immigrant communities. Trump had energized his campaign by promising to build a wall on the México/US border and deport Mexicans, whom he claimed were rapists and murderers. His attacks included plans to increase the deportations of immigrants, which were already at all-time highs under the Obama administration. Trump's rhetoric sent chilling messages to immigrant communities about their security, with one dual-language teacher reporting on the day after the election that her students said goodbye with a half-joke that they might not be back tomorrow because they and their parents might be deported.

At the school, the mood was somber. Even the atmosphere in the hallways, which usually teemed with people excitedly chatting and rushing to their first destinations, was subdued. Having observed Borane dual-language classrooms for two months by then, I anticipated that most of the teachers and staff would attend to their kids' emotional well-being, especially the well-being of Latinxs and other racialized-Othered youth given the racist rhetoric of the election. Borane's largest racial group was Latinx students (approximately 34 percent), and its dual-language program was closer to 55 percent Latinx.

That day, I first visited Ms. West's English language arts dual-language class. Ms. West's firm, rigorous, and fun demeanor made her well-liked by her students. She was also one of the teachers likely to discuss difficult issues with her sixth graders.

Ms. West's homeroom classroom students sat in a circle, talking about the election in serious tones. When they transitioned to the day's English language arts period, Ms. West asked her students at what time they had gone to bed the night before, and students' responses included midnight, 1 a.m., and 2 a.m.—even later than I had endured. One of the students asked Ms. West: "Are you wearing all black like Ms. Green [another teacher] because you're sad? And who did you vote for?" Ms. West responded gently that it was not polite to ask people for whom they voted. Then she added, "But I'm not happy." She reminded them about what they had mentioned in homeroom, to "be extra kind to each other because some people are very disappointed and also tired because they went to sleep late." Unusually, the principal walked in, and Ms. West shared that they "had a really good circle that morning." The principal expressed his approval and promptly left. Ms. West directed the attention of the class to their scheduled visit to the school library for its book fair. She shared with the students that although she cared about their feelings, she also wanted to get them the schooling they needed.

As we left in a group to the library, a White woman approached me to introduce herself. We shook hands and she told me she was "just a mother" volunteering once a week or so. In the hallway, as Ms. West and I walked together to the library, Ms. West whispered to me that she was the mother of the only boy in the class who was a Trump supporter. Ms. West shared with me that the school had "a post-election coordinated plan for ____ students." I did not catch what word she said before "students" because her whisper trailed off as she continued. I thought I heard "undocumented students," but after I asked for clarification—"For whom?"—she whispered, "Trump supporters."

Trump supporters—I was taken aback. I assumed the school would formulate a plan to support its immigrant, Latinx, Muslim/Arab, and other students from marginalized groups in the event of Trump's victory. I had not expected Trump-supporting White students to be their main concern! Maybe the school's educators did not anticipate Trump winning, thus planned for supporting its Trump-supporting students? Yet after spending the day hearing some students worry that they would be separated from their families, it was difficult not to interpret the situation as a disregard for the severe consequences for the most vulnerable students, some of whom came from communities with histories of family separation.[1] Indeed, Trump's racist rhetoric had fueled assaults against immigrants and people from racialized groups, increasing hate crimes' visibility and number during the presidential campaign.[2] And these students would suffer from the president-elect's promised policies. In contrast, Trump-supporting families did not expect to face equivalent harms had Hillary Clinton won. Given the distress and realities of students from mixed-status families, the school's coordinated plan and the time and attention dedicated to the Trump-supporter students seemed misguided or ill-conceived at best. The school practice decision left the individual teachers with the task of including in their classroom instruction any efforts centered on the concerns of racialized-Othered students. It also left teachers without guidance on how to develop students' critical consciousness to understand the outcome of the election.

Later, during our lunch break, Ms. West shared that the school had held a mock election and that only 25 out of Borane's 650 students had voted for Trump. She said that boy was one of those students, and maybe the only one from a Republican family in the school's dual-language program. Then I remembered that, as he was leaving the classroom earlier that morning, I had heard Ms. West praise him because he did a good job at today's circle discussion, again demonstrating the attention to Trump supporters.

The adults at Borane strove to support students in the wake of the election. Borane's principal checked in on all the classrooms that morning. Adults fielded students' questions in and outside of their class time. They listened and consoled students. People did what they could. Yet the attention seemed skewed. The school plan's focus on Trump-supporting (White) students reinforced racial hierarchies. And the explanations about how Trump was elected—"Some people are ignorant"—seemed devoid of structural considerations.

In this chapter, I continue to connect how structural forces shaped the bilingual education program primarily for the material advantage of White students rather than for Latinx equity, while also spotlighting relevant district and state policies. I demonstrate how state funding policies, for example, pushed the program to prioritize Whites' concerns over those of racialized Others, thereby distributing resources along racial lines. I reveal how the program, as a racial project, structurally privileged whiteness and, consequently—although not intentionally—reinforced racial inequities, perpetuated a white supremacist racial hierarchy, and ultimately "made race."

LATER THAT NOVEMBER AFTERNOON

Like many other classrooms, posters decorated the walls of Mr. Ochoa's classroom. Mr. Ochoa was one of Amlie's social studies/history teachers and an immigrant from Spain who identified as White and culturally Hispanic.

Many of the posters had some political message, like "The fact that we have to debate whether or not racism still exists is proof that it does!" On Wednesday, November 9, 2016, the day after the presidential election, I visited his dual-language tenth-grade World History class. I decided to make this the last class I visited that day because I perceived Mr. Ochoa as a caring teacher, and I felt he would be sensitive to so many being emotionally drained and vulnerable after the news of Donald Trump's election. That day had indeed been tough. Students and teachers cried together.

Mr. Ochoa started his class with an activity that asked the students to check in with their emotions. He asked each student to write down a single word describing how they felt at that moment. Following this, he instructed students to walk around the classroom and share their chosen words with at least three classmates. Common choices emerged, including "angry," "confused," and "disappointed." After this exchange, the students regrouped to share with the whole class the words they had heard. Wanting to validate the mood, Mr. Ochoa then took a moment to implore his students to be kind and understanding toward each other.

After drawing a brief parallel between Pericles' concept of Greek democracy and its influence on US democracy, Mr. Ochoa turned his attention to the looming topic of the recent presidential election. He played a video for the sophomore class featuring political analyst Van Jones. Jones referred to the election outcome as a "whitelash against a changing country," a comment that aimed to capture the complex social and racial dynamics at play.[3] As the video played, a heavy silence descended on the room. The students, usually buzzing with chatter, were unusually still under the weight of the topic.

After the video ended, one Latino student exclaimed, "But why do we have an electoral college?" Mr. Ochoa responded that he did not know but that it was the design a long time ago and it has stayed that way.[4] Then the class's sole Black male student grumbled, "I don't want to talk about the election!" His weariness appeared to stem from the day's unrelenting focus on this topic.

Mr. Ochoa's last activity for the class was:

Write down:
One thing you are going to do to stay positive
One way in which you are going to try to support others
One thing you are going to do to stand-up for what you believe in the community

---

As the period neared its end and the students were chattier, Mr. Ochoa responded to a remark that I did not catch, addressing a vocal White male student, "You of all people should be happy right now." The boy was wearing a red baseball cap with the American flag. He replied feeling surprised, that the news was unexpected, but that he was pleased, given he would have voted for Trump.

Students wanted to understand the rationale behind the Electoral College's existence, but Mr. Ochoa's own educational background had not prepared him to answer the question. His training and the design of the curriculum limited his ability to help students understand the consequences of the United States' racist legacies and structures. That November day illustrated the school's and the program's shortcomings in educating students, particularly Latinxs. They inadequately accounted for Latinxs' fears regarding the possibility of family separation, and they did not help advance all students' understanding of structural racism. The US K–12 schools' noncommitment (at times hostility) when it comes to dealing with racial histories and their contemporary consequences miseducates and disadvantages students, particularly those who are racialized as Others.[5]

WHITE FLIGHT

Oakville, a bustling and thriving urban progressive city, promoted its image of being good on "diversity issues" (meaning race). Yet, some Black and Latinx community members scoffed at this characterization. These community members shared that when they organized to voice complaints about the city's racial disparities and to demand better services, they noticed many White folks on the defensive.

While these communities organized for attention, the district also faced another racial problem, one that the district did proactively tackle. As the district's population of racialized Others increased, district officials grew concerned about a trend: an exodus of White families from the school district (see figure I.1 showing a decrease in number of White students, from approximately eighteen thousand in 1990–1991 to eleven thousand in 2015–2016). To prevent white flight from intensifying, the district administrators looked to implement dual-language programs.

While some people did not consider the schools with dual-language programs as good as other schools, district administrators believed that the opportunity for White and/or middle-class students to become bilingual would serve as an incentive for their parents to keep their children in the district, even if the school was in a less desirable attendance area of the district. To attract families and extend the program to more elementary schools, the district used language from the national discourse on bilingualism's benefits, such as cognitive development.[6]

The district responded to racial disparities and changing demographics through several policy reforms, which brought other tensions. For example, one elementary school with a large Latinx population rejected a proposed district expansion of the ELL plan. The opponents of the dual-language strand program noted that the plan would require changing personnel; for example, some staff (likely non-Spanish-speaking teachers) would lose their positions and/or be transferred to a different school. Opponents also noted that the program would segregate Black children and special education children into non-dual-language classrooms, like it did in other schools. Some dual-language teachers agreed that this had happened in previous cases; for example, Ms. Thomson shared, "One of the big issues is that [the program] is kind of segregating schools."

The result of these objections was that the district decided to not offer a dual-language program in that elementary school. Instead, parents of Spanish-speaking ELLs in that school who wanted the dual-language option had their children transported free of charge to a nearby school with a dual-language program.

The district's policy choices affected the various racialized groups differently and in relation to one another. Indeed, the debate and district decision positioned Latinx interests against Black interests. Arguments against a proposed dual-language expansion in schools with many Latinxs ignored the possibility of increasing Black participation and decreasing White participation in the dual-language program. The controversy over expanding dual language also distracted people from seeing that the program—which was supposed to mitigate racial inequities—was helping Whites accumulate material advantages, like awards and recognitions, over racialized Others.

"DUAL LANGUAGE IS REALLY MEANT FOR THE WHITE FAMILIES"

One of the ways the district's dual-language program was not serving Latinxs was in how and to whom it promoted the program. Because the program needed to include half Spanish-dominant students, dual language enrolled more Latinxs than Whites relative to the overall district percentages, though it became clear that dual language was primarily tailored to the latter and their parents. According to parents and teachers, the district easily attracted

White families to enroll their children in the elementary-level dual language program.

Ms. Rita, a White former staff member in charge of recruitment, shared, "There was always a *huge* waiting list for the non-native-Spanish speakers, so the White kids trying to get in. They had a really hard time filling the Spanish half." She elaborated, "The district does a really great job promoting [dual-language education] with non-Spanish speaking families. [The district] talks about the importance of, 'If you're White, here's why it's great to have your child exposed to another language.'" She added, "I think the way we talk about [dual language] is really meant for the White families, the educated upper-middle-class White families, to understand language acquisition."

Ms. Rita believed the district saw White parent buy-in as a necessity for the dual-language program, and thus needed to educate them about the utility of bilingualism for their children. This resulted in the district's marketing efforts not specifically targeting Latinx families. Ms. Rita, for instance, noted that the concerns commonly raised by Latinx families, such as "Will my child learn English?" were not adequately addressed. This issue was particularly evident at the secondary level, where a higher number of youth tended to drop the program. She stated, "It's not specific for Latino communities. [What's] lacking is something that's specifically for Latino families to talk about the importance of having two languages and that you don't have to give up one to learn the other." Perhaps because politically active Latinxs (who were mostly middle class) pushed for bilingual education, the district functioned as if the program did not have to recruit or market to Latinxs, the majority of whom were working class.[7]

Others also perceived that the district offered dual language because the White families supported it. The program indeed had investment from White parents, as Mrs. Nadia had observed in district meetings proposing dual language:

> It's really interesting to see how many White privileged families stood up and said, "We want our kids to have this," and see how many Latino families were there telling them this is important. There were a lot of middle-upper-class White families saying, "This is important," and that's why they passed it.

Teachers and administrators saw much White investment in the program and felt obliged to cater to it. For example, the district hosted an information session for parents and youth about the Seal of Biliteracy award to high school graduates who met the state's biliteracy requirements (see chapter 5). Almost all the families in attendance that evening were White, so the district staff member gave the presentation in English, and the White parents asked most of the questions (in English).

These two factors—the district's promotion of bilingualism's benefits and White parents' advocacy for the program—amplified a message. They projected the idea that the program's purpose (learning Spanish) and its rewards, such as better job prospects and exposure to diversity, were commodities for all, but especially for Whites without ties to Spanish or a Latinx identity. This message contributed to the program having a longer waiting list for the English-dominant spots than for the Spanish-dominant spots. Latinxs' lower demand for the program resulted from the district's promotion of the program as beneficial for English-dominant students—and its neglecting to offer a similar campaign targeting Latinx parents. No campaign looked into or targeted the concerns of Latinx families. This lack may have precluded dual language from being more popular with Latinx families. Ultimately, the district's prioritizing the needs and narratives of White families gave them more power in the district, which perpetuated inequities in educational access.

SOMOS BILINGÜE ELEMENTARY SCHOOL

The school that started the dual-language model in Oakville, Somos Bilingüe Elementary School, was born from community struggle. Latinx and other community activists pressured the district to open one bilingual elementary school. Ms. Aguirre, an advocate and founder of the school, described the school as an "institutional change:" Spanish-speaking students had the option to be in classrooms that continued developing biliteracy. She and other activists opposed the practice of placing Latinxs in transitional bilingual programs, which disregarded bilingualism and aimed to move students to all-English classrooms once they had achieved proficiency in English.

Ms. Aguirre and other advocates lobbied for the school district to allow them to open a charter dual-language school because it would offer more continuity and be easier for Latinx families, unlike the Saturday morning academy that offered the Afro-centric courses in town. The founders and advocates saw providing the dual-language school through the district as lending legitimacy to their effort. They succeeded and opened a school that was affiliated with the public school district but had its own board and governing structure. They decided that the elementary school would have four goals: to develop biliteracy, foster global citizens, ensure community control of the school, and uphold a social justice mission.

I asked a few dual-language advocates and founders why the secondary-level dual-language program did not follow the charter model of the elementary school—that is, have its own school, instead of being a strand program in the nearest middle school and then high school. Most answered that the community did not continue to advocate for or be involved in decisions at the secondary level, and the lack of attention left the question of continuation of the program into secondary-level schools for the district to manage.[8] Having the dual-language program housed in a district school, instead of following the charter school model, meant losing parent and community control.[9] Without community attention to the secondary-level program, the district made decisions for the dual-language programs that followed its status quo practices and that addressed its larger issues, like curtailing white flight. Ultimately, Oakville's abandonment of the community-controlled bilingual education model at the secondary level hindered the achievement of the community's initial goals, including its social justice ideals.

"ON THE BACKS OF LATINO STUDENTS"

Ms. Nader had doubts about whether dual language catered to Latinxs' needs. Even though some dual-language teachers saw the program as a means for improving Latinx achievement, Ms. Nader, who identified as a teacher of color, was skeptical:

> One of my main frustrations with the [dual-language] program is that native Spanish-speaking Latino students make it possible, and they aren't benefiting as much as I think that they should be. So it really appears to me as though it's on the backs of Latino students. . . . It doesn't appear to me that they're benefiting as much as they're contributing to it.

Like other dual-language educators, Ms. Nader recognized Latinx students as integral to implementing a dual-language program because of English's dominance in the United States. This dominance and factors like residential segregation meant that most White students would have insufficient exposure to Spanish without being in a dual-language classroom with Spanish-speaking Latinxs. For example, Mrs. Blair shared that her son had been in a bilingual program with no student speakers of the target language (Japanese), and his Japanese had not progressed. Returning to the issue of Latinxs needs,

Ms. Nader said she grew disheartened when she saw that Latinx students were not benefiting from the program in the same way as their White counterparts.

Some Latina mothers like Mrs. Vero concurred with this concern. Mrs. Vero felt that the program took more from the Latinxs than it delivered. "Lo que no me gusta del programa es de que siento que utilizan a los latinos, los utilizan mucho." (What I dislike about the program is that I feel it uses Latinos, it uses them a lot.) She explained that the program made "muchas promesas y esas promesas no las han cumplido" (lots of promises and these haven't been kept). She recalled hearing promises from bilingual education advocates that the program would get Latinx student achievement on par with that of their White counterparts. People did not see Latinxs benefit as much from the program as their White counterparts, and often this benefit was in terms of Latinxs not achieving on par with their peers.[10]

USING FUNDS FOR ENGLISH LEARNERS (PERPETUATING HIERARCHIES)

The concerns described above were well-founded, especially when one saw how money and resources were allocated. The state of RedRock professed a "bilingual-bicultural" conception of educating students it labeled ELLs. RedRock had historically been following national trends in providing inadequate education to language-minoritized students; however, the recent population increase had put added pressure on the state to improve schooling to these students.[11] Not following the lead of California, Arizona, and Massachusetts in outlawing bilingual education in its public schools, RedRock promoted bilingualism and bilingual education programs by passing a Bilingual-Bicultural Education Statute and by offering a Seal of Biliteracy on diplomas of its qualifying high school graduates.

However, while the statute promoted bilingualism and bilingual education, RedRock's language policies and support for bilingual programs still emphasized students' learning English. Additionally, one could wonder whether this statute was an unfunded mandate, because, like the rest of the nation, RedRock suffered since the 1994–1995 school year from a shortage of ESL/bilingual education teachers.[12]

The Bilingual-Bicultural Education Statute stipulated that a district's ELL numbers prompted state supplemental aid. Oakville, having the sufficient ELL pupil count, applied for the modest state funds to support ELLs' bilingual education. The statute allowed each district flexibility in establishing programs suited to its needs. While the statute was meant to improve the educational outcomes of ELLs, the district elected to offer dual language, a bilingual model popular with White families, instead of opting for and promoting a bilingual model traditionally for Latinxs, such as Spanish for heritage speakers. Under the provisions of the statute, the district partially financed its dual-language program using the state's reimbursement for associated costs, such as personnel and supplemental books. However, by allocating these resources to provide dual-language education to non-ELLs—predominantly the more politically powerful White families— it ended up stretching these resources thin. This distribution of the funds is troubling for several reasons.

First, education for ELLs and Latinxs is not funded equally, let alone equitably.[13] Second, the percentage of state supplemental aid that districts received for ELLs has decreased in the past decade.[14] Third, the modest reimbursement for ELLs represents one of the few funding sources for secondary-level bilingual education. It is also one of the few funds that benefit Latinxs (albeit indirectly). This is so because these funds are based on language, not race, and thus are considered *race-neutral*, consequently avoiding the challenge of strict judicial scrutiny. Having this money used for dual language— which results in sharing the scarce resources meant for ELLs with White and already privileged youth—lessens the beneficial impact on the marginalized group for which these funds were intended. This thwarts their prospect of ameliorating inequities, as happens with other race-neutral policies.[15]

RESOURCES SPREAD THIN

Oakville's district spread its scarce bilingual teachers and resources even thinner by opting for a model that White families supported, which caused some Latinxs to be excluded from bilingual schooling. For example, because of a lack of bilingual teachers, once Amlie High adopted dual language, teachers of Spanish-heritage courses (which serve Latinxs keen on learning Spanish) were reassigned to teach dual language, canceling the heritage courses.

Spanish-heritage courses are among the few language models that specifically cater to Spanish speakers; thus, discontinuing them negatively and disproportionately affected Latinxs, especially the many Latinxs who had not been enrolled in elementary-level dual language. Ms. Thomson explained that non-dual-language Spanish-heritage Latinxs were "falling through the cracks, and nobody's really catching them." She elaborated, "The point of heritage classes is to serve our heritage speakers, and the whole point of the program is an equity strategy. Yet I feel like there's no focus on the heritage speakers." The only biliteracy options for the sizeable non-dual-language Latinx student population were the Spanish world-language courses, which were not suited for Spanish-heritage learners. Indeed, bilingual programs that served only Latinx youth, such as heritage, developmental, and maintenance bilingual models, were not considered an option because of the need for bilingual models that provide White students access to biliteracy. Consequently, the program distributed resources along racial lines in ways that did not challenge whiteness, let alone challenge the patterns that perpetuate racialized categories.

WHITE "POLITICAL REALITIES"

Despite the inequitable funding, some people acknowledged that including White children in dual language was the political reality that enabled the district to offer bilingual education. Mr. Pérez felt that having White students was a necessary trade-off: "Some political realities are that when you have 50 percent Anglo speakers, they bring a certain level of involvement in political clout to [dual language.] It would be more difficult with just Latino speakers." He believed that offering biliteracy to Latinxs was "one of the good things" that ensued from including White students, that this was the only way this program could run. Additionally, having middle-class White students brought a certain level of prestige to the program, which also attracted families of various backgrounds. Although this political reality may be true, making the dual-language program the only bilingual option positioned White students' access to biliteracy as a precondition for bilingual schooling's existence, and again solidified their status in the racial hierarchy.

In a conversation with Ms. Lucas about funding and students, she agreed with having White students in the program, but was bothered that people misunderstood the program as not being for Latinx children. Ms. Lucas believed the funding was meant for ELLs who had a right to a bilingual education by state law. She stated that ELL "students have these legal rights to certain types of education they're supposed to have access to. Except those programs are looked at by some people [as], 'Oh, those are programs for White kids to learn Spanish.'" Indeed, her insight reflected what many participants believed.

Mr. Pérez mentioned "political realities" necessitating the inclusion of Whites in dual-language programs, which hindered the possibility of reallocating resources primarily for Latinxs. For example, instead of using these resources to promote bilingualism and dual-language programs that included White middle-class families, these resources could have been employed to develop and publicize bilingual models tailored specifically for Latinx communities. This district decision, which offered biliteracy recognition only under conditions that allowed Whites to earn this distinction, dispensed resources according to Whites' expectations. By selecting bilingual programs and policies dependent on White support, the district prioritized Whites' interests over Latinxs' needs, thereby reinforcing the high status of whiteness.

"PROBABLEMENTE FUNCIONARÍA PERO . . ."

All the adult participants expressed frustration with the program's underfunding. But no one, except two Latina mothers, thought to use the funds exclusively for Latinxs. When I asked one of these mothers, Mrs. Teresa, what she thought about the program having White students, she answered, "Probablemente funcionaría pero entonces estaríamos hablando de que hay recursos para la comunidad latina, y no hay recursos." (It would probably work, but then we'd be talking about having resources for the Latino community, and there aren't resources.) The two Latina mothers felt that using the funds for ELLs to teach White students was troubling because the program was not adequately funded to serve the Latinx youth.

Though Latinxs (especially the few who were middle class and politically active) fought for the program's funding and supported dual language, the policies and practices added to the advantages that perpetuate Whites' status in the racial hierarchy.

. . . CATERING TO WHITES' NEEDS

The dual-language program required support from Whites, but some saw it as co-opted by the capital of White families, who expected schools to grant their college-bound children the advantages of the program. Oakville's situation also illustrates that the underfunding of schools serving racialized-Othered communities, as a material consequence of racism, also ends up negatively affecting White students, although in distinct ways.[16] Had the history of bilingual education and schools serving racialized-Othered communities not been marred by systemic disinvestment due to racism, perhaps the resource of bilingual education would be more robust and widely accessible, rather than being a limited and highly sought-after commodity. The reality of underfunding puts White families in a position where they might feel stuck in a double bind. On the one hand, they want to expose their children to other cultures and experiences and to learn a different language. On the other hand, their children's participation in the program would mean diverting scarce resources away from children who are more disadvantaged.

Instead, in this racial context, biliteracy schooling was available to Latinxs only as long as Whites could use dual language according to their needs. Consequently, the program policies and practices responded to the needs of its White students in ways that prioritized them above those of Latinx students. This meant that Latinx students' needs were secondary. One could even consider the presence of Latinx students as in service of Whites' biliteracy because their attendance enabled White youth to acquire Spanish. These policies and practices resulted in inequitable benefits for Latinxs and differential academic outcomes, which perpetuated the perception that certain groups were inferior and implicitly reinforced the white-supremacist racial hierarchy.

That White students received a more enriching bilingual/biliterate education and opportunities compared with their Latinx peers helped White students secure a privileged position. White students enhanced the program's prestige; for example, some people opined that the Borane program's desirability remained high because it included White students. The program sought the cachet provided by Whites, creating a cycle of perpetuating White students' high standing compared with other racialized groups. The few Black students in the program (mostly already high achievers) also provided status to the program.

These policy decisions resulted in not giving Latinxs their due resources, thus producing the group's lower achievement, which perpetuated the common sense of racialized distinctions in intelligence existing, the common sense of having a racial hierarchy, and the Latinx group's inferior status. The patterns also reinforced our larger society's white-supremacist racial hierarchy. These chapters have shown with a relational analysis the construction and privileging of whiteness to benefit white supremacy at a structural level.

For a program to really live up to people's expectations of providing educational equity, it must disrupt these racial patterns. These patterns demonstrated to teachers like Ms. Nader and mothers like Mrs. Vero that the program had not kept its promise to eliminate inequities, to dismantle the racial hierarchy of how resources are distributed. Additionally, while the program enhanced educational outcomes for a limited segment of the Latinx population, it acted more as a token concession, offering minimal material and occasional representational advancements for Latinxs. Ultimately, the program, teachers, and curriculum constructed and privileged whiteness in a racial hierarchy with Latinxs. In a cyclical process, the dual-language program reflected and reinforced society's ideas and patterns about race; that is, it worked as a racial project—teaching what is race and the hierarchical place of the racialized groups through distributing resources along racial lines.

Conclusion

The graduation of Amlie High's first dual-language cohort transcended a mere ceremony for its students. It marked a notable accomplishment for Oakville's Latinx community in their quest for educational justice. Their struggle for bilingual education was not just commendable, it was a necessary fight to realize a vision of public schooling that honors Latinxs' languages and cultures.

But despite its achievements, the program grappled with structural constraints that hindered the full realization of an equitable education for Latinx students. Additionally, the program inadvertently advanced ideas that it did not intend to promote. For instance, implementing the dual-language program in response to pressure from the Latinx community unintentionally furthered the notion that language education was the primary educational challenge for Latinx students. Indeed, many in the community echoed this idea, perceiving that the program provided access to biliteracy and cultural representation as a path to educational equity for Latinxs.[1] During the eighteen community meetings I attended and the parent interviews I conducted, a common theme emerged: the belief that a robust bilingual program would enable Latinx students to appreciate their heritage and gain economic advantages from their biliteracy. This suggested an underlying belief that effective language education could counteract racial discrimination. However, discussions rarely ventured beyond this; I did not hear bilingual education advocates or parents speak about the need for the program to teach racial ideas beyond multiculturalism. Despite some teachers' efforts to advance students' critical consciousness about racism, the predominant focus on language seemed to obscure other needs. Specifically, it neglected the need to address the contradictions about race expressed by students like Andrea and Mia.

In this concluding chapter, I present two main sections. The first advocates for embracing ambitious teaching about the ambivalence of race. Toward this end, I discuss three recommendations that aim toward reconnecting bilingual education to its race-radical roots and thus enhancing students' critical-racial consciousness. The second section addresses the question of whether language can delineate a racialized group, thus contributing to the specificity of Latinx racialization.

RECOMMENDATIONS

Different forces struggle over how bilingual education as a racial project can function. Bilingual education has the potential to either perpetuate or challenge dominant ideas about concepts like race, the Latinx racialized group, and Latinidad. To advance bilingual education as a race-radical intervention, I invite educators to *embrace ambitious teaching about the ambivalence of race*. I describe this approach through three recommendations: embracing theory, grounding bilingual education in ethnic studies, and reconceptualizing Latinx and Latinidad.

Embracing Theory

During a conversation with Ms. West between her classes, she shared with me that she designed lessons that centered racism in police shootings and the district's discipline plan because she felt the urge to explore and talk about these issues with students:

> I used to shy away from [controversial issues] as a younger teacher because I thought that I needed to have answers as the authority person in the classroom, and now I'm totally, "No, I don't have the answers either, but I care about this issue, and I want to talk through it. We don't have to answer all the questions right now."

Indeed, individual teachers cannot have all the answers; that is just the nature of the teaching profession. Taking a stance like Ms. West's—of talking through questions—can help one think expansively and move toward options of what to do. For teachers, adopting an inquiry stance and learning in community with other teachers can support learning and teaching ambitiously about race and other taboo topics.[2]

Taking an inquiry stance toward teaching and learning about race, for this book's purposes, also means embracing theory. Scholars like Bettina Love have called on teachers to "embrace theory" and offer lessons that teach about historical and contemporary structural oppression.[3] Similarly, I invite teachers (and education researchers) to embrace theory about race and thus *embrace ambitious teaching about the ambivalence of race.*

Ambivalence of Race

Race is a complex concept full of contradictions. Thus, my call for embracing theory involves engaging in contradictory ideas about race; that is, the ambivalence of race. By *ambivalence of race*, I draw from Zeus Leonardo's race ambivalence, which decidedly rejects race evasiveness while being anti-race.[4] I elaborate on this idea by contrasting three race perspectives: pro-race, anti-racism, and anti-race.

A pro-race stance rejects race evasiveness/colorblindness, celebrates multiculturalism's inclusivity of racial diversity, and supports being proud of racial identities. This stance is evident in bilingual schooling's approach of ensuring cultural relevance by teaching students Spanish and their histories. It also appears in the cross-racial coalitions that facilitated the establishment of bilingual education.

An anti-racism stance recognizes that racism and racial categories do affect human experience. An anti-racism stance entails teaching beyond multiculturalism into exposing structural racism. This helps direct attention from the individual to the institutional and to moving toward collective action in solidarity with movements for community self-determination.

But even teachers who recognize society's structural racism and the importance of an anti-racism stance might not approach teaching with the perspective that the concept of race itself is inherently nefarious. Without educators challenging mainstream ideas of multiculturalism and what race is, schooling risks oversimplifying the complexities and contradictions of race, and thereby may struggle to effectively address racism.

Embracing ambitious teaching about the ambivalence of race means teaching to develop *critical-racial consciousness*, a consciousness that includes rejecting race evasiveness, complicating a pro-race stance, engaging in anti-racism, and adopting an *anti-race* stance.[5] To understand what this means, we return to Leonardo's concept of *anti-race*, a stance that recognizes the category of race itself as dehumanizing and thus aspires to abolish race. While an anti-race stance recognizes race as a nefarious invention, it does not dismiss race as an illusion or as unreal. An anti-race stance, like the pro-race and anti-racism stances, acknowledges that people are ascribed a race and that this affects their experiences. Thus, an ambitious approach to teaching about the ambivalence of race involves exposing race as a social construct.

This requires teaching about the process of racialization, where racial categories were invented to essentialize, dehumanize, and create hierarchies.[6] Moreover, this approach teaches about how people resist racial oppression by forming alliances and coalitions across racial lines to organize movements against racism.[7] Such resistance often entails embracing racial ascription—which, paradoxically, reinforces the existence of racialized groups.

An anti-race teaching stance grapples with the issue that "Latinx" is a cherished identity for some, despite being a category that results from racialization, a process in service of colonialism and imperialism. An anti-race stance complicates racialized identities by not simplifying them as inherent or minimizing their nefarious origin and quality. Thus, ambitious teaching about the ambivalence of race dually holds the ideas that individuals cannot escape racial ascription and that racialized identities are not innate—thus people *learn* racialized categories and identities.[8] It means that educators introduce the idea that racialized categories and identities (including people contesting these) happen in human interactions and institutions such as schooling. It entails showing that society has constructed expected roles and behaviors associated with different racialized groups that restrict people's actions and ideas. And it includes acknowledging that these concepts shape the possibilities of what people can be and how they can act in the present and future.[9]

Embracing ambitious teaching about the ambivalence of race presents educators with what might seem like a double (or triple) bind of simultaneously taking a pro-race, anti-racism, and anti-race stance. For example, a pro-race position strives toward a positive racial self-identity—creating one's identity as inherent to the person—which may make racial identity as something beloved, as something essential to our person. One problem with this position is that it may result in the idea that race is intrinsic and unchanging. If race is our identity, our self, how could we move for society to rid itself of race? (Both a pro-race and an anti-racism stance—while the latter contests racism—do not trouble race and project race in perpetuity.[10]) In contrast, an anti-race stance points out that racial identities are linked to restricting roles and activities. Yet we cannot escape being racialized, nor is race evasiveness productive. This contradiction is not simply an unsustainable position—it speaks to the construction of race itself.[11] Ambitious teaching about the ambivalence of race nudges toward seeing that being both anti-racist and anti-race is not a contradiction, but a stance that recognizes race as discordant and full of ambivalence.[12]

Schools should teach the ambivalence of race to enhance students' critical-racial consciousness and lean into considering complicated ideas. These ideas would include exploring what it means to have a racial identity and community that one cherishes because of its struggle and resilience but be aware of racialization's intended oppressive purposes, outcomes, and contradictions. They would include acknowledging that individuals cannot escape racial ascription while remaining wary of attaching to racial identity.[13] Other ideas schools could teach include how individuals experience racism differently, such as through colorism.[14] This could lead to recognizing the various dimensions of race and racist structures, and examine how these affect an individual and a group differently.[15] Embracing an ambitious teaching about the ambivalence of race rather than oversimplified views will help students develop nuanced perspectives, better understand our racialized society, and more effectively equip them to join others in struggle against the inequitable distribution of resources along racial lines.

Ambitious Teaching

Education experts on critical-race pedagogy have undertheorized the concept of ambitious teaching when it comes to teaching about race.[16] Ambitious teaching about race is intentional, sustained, strategic, and explicit about racialization and the ambivalence of race.

Ambitious teaching about race includes critical-race pedagogy that is purposeful in enhancing racialized-Othered students' thinking and in complicating dominant ways of thinking of race, including a pro-race and anti-racism stance.[17] It moves racialized-Othered students beyond a liberal-whiteness's perspective on race, a perspective that often endorses multiculturalism and stops short of advocating for structural change.[18]

In ambitious teaching about race, teachers, as institutional agents, recognize that schools make race. This is not limited to the racial ideas that are either ignored or explicitly presented. Acknowledging this role of schools requires the development of lessons that scaffold the understanding that schools—among other institutions—make race through its policies, practices, and discourses reproducing racialized patterns. These patterns, in turn, reinforce racialized categories and the resultant material consequences, often presenting them as natural or neutral.

Grounding Bilingual Education in Ethnic Studies

As I have established, dual-language education, a widely available option for Latinxs to obtain biliterate schooling, contends with different ways of being a racial project. For one, it could be a racial project that offers inclusivity yet lacks accompanying efforts to ensure an equitable education to Latinxs.[19]

The history of language education policy perpetuating racist settler colonialist ideas and US imperialism pulls bilingual education toward being framed as solely a language intervention that celebrates bilingualism and multiculturalism.[20] This status quo framing perpetuates dual-language education as a racial project that is race evasive and obstructs programs from cultivating students' critical-racial consciousness.[21] To not undermine the potential of dual language, bilingual education advocates, parents, and educators should lobby for an expansive bilingual education, one grounded in ethnic studies.

Ethnic studies—with its focus on developing youths' critical consciousness about racism, capitalism, imperialism, and colonialism—can guide dual language to being a racial project that moves toward ambitious teaching about race.[22] Infusing an ethnic-studies curriculum into bilingual education can move the latter beyond merely being a linguistic intervention to cleaving to bilingual education's anti-racist, race-radical roots. Ethnic studies can offer lessons on teaching the intertwined histories of Latinx communities with other communities. Grounding bilingual education in ethnic studies could lead to teaching that schooling in the US settler state seeks to erase peoples' ties to the land and promotes education as about improving one's opportunity to consume. It could lead students to act in solidarity with others by relating to other groups based on interlinked struggles against white supremacist racial hierarchies, capitalism, colonialism, and imperialism. It could provide Latinx students an education aimed for their communities to self-determine their future *in relation with* other communities.[23] Thus, any success Latinxs have in obtaining bilingual education must be accompanied by building complex alliances in a multiracial democracy.[24]

Offering bilingual education and ethnic studies should not be mutually exclusive.[25] Rather, they should accompany each other to provide students an equitable education. And it can be done. This book offers some examples of bilingual education teachers expanding beyond language and working toward a race-radical approach in dual language. But these examples came mostly from individuals' prerogative and political clarity.

Institutional support for teachers to teach ambitiously about race would help achieve improved results. Policymakers and school leaders should work toward and implement institutional policies and structures to help teachers do this work. As history shows, implementing policies and practices that challenge racial hierarchies is a prerequisite for eradicating racist ideas and outcomes and to affecting material consequences.[26] Districts must commit to intentional curriculum planning and sequencing for teaching about race. This need is especially apparent when we compare how US schools have decided to organize the teaching of a subject like math versus the topic of race.[27] We have, as a society, accepted that it is important to teach students to understand our mathematical world; and math education, however imperfect, has a general sequence of how concepts should be ordered throughout primary, secondary, and tertiary education. The same is not true for teaching about race.

To incorporate ethnic studies, lessons would need to be sequenced throughout primary and secondary education, with different levels of complexity by age. For example, secondary-level teachers could address the ambivalence of race through having youth research their community's understandings of race and explore how people's ideas about race and ethnicity are based on context and change and adopt, oftentimes strategically. Perhaps students could study how people in their community perceive a person's race based on speech. Therefore, embracing an ambitious teaching of the ambivalence of race includes guiding students to denaturalize race and to recognize that racial oppression and the different experiences with racial oppression make racialized groups.

Teachers face many institutional restraints in attempting to infuse ethnic studies into bilingual education. To alleviate these challenges, broad community support is essential. This support should encompass school communities, parents, education researchers, and teacher training programs. For example, teacher training should empower educators to adopt an inquiry-based approach, an essential part of learning how to scaffold lessons that enhance critical-racial consciousness.

Reconceptualizing Latinx and Latinidad

Teaching Latinidad as an ethnicity linked by a common culture, by Spanish, often employs a multicultural stance and disregards racialization. In contrast, an ambitious teaching of the ambivalence of race teaches students that a racialized group, like Latinx, exists in a society like the United States because of its inequitable distribution of resources (regardless of whether the US census notes that group as a race category).[28] Importantly, ambitious teaching about race should include the idea that the racial oppression and categorization Latinxs face *makes* the Latinx racialized group, as happens with other racialized groups.[29]

Instead of teaching Latinidad as about a shared language and culture, an ambitious teaching of race explores the dual histories of the term "Latinx" and contrasts the racial ideas between the United States and Latin America.[30] "Latin America" as nomenclature emerged from the imperialist project of non-Anglo-European elites wanting to counter British/American imperialism.[31] This history emerged alongside another history that involves a coalition of Mexican Americans, Puerto Ricans, and Cuban Americans wanting a label besides "Spanish speakers," first settling on "Hispanics," and then (some) rejecting the term's ties to Spain by using "Latino."[32] As a US-imposed racialized category, "Latinx" ignores the diversity within those labeled "Latino/Latina/Latine/Latinx." Yet an ambitious teaching of race rejects a narrow understanding of the Latinx lived experience, centers Blackness and Indigeneity, and cultivates a capacious conceptualization of Latinidad.[33]

The recognition of "Latinx" as a racialized term does not intend to legitimize the term or give it panache. Rather, teaching the concept as a racialized category would help to teach students why being ascribed the label Latinx can perpetuate erasure for some individuals. It acknowledges that racial categories are meant to disregard the variety in people's cultural practices and human experiences by lumping them together and then placing them into a racial hierarchy.[34] Thus, unsettling the Latinx concept from ethnicity could lead to complicating race.

To reconceptualize Latinidad with an ambitious approach to teaching race brings to light the anti-Indigeneity, anti-Blackness, and anti-whiteness in the Latinx term's history, and further complicates other racial categorizations. It challenges bilingual education's anti-Black and anti-Indigenous elements. Additionally, it exposes the different understandings and experiences individuals and ethnic communities assigned "Latinx" may have with racism, colonialism, and imperialism.

An ambitious approach to teaching race recognizes that racial oppression pushes some people to see their commonalities and join in solidarity with communities against their oppression.[35] It teaches that being racially targeted contributes to forming racialized groups and can mobilize people; it does not romanticize racialization because forming racial categories is fundamentally about dominating and justifying some groups as less worthy, less human.

These recommendations are oriented toward the goal of reestablishing bilingual education's foundations in race-consciousness, ultimately providing an education that fosters the development of students' critical-racial awareness.

Teaching with a pro-race, anti-racism, and anti-race stance is no simple matter, particularly given society's inclination to oversimplify race and avoid teaching about racism and race directly. Oakville's educators, community members, parents, and youth took time and energy to share with me the successes, contradictions, and challenges of their bilingual education experiences, many with the hope of improving schooling in times of racial reckoning. Making bilingual education into a racial project that combats racist ideas requires reimagining an equitable education to include ambitious teaching about the ambivalence of race. How schools approach the work of developing critical-racial consciousness will inform ideas about race—ideas that have real consequences through US structures, institutions, and stories connecting these ideas to power and distributing resources along racial lines.

DELINEATING THE LATINX RACIALIZED GROUP

Learning about how our schools construct and conceptualize the Latinx racialized group illuminates how our society thinks about race and engages in racialization. While schools may teach that race is "skin color"—indicative of how our society simplifies to only one dimension of race to make sense of it while keeping the racial order—our societal ideas and racialization processes are much more complex and have multiple dimensions given that, in this country, racial oppression is founded on capitalism, imperialism, settler colonialism, anti-Blackness, and white supremacy.[36] Sociologists Michael Omi and Howard Winant describe racialization as a process of othering through "immediately visible corporeal characteristics facilitat[ing] the recognition, surveillance, and coercion of . . . Native Americans and Africans from Europeans."[37] However, they also note that "once specific concepts of race are widely circulated and accepted as a social reality, racial difference is not dependent on visual observation alone."[38] In other words, US society has so ingrained racial organization and logic that racial delineations are not drawn only by the visual.[39] Indeed, reducing race to physical characteristics ignores historical and social science research showing the variability of racialization, racial logics, and the instability in the concept of race itself.[40] Thus, skin color (or another phenotypic element) is but one part of racialization, a process that interrelates aspects like language, citizenship, immigration, and religion to racialize people.[41]

Given the instability of the concept of race, I submit that racialized categories can have different *types* of boundaries for distinguishing one from another. These boundaries can change and vary, influenced by specific racial and colonial logics, and they serve to mark and sort bodies into groups in different ways in particular sociohistorical contexts. For some racialized groups, visual traits like skin color may be the defining markers. For others, nonvisual characteristics, such as language, could delineate the group.[42]

In my previous works, I have argued that the Latinx racialized category has the signature boundary of an *imagined* Spanish.[43] This book's findings lead me to a more specific conclusion: the dual-language program, as a racial project, reinforces the Spanish language as the signature boundary that delineates and binds the Latinx racialized group.[44] This reinforcement by the dual-language program both mirrors and strengthens societal perceptions of the group, while also aligning with research suggesting that people's visual and auditory judgments collaboratively inform their conceptions of racialized groups.[45]

CONCLUSION

For Latinx education spaces like Oakville's bilingual program to not expand the concept of race beyond skin color—especially given the phenotypic diversity within the Latinx group—represents a significant omission, indicating a lack of consideration of racialization. Not teaching about racialization also limited the dual-language program's ability to explore why there is even a "Latino" category in the first place: to incorporate people into a white supremacist racial hierarchy and settler colonial nation-state. Neglecting this nefarious aspect of race prevented the program from effectively teaching about the contradictions of race and Latinidad. One such contradiction involves the role of the "Latino" racialized category in essentializing individuals and categorizing them within a white supremacist racial hierarchy; as people cannot escape racialization, some develop group affiliations and join with others to resist racism; yet paradoxically, these anti-racist movements can sometimes inadvertently reinforce racially organizing our society.

Given the contradictions inherent in race, schools inadvertently contribute to the racialization of the Latinx group, including through offering dual language, which some individuals employ as an anti-racist intervention. I highlight this point not to suggest that eliminating bilingual education would reduce the racialization of Latinxs or solve the inherent dilemmas of race's contradictions. Instead, my aim is to encourage recognition of these contradictions and the understanding that bilingual education is a racial project. By acknowledging this, we can work toward ambitious teaching about the ambivalence of race and, in doing so, reconnect bilingual education to its race-radical roots to make justice.

Methodological Notes on Studying How a Bilingual Education Program Makes Race

T hree years before formal data collection, I joined organizations that advocate for Latinx education issues. I also gathered local newspaper stories that focused on Latinx youth and families, school-board meeting minutes, and demographic data from the (anonymized) state's department of education. For the study's formal data collection (fifteen months; February 2016–June 2017), I amassed document data, participant observations, post-observation discussions with teachers, and interviews.

I conducted my fieldwork in the two schools and the community, talking in and out of the classroom setting with teachers, staff, parents, community members, and students. The data collection in schools resulted in 180 hours of classroom observations of teachers' curriculum and instruction. I also drew from my researcher fieldnotes, over 51 hours of interviews, 29 hours of informal discussions with teachers, 18 community meetings (34 hours), and various district documents.

I carried out one semistructured, open-ended ethnographic interview that elicited narrative responses with each study participant. Interviews ranged from sixty to ninety minutes, with most around sixty minutes. I tailored all interviews to the interviewee's district role and audiorecorded and transcribed them. Interviews allowed me to notice similarities and differences in how participants experienced the dual-language program and their understanding of how the program affected the educational experiences of diverse youth. I invited teachers to participate in a second interview after the school year ended (three were unavailable). I also invited students for a second interview, and three accepted. In this second interview, I asked participants about their reflections and/or changes regarding our previous conversations; I shared preliminary, recurring, and singular ideas that I had identified from my first analysis and elicited their insights. In interviews and other interactions, I attempted to demonstrate an equanimous nonjudgmental disposition with all participants.

PARTICIPANTS

I recruited teachers, school staff, youth, parents/guardians, and community members (n = 39). I selected participants to support the inclusion of various stakeholders who were in some way involved in and had opinions about the dual-language program. I contacted potential participants via email, phone, and/or in-person to invite them to participate. I contacted them on a rolling basis through snowball sampling and/or purposive sampling. As I collected data, speaking with participants pointed me to potential participants whom I later contacted to provide further information. Speaking with participants also helped me identify events for me to attend that may contribute data to the study.

WHAT I PAID ATTENTION TO WHILE IN THE FIELD

During my observations of classrooms, I paid attention to teachers' engagement of *racial-literacy practices*, or the sociocultural practices around text and discourse that people use—even if unintentionally or by propagating race evasiveness—to make meaning of racial ideologies.[1] I focused on the opportunities provided to help youth develop critical-racial consciousness, which includes understanding race as a social construct and determinant, interpreting the racial issues in a given situation, and taking anti-racist actions. I examined how a so-called progressive schooling reform, in this case dual-language education, racializes through the relational ways in which discourses, ideologies, and practices affect different racialized groups, with particular attention on Latinxs.

I paid attention to *raciolinguistic ideologies*, which refers to how race and language intersect to influence, for example, how race is constructed and how language is used.[2] And I looked at how the curriculum and instruction offered opportunities for youth to develop their critical-racial consciousness. Doing all this while focusing on the Oakville school district's dual-language program helped me understand how schooling teaches about and engages in racialization. I examined the decisions made in policy, program, and pedagogy, focusing on how these decisions affect the positioning of racialized groups. This included considering aspects such as classroom composition and the content of teaching and discussions. Additionally, I noted the role of racialization in determining the outcomes and material consequences of schooling, including the allocation of resources, access to rigorous curriculum, and distribution of awards.

ANALYSES

I adapted LeCompte and Schensul's recursive analytic process.[3] Stage 1 took place during data collection. Soon after collecting each interview transcript, document, and extended fieldnote, I employed a sentence-by-sentence "in vivo" coding practice.[4] As I read the data, I highlighted words and phrases from each sentence that spoke to its idea(s). I then reread the in vivo codes, attending to my ethnography's overarching questions.

As I compiled more data from each technique, such as interviews and observations, I began to identify salient patterns and discrepancies. These I observed both within and across the different techniques. In my analytic memos, I documented these patterns and discrepancies along with reflections on how the data answered my research questions.

Soon after my formal data collection ended, I selected recurring data and formed these into inductive gerund codes that denote action and interaction ("process coding").[5] For this Stage 2 coding, some examples of these codes include:

- Repeating curriculum
- Talking openly about racism/race
- Evading race
- Comparing Latinxs to other groups
- Focusing on ethnicities in/from Latin America
- Essentializing Latino culture

Both Stage 1 and Stage 2 coding practices helped me to familiarize myself with and condense the data, and to make initial comparisons across data.

I started the Stage 3 analysis in July 2020. This stage focused on a relational racialization analysis. I reviewed the whole corpus of data and Stage 1 and Stage 2 codes, including all analytical fieldnotes and memos using deductive theoretical codes that I created. These codes included:

- Boundaries/differential/relational racialization
- Racial patterns/hierarchy
- Material consequences
- Raciolinguistic ideology
- Settler colonialism
- Mestizaje/mestizo
- Indigeneity/Native
- Afro-Latinx/Asian-Latinx
- Blackness/Black people

As I coded the data, I wrote memos on the trends and divergences I noticed. I examined discourses, the program's curriculum and instruction, policies of resource allocation, and racial literacy practices to get at the connections between the group relationships.

PRESENTATION

Because I did not audio record classroom observations or informal conversations with teachers, I reconstructed the vignettes from field notes, analytical memos, informal conversations with teachers and students after observations, follow-up conversations with participants for specific information, and my memory. Apart from this, participant's quotes are from their audiorecorded one-on-one formal interview(s).

Instead of confining my background and viewpoint to a separate positionality section, I have woven them throughout the book. These snippets show how my experiences, education, and educator trajectory have shaped my methodological choices, research methods, and analyses. This approach allows for narrative explanations when relevant and reflects my awareness that a researcher influences the interpretation and presentation of the research.

Notes

Preface

1. To protect anonymity, I have changed some details, limited teachers' physical descriptions, and used pseudonyms for names of the research study's location, including the US state, schools, and participants. I also use pseudonyms to move from thinking about a particular program to thinking about schooling in general.
2. Throughout the book, I deliberately chose "Latinx," "Hispanic/Latino," or other variations, a practice that extended to my choices of other categories such as "Native American," "Indian," and "Indigenous." This variability does not imply the conflation of these terms; rather, it reflects my deliberate choice of terminology tailored to the specific context—whether it involved referencing government population surveys or historical documents or conveying my political inclinations.

    I use "Latinx" for political reasons that I explain in another section; however, none of my study's participants identified as "Latinx" with an "-x"; instead some identified as Latina or Latino. I describe participants based on their self-identifications (e.g., White woman).
3. Dual language is an *additive* bilingual education model, meaning students acquire another language (e.g., English) while developing their home language(s) and learning academic content. Students in additive bilingual education are likelier to succeed academically compared with students in *subtractive* language programs, such as ESL, which center English learning, operate on deficit ideas, and usually provide remedial content; see, e.g., Collier and Thomas, "Astounding Effectiveness of Dual-Language."
4. For another example of interests converging in dual-language education, see Palmer, "Race, Power, and Equity."
5. Scholars have examined with different foci the question of how dual-language education advances equity. Some research centers the language-learning aspect and challenges the rigid language separation of dual language, noting translanguaging as a better approach; see Nuñez et al., "They Are"; Sánchez, García, and Solorza, "Reframing Language Allocation Policy." Other research focuses on dual-language education's development of critical consciousness (e.g., Palmer et al., "Bilingualism, Biliteracy, Biculturalism, and Critical Consciousness for All").
6. Lewis, *Race in the Schoolyard*.
7. For scholarship on "making race," see Carpio, *Collisions at the Crossroads*; Molina, *How Race Is Made*.
8. Omi and Winant, *Racial Formation in the U.S.*
9. Cabrera et al., "Missing the (Student Achievement) Forest for All the (Political) Trees."
10. Omi and Winant, *Racial Formation in the U.S.*
11. Omi and Winant, *Racial Formation in the U.S.*
12. HoSang and Molina, "Introduction"; Lewis, Hagerman, and Forman, "Sociology of Race." Also see Warmington's call to examine "associations, values, qualities and representations

[that] are placed within particular raced categories" and "their consequences for groups and individuals" (Warmington, "Taking Race Out of Scare Quotes," 290).
13. By "the ambivalence of race," I refer to education scholar Zeus Leonardo's "race ambivalence," which I describe in the conclusion; see Leonardo, *Race Frameworks*.

Introduction

1. Barreto and Segura, *Latino America*.
2. Clemetson, "Hispanics Now Largest Minority."
3. To protect anonymity, I use a pseudonym for the US state and I have omitted citations of references that disclose state/city demographics and other location-specific information and could reveal the location of my research. For information on Latinx settlement in recent decades see, Vásquez, Seales, and Marquardt, "New Latino Destinations."
4. Hamann, Wortham, and Murillo, *Revisiting Education in the New Latino Diaspora*.
5. Citations withheld to not identify the state.
6. To not identify the state, I give approximate percentages and withhold the US Census Bureau citation.
7. Dondero and Muller, "School Stratification in New and Established Latino Destinations."
8. Dondero and Muller, "School Stratification in New and Established Latino Destinations."
9. For a similar perception in another context, see Flores, "Controlling Images of Space."
10. Because Oakville is not as racially segregated compared with other US cities, Oakville's secondary schools have a higher racial diversity and better reflect the racial composition of the city than its elementary schools. This pattern of more racial segregation in elementary schools is due to some neighborhood class and racial segregation, patterns common in US cities, and because the attendance lines of secondary schools draw from a larger area than elementary schools.
11. Bilingual programs that create classrooms that balance the languages (e.g., 50 percent Spanish-dominant students, 50 percent English-dominant students) are "two-way" programs instead of the more general "dual language." I use "dual-language" instead of "two-way" to follow Oakville's nomenclature.
12. Christian, Howard, and Loeb, "Bilingualism for All."
13. This contrasts with places with high concentrations of Latinxs (e.g., California, Florida, Texas), where there are many Latinx students who are English-dominant. In locations with an established Latinx population, Spanish-English dual-language classrooms could have all Latinxs.
14. Orfield and Frankenberg, "Brown at 60."
15. I have noted some problems with the logic of seeing the dual-language model as helping to racially integrate Latinxs through the model's linguistic enrollment, Chávez-Moreno, "Raciolinguistic and Racial Realist Critique." Also see Lewis, Diamond, and Forman, "Conundrums of Integration."
16. Molina, HoSang, and Gutiérrez, *Relational Formations of Race*.
17. HoSang and Molina, "Introduction."
18. In 2016, at the beginning of this study, Hispanics/Latinxs were 18 percent of the US population; Flores, "How the U.S. Hispanic Population is Changing."
19. Dávila, *Latino Spin*.
20. Other scholars also have called for and/or provided insightful studies of structural racism in education, e.g., Kohli, Pizarro, and Nevárez, "New Racism"; Ladson-Billings and Tate, "Toward a Critical Race Theory of Education."
21. Lewis, *Race in the Schoolyard*.

22. Pollock, *Colormute*.
23. I use "race evasive" instead of "colorblind" to unsettle ableism and avoid propagating the idea that racialization is solely based on skin color and physical characteristics. For more on attributing "Latino academic underperformance" to "Latino culture," see Chávez-Moreno, "Raciolinguistic and Racial Realist Critique."
24. I add the quotes to "CRT" because the anti-CRT campaign has intentionally, disingenuously distorted the term.
25. For examples of the anti-CRT movement, see Alexander et al., "CRT Forward"; Cammarota, "Race War in Arizona."
26. See, e.g., Chávez-Moreno, "Dual Language as White Property"; Chávez-Moreno, "Raciolinguistic and Racial Realist Critique"; Ladson-Billings and Tate, "Toward a Critical Race Theory of Education."
27. Brown and Brown, "Teaching K–8 Students about Race"; Chávez-Moreno, "Critiquing Racial Literacy"; Skerrett, "English Teachers' Racial Literacy."
28. Love, *We Want To Do More*, 148.
29. For some examples, see Chávez-Moreno, "Continuum of Racial Literacies"; de los Ríos, López, and Morrell, "Critical Ethnic Studies."
30. For more on critical consciousness, see the work of Paulo Freire, including *Education for Critical Consciousness*.
31. Cochran-Smith and Lytle, *Inquiry as Stance*.
32. See for example, Chávez-Moreno, "Race Reflexivity"; Chávez-Moreno, "U.S. Empire and an Immigrant's Counternarrative."
33. Nor does it uncover the "unitary core that binds" Latinxs; Beltrán, *Trouble with Unity*, 161.
34. Mora, *Making Hispanics*.
35. Omi and Winant, *Racial Formation in the U.S.*
36. Smedley and Smedley, "Race as Biology Is Fiction, Racism as a Social Problem Is Real."
37. For an insightful discussion of race as a mediating tool that affects us and that we shape, see Warmington, "Taking Race out of Scare Quotes."
38. Hall, "Race, the Floating Signifier"; Lacayo, "Perpetual Inferiority." I owe my use of "allusion/allude" to Leonardo, "Ideology and Its Modes of Existence."
39. For many scholars, race is a sociocultural relation, not in the anthropological or ethnic sense, but as a discursive relation with material consequences; see, e.g., Goldberg, "Racial Comparisons"; Hall, "Race, the Floating Signifier"; Leonardo, *Race Frameworks*.
40. Kendi, *Stamped from the Beginning*; Quijano, "Coloniality of Power and Eurocentrism in Latin America"; Wolfe, *Traces of History*.
41. For an account of how the category Arab/Muslim has been racialized, see Merseth, "The Relational Positioning of Arab and Muslim Americans."
42. Fields and Fields, *Racecraft*, 40–41.
43. Fields and Fields, *Racecraft*.
44. Baker et al., "School Funding Disparities."
45. Hochman, "Racialization"; Omi and Winant, *Racial Formation in the U.S.*
46. Hochman, "Racialization"; Omi and Winant, *Racial Formation in the U.S.*
47. Molina, HoSang, and Gutiérrez, *Relational Formations of Race*.
48. Omi and Winant, *Racial Formation in the U.S.*
49. Gómez, *Inventing Latinos*.
50. I do not use the term "panethnicity" to describe Latinxs because, in the United States, this term is usually reserved for Latinxs and Asians. This usage, along with other practices,

signals that "panethnicity" often serves as a euphemism for race. However, researchers could conceptualize "Latinx" as a panethnicity, a suggestion that does not preclude it from also being a racialized group.

51. Smedley and Smedley, "Race as Biology Is Fiction, Racism as a Social Problem Is Real."
52. Cobas, Duany, and Feagin, "Racializing Latinos," 8.
53. Almaguer, "Race, Racialization, and Latino Populations."
54. Golash-Boza and Darity, "Latino Racial Choices."
55. Chávez-Moreno, "The Problem with Latinx"; Gómez, *Manifest Destinies*; Haney López, "Race, Ethnicity, Erasure"; Roth, *Race Migrations*.
56. Fergus, Noguera, and Martin, "Construction of Race and Ethnicity for and by Latinos"; Torres-Saillant, "Inventing the Race."
57. See Gómez, *Manifest Destinies*; Martinez, "The Legal Construction of Race."
58. This is particularly true when conclusions rely on a single variable, be it how Latinxs racially identify themselves or their use of the Spanish language; Dávila, *Latino Spin*.
59. Gómez, *Manifest Destinies*; Gómez, *Inventing Latinos*; Haney López, "Race, Ethnicity, Erasure"; Chávez-Moreno, "The Problem with Latinx."
60. Compare Beltrán, *Trouble with Unity*; Dávila, *Latino Spin*; Milian, *LatinX*; Roth, *Race Migrations*.
61. See, e.g., Alberto, "Coming Out as Indian"; Flores, "Latinidad Is Cancelled"; LeBaron, "When Latinos Are Not Latinos."
62. See, e.g., Gómez, *Manifest Destinies*; Molina, HoSang, and Gutiérrez, *Relational Formations of Race*.
63. For more on the diversity within racialized groups, see, e.g., Gómez, *Inventing Latinos*; Harris and Khanna, "Black Is, Black Ain't"; Philip, "Asian American as a Political-Racial Identity."
64. I recognize that some scholars use "ethnoracial" to signal the complexity of the interaction between ethnicity and racialization, but that is not my book's project. For an example in education, see Busey and Silva, "Troubling the Essentialist Discourse of Brown."
65. Mignolo, *Idea of Latin America*.
66. Chávez-Moreno, "The Problem with Latinx."
67. This last reason is inspired by Milian, *LatinX*.
68. In the same way that, for example, not all White folks are always guided by whiteness, not all Latinx folks always ascribe to Latinidad. For more on whiteness, see Leonardo and Zembylas, "Whiteness as Technology of Affect."
69. For critiques of the Latino/a/x or Latinidad concepts, see, e.g., Beltrán, *Trouble with Unity*; Flores, "Latinidad Is Cancelled"; Milian, *LatinX*.
70. National Center for Education Statistics, "Racial/Ethnic Enrollment in Public Schools."
71. US Department of Education, "Our Nation's English Learners."
72. See, e.g., Collier and Thomas, "Astounding Effectiveness of Dual-Language."
73. Chávez-Moreno, "Researching Latinxs, Racism"; Chávez-Moreno, "Literature Review of Raciolinguistics"; Lewis, Hagerman, and Forman, "Sociology of Race."
74. Alemán, "Situating Texas School Finance Policy"; Baker et al., "School Funding Disparities."
75. Lewis, *Race in the Schoolyard*; Rodríguez and Conchas, *Race Frames*.
76. Lewis, *Race in the Schoolyard*.
77. Lewis, *Race in the Schoolyard*, 95.
78. Rosa, *Looking Like a Language*.
79. Latinx studies is experiencing a turn toward examining racialization processes in more recent gateways. As sociologist Néstor Rodríguez notes:

More than just becoming the largest minority group in the United States, in many ways Latinos are restructuring the social landscapes in the areas where they settle. Yet, Latino research has not adequately analyzed the underlying social forces of this development.

Rodríguez, "Theoretical and Methodological Issues of Latina/o Research," 7; Vásquez, Seales, and Marquardt, "New Latino Destinations."

80. See political scientist Pedro Cabán's "Moving from the Margins to Where?," 31.
81. Hamann, Wortham, and Murillo, *Revisiting Education in the New Latino Diaspora*.
82. Hamann, Wortham, and Murillo, *Revisiting Education in the New Latino Diaspora*.
83. Cheng, *Changs Next Door to the Díazes*.
84. Hamann, Wortham, and Murillo, *Revisiting Education in the New Latino Diaspora*.
85. Lowenhaupt, "Bilingual Education Policy"; Vásquez, Seales, and Marquardt, "New Latino Destinations"; Wortham, Mortimer, and Allard, "Mexicans as Model Minorities in the New Latino Diaspora."
86. Darder, *Culture and Power*; Sleeter and Delgado Bernal, "Critical Pedagogy, Critical Race Theory, and Antiracist Education."
87. See, e.g., Fallas-Escobar and Deroo, "Latina/o Bilingual Teacher"; Lima Becker and Oliveira, "'This Is a Very Sensitive Point.'"
88. See, e.g., Babino and Stewart, "Remodeling Dual-Language Programs"; Morales and Maravilla, "Problems and Possibilities of Interest Convergence in a Dual Language School."
89. See, e.g., Scott and Bajaj, "Introduction"; Wills, "Silencing Racism."
90. See, e.g., these literature reviews: Brayboy, Castagno, and Maughan, "Equality and Justice for All?"; Cabrera, "Where Is the Racial Theory in Critical Race Theory?"; Chávez-Moreno, "Examining Race in LatCrit"; Dixson and Rousseau, "And We Are Still Not Saved"; Harper, "Race without Racism"; Kohli, Pizarro, and Nevárez, "New Racism"; Lynn and Parker, "Critical Race Studies in Education."
91. For a research study using a relational-race approach, see Singh, "Negotiating Antiblackness."
92. For a notable exception, see Lewis, *Race in the Schoolyard*.
93. Chávez-Moreno, "Examining Race in LatCrit."
94. Although Leonardo's critique is specific to CRT, it raises significant concerns, given CRT's status as the predominant theoretical framework for studying race in the field of education. For Leonardo's argument of how education's dominant race theory (critical race theory in education) has neglected defining race, see Leonardo, *Race Frameworks*, 28.
95. Leonardo, "Dialectics of Race Criticality."
96. Bartlett and Brayboy, "Race and Schooling," 365.
97. Chávez-Moreno, "Examining Race in LatCrit." For examples of education research examining racial projects and racialization, see Rodríguez and Conchas, *Race Frames*.
98. Johnston-Guerrero and Tran, "Born This Way?"; Roth et al., "Do Genetic Ancestry Tests Increase Racial Essentialism?"
99. Chávez-Moreno, "Literature Review of Raciolinguistics."
100. Chávez-Moreno, "Examining Race in LatCrit." For an education study on how a college course impacts individuals' development of a Latinidad identity, see Castillo-Montoya and Verduzco Reyes, "Learning Latinidad."
101. Addressing the call by Lewis, Hagerman, and Forman, "Sociology of Race."
102. Lewis, *Race in the Schoolyard*.

103. Alim, Rickford, and Ball, *Raciolinguistics*; Rosa, *Looking Like a Language*.

104. Chávez-Moreno, "The Problem with Latinx"; Rosa, *Looking Like a Language*.

105. Alim, Rickford, and Ball, *Raciolinguistics*; Flores and Rosa, "Undoing Appropriateness."

106. For examples of race-conscious education uplifting academic achievement, see Cabrera et al., "Missing the (Student Achievement)"; de los Ríos, López, and Morrell, "Critical Ethnic Studies."

107. Some research on secondary-level dual language includes: de Jong and Bearse, "Same Outcomes for All?"; Hernandez, "Are They All Language Learners?"

108. Desmond, "Relational Ethnography," 561.

109. Molina, HoSang, and Gutiérrez, *Relational Formations of Race*; Desmond, "Relational Ethnography"; Goldberg, "Racial Comparisons."

110. Lewis, Hagerman, and Forman, "Sociology of Race"; Molina, *How Race Is Made*.

111. HoSang and Molina, "Introduction"; Molina, "Examining Chicana/o History."

112. Notable exceptions include: Enriquez, "Border-Hopping Mexicans"; Lewis, *Race in the Schoolyard*; Merseth, "The Relational Positioning of Arab and Muslim Americans."

113. For examples of this conversation with education scholars problematizing "Brown" and mestizaje, see Busey and Silva, "Troubling the Essentialist Discourse of Brown"; Calderón and Urrieta, "Studying in Relation"; López and Irizarry, "Somos Pero No Somos Iguales."

114. Desmond, "Relational Ethnography," 558.

115. DuBord, "Language Policy and the Drawing of Social Boundaries."

116. San Miguel, *Chicana/o Struggles for Education*.

117. Macías et al., *Educación Alternativa*; San Miguel, *Chicana/o Struggles for Education*.

118. Hurie and Callahan, "Integration as Perpetuation."

119. San Miguel, *Chicana/o Struggles for Education*.

120. Flores, "Deficit Perspectives and Bilingual Education"; Sung, "Accentuate the Positive."

121. For a critique of multicultural education, see Ladson-Billings and Tate, "Toward a Critical Race Theory of Education."

122. Sleeter and Delgado Bernal, "Critical Pedagogy, Critical Race Theory, and Antiracist Education."

123. García and Sung, "Critically Assessing the 1968 Bilingual Education Act."

124. *Lau v. Nichols*, 414 US 563 (U.S. Supreme Court 1974).

125. Cammarota, "Race War in Arizona"; Gándara and Hopkins, *Forbidden Language*.

126. Center for Applied Linguistics, "Growth of Two-Way Immersion Programs."

127. For more on bilingual education's negative connotations and on racial integration, see Chávez-Moreno, "Raciolinguistic and Racial Realist Critique." In Arizona, ELLs were prohibited from enrolling in dual language, a policy that contributed to distancing dual language from the stigma of being seen as an educational intervention for "at risk" students; Combs et al., "Bilingualism for the Children."

128. Palmer, "Race, Power, and Equity."

129. Collier and Thomas, "Astounding Effectiveness of Dual-Language," 1; Kim and Son, "What Is Visible and Invisible."

130. Darder, *Culture and Power*; Pacheco and Chávez-Moreno, "Bilingual Education for Self-Determination"; Palmer et al., "Bilingualism Biliteracy, Biculturalism, and Critical Consciousness for All."

131. I further define "critical-racial consciousness" in the book's conclusion; Chávez-Moreno, "Continuum of Racial Literacies"; Palmer et al., "Bilingualism Biliteracy, Biculturalism, and Critical Consciousness for All."

132. Cabrera et al., "Missing the (Student Achievement)"; de los Ríos, López, and Morrell, "Critical Ethnic Studies."
133. Although, some call for canceling Latinidad altogether, see, e.g., Flores, "Latinidad Is Cancelled."
134. Orellana and Gutiérrez, "At Last."
135. Lipsky, *Street-Level Bureaucracy.*

Chapter 1

1. Borane's total enrollment was approximately 650, with 33 percent of the students labeled as ELLs and 19 percent designated as special education.
2. In block scheduling, each class is an hour and a half; in the high school, this meant students had four classes per day. Most classes complete in one semester, and then a new set of four classes begins in the spring semester, meaning a student would take a total of eight classes per year.
3. I provide all translations.
4. For a discussion about White students and racialized students having different understandings of racism and thus requiring different racial pedagogy, see Leonardo and Manning, "White Historical Activity Theory."
5. Santiago, "Diluting Mexican American History for Public Consumption."
6. Orozco and López, "Impacts of Arizona's SB 1070"; Santos, Menjívar, and Godfrey, "Effects of SB 1070 on Children."
7. Sesame Workshop, "Explaining Race: #ComingTogether," YouTube, accessed November 8, 2022, https://youtu.be/Dk_HYAiS26I.
8. Cammarota, "Race War in Arizona."
9. For racialization as a transnational process, see Roth, *Race Migrations*; Zamora, *Racial Baggage.*
10. In terms of scaffolded race instruction, Leonardo and Manning argue that Whites have a different zone of proximal development in terms of learning about race than racialized Others because whiteness obscures the racial aspects of one's experiences and Whites start from being immersed and invested in whiteness. Leonardo and Manning, "White Historical Activity Theory."
11. This dissonance happens in other contexts too; e.g., Aranda and Rebollo-Gil, "Ethnoracism and the 'Sandwiched' Minorities."
12. Fields and Fields, *Racecraft*; Gómez, *Manifest Destinies*; Kendi, *Stamped from the Beginning*; Carbado, "Racial Naturalization"; Omi and Winant, *Racial Formation in the U.S.*
13. See the concept of "racial scripts" in Molina, *How Race Is Made.* Also see Nasir, *Racialized Identities.*

Chapter 2

1. See, e.g., Cabrera et al., "Missing the (Student Achievement)"; Collier and Thomas, "Astounding Effectiveness of Dual-Language"; de los Ríos, López, and Morrell, "Critical Ethnic Studies."
2. Gómez, *Manifest Destinies*; González, *Harvest of Empire.*
3. Zentella, "'Limpia, Fija y Da Esplendor.'"
4. For an empirical study and critique of hiring foreign teachers, see Dunn, "Global Village versus Culture Shock."

5. Lozano, *American Language*.
6. Pérez Huber et al., "Theorizing Racist Nativism"; Gómez, *Inventing Latinos*.
7. Citation withheld.
8. Orozco and López, "Impacts of Arizona's SB 1070"; Santos, Menjívar, and Godfrey, "Effects of SB 1070 on Children."
9. Roth, *Race Migrations*; Zamora, *Racial Baggage*.
10. I never heard any program participant mention "Latinx" as a panethnicity. That designation, like that of being an ethnic group, would not preclude "Latinx" from also being a racialized group. Compared to the "ethnic" label, panethnicity may be a more appropriate description of "Latinx" when conceptualized as Okamoto and Mora do: "Panethnicity is characterized by an acknowledgement of subgroup diversity as well as a broader sense of solidarity" (Okamoto and Mora, "Panethnicity," 221).
11. Media, corporations, etc., do work to create a sense of "Latino culture," e.g., by promoting Día de los Reyes or Dora the Explorer as "Latino."
12. It was easy for high-school students to drop the dual-language program. Students self-selected to continue participating by enrolling in the Spanish dual-language (DL) classes (Spanish DL 1, Spanish DL 2, Spanish AP Language & Culture, Spanish AP Literature & Culture, US History 9th, World History 10th, Ethnic Studies, and Latin American Studies). Because students selected their courses, they easily could self-select out of the program by not enrolling in any dual-language courses, as happened in some cases.

      Other general classes (such as English, science, art, music, computers, and other electives) were open to all students thus had a mix of dual-language and non-dual-language students. Teachers of those general classes did not know which students participated in the dual-language program. Students selected and/or were placed into tracked courses (e.g., remedial, honors, or AP mathematics).
13. See another example showing the focus on skin color and the decoupling of race from racism in Wills, "Silencing Racism."
14. Omi and Winant, *Racial Formation in the U.S.*
15. For a discussion on the instability of race and racialized categories, see Omi and Winant, "Racial Formation Rules."
16. Leonardo, *Race Frameworks*.
17. Omi and Winant critique the reduction of race to skin color; see Omi and Winant, *Racial Formation in the U.S.*
18. Fields and Fields, *Racecraft*; Gómez, *Inventing Latinos*; Kendi, *Stamped from the Beginning*; Hochman, "Racialization"; Zepeda-Millán and Wallace, "Racialization in Times of Contention."
19. Omi and Winant, "Resistance is Futile?"

Chapter 3

1. Gómez, *Inventing Latinos*.
2. Bang et al., "Undoing Human Supremacy and White Supremacy"; Chávez-Moreno, "U.S. Empire and an Immigrant's Counternarrative."
3. Stone, "Centering Place in Ethnographies of 'Latinx' Schooling."
4. For an example of how language teaching programs of Indigenous peoples worked from racial settler logics that described them as less than human, see Marquez and Kunkel, "The Domestication Genocide of Settler Colonial–Language Ideologies."
5. Alberto, "Coming Out as Indian"; Martínez, "Dual-Language Education and the Erasure of Chicanx, Latinx, and Indigenous Mexican Children."

6. Blackwell, Boj Lopez, and Urrieta, "Critical Latinx Indigeneities."
7. I use the term "diaspora" to describe the dispersion of populations due to globalization, transnationalism, and imperialism; Brah, "Thinking Through the Concept of Diaspora"; González, *Harvest of Empire*; Hamann, Wortham, and Murillo, *Revisiting Education in the New Latino Diaspora*. For racial diasporas and Indigeneity, see Bang et al., "Undoing Human Supremacy and White Supremacy."
8. Leonardo and Manning, "White Historical Activity Theory."
9. Mestizaje (racial mixing/mixture) is used to conceal persistent inequalities and systemic racism; see Ríos, "Mestizaje." For a cogent critique of *la raza cósmica* and an intellectual genealogy, see Palacios, "Multicultural Vasconcelos."
10. Patel, *Decolonizing Educational Research*.
11. Gómez, *Inventing Latinos*; González, *Harvest of Empire*.
12. Lee, *Unraveling the "Model Minority" Stereotype*.
13. Chang and Au, "You're Asian"; Lee, *Unraveling the "Model Minority" Stereotype*.
14. On the "model minority" in other contexts, see Cheng, *Changs Next Door to the Díazes*; Lee, *Unraveling the "Model Minority" Stereotype*.
15. Romero and Escudero, "Asian Latinos."
16. For readings on the racialization of Mexican Americans specifically, see Gómez, *Manifest Destinies*; Massey, "Racial Formation in Theory and Practice."
17. Urciuoli, *Exposing Prejudice*.
18. Flores and Rosa, "Undoing Appropriateness"; Zentella, "'Limpia, Fija y Da Esplendor.'"
19. For how ideas about perfect Spanish affect Latinx teachers, see Briceño, Rodríguez-Mojica, and Muñoz-Muñoz, "From English Learner to Spanish Learner."
20. Briceño, Rodríguez-Mojica, and Muñoz-Muñoz, "From English Learner to Spanish Learner."
21. Blackwell, Boj Lopez, and Urrieta, "Critical Latinx Indigeneities."

Chapter 4

1. For an overview of Chicano and some Puerto Rican desegregation cases, see chapter 3 in Gómez, *Inventing Latinos*.
2. For an example of Mexican American school segregation in the Midwest, see Donato and Hanson, "'In These Towns, Mexicans Are Classified as Negroes.'"
3. McCormick and Ayala, "Felícita 'La Prieta' Méndez," 13.
4. For more on curricular simplification of the *Méndez* case, see Santiago, "Diluting Mexican American History for Public Consumption."
5. For an autoethnography on bilingual education and Black erasure, see Cioè-Peña, "Writing, Rioting and Righting Como Negra."
6. The book's Introduction has the district's population information.
7. Howard, *Why Race and Culture Matter in Schools*; Milner, "Disrupting Punitive Practices and Policies."
8. Although my study did not focus on capturing students' use of Black American English (BAE), I did hear some Black dual-language students use BAE.
9. For more on Black languaging in a Spanish/English dual-language program, see Presiado and Frieson, "'Make Sure You See This.'"
10. The fact that the program's teachers never mentioned BAE likely influenced whether students regarded BAE as adding to their bilingual abilities.
11. This is similar to other research findings that examine student perceptions, see, e.g., Sung, "Raciolinguistic Ideology of Antiblackness."

12. This suggests that the "impartial" science that examines how bilingualism provides "cognitive development" arises from ideological and value-laden decisions about what counts as a language and as cognitive development. See Alim, Rickford, and Ball, *Raciolinguistics*; Flores and Rosa, "Undoing Appropriateness."

13. For relational racialization of Latinxs in a California schooling context, see Cheng, *Changs Next Door to the Díazes*.

14. For an example of Mexicans as a model minority, see Wortham, Mortimer, and Allard, "Mexicans as Model Minorities in the New Latino Diaspora."

15. The findings with respect to how Latinxs were positioned above Black folks is consistent with other research, e.g., Gómez, *Manifest Destinies*; Gómez, *Inventing Latinos*.

16. On Black immigrants as a Black model minority, see Wallace, *Culture Trap*.

17. Carter et al., "You Can't Fix What You Don't Look At."

18. Annamma et al., "Black Girls and School Discipline."

19. For other examples of anti-Blackness in the Latinx community, see Hernández, *Racial Innocence*.

20. For research showing Latina/Latino teachers and (anti)Blackness, see Flores, "Controlling Images of Space"; Singh, "Negotiating Antiblackness."

21. Annamma et al., "Black Girls and School Discipline"; Stovall, "Killing You Is Justice"; Winn, *Girl Time*.

22. For research showing that predominantly Hispanic/Latinx spaces are not necessary free from anti-Blackness, see Pirtle et al., "'I Didn't Know What Anti-Blackness Was Until I Got Here.'"

23. For other contexts, see Gamez and Monreal, "'We Have That Opportunity Now'"; Singh, "Negotiating Antiblackness."

24. To see how the model minority discourse, even when Black folks are the model, is fundamentally anti-Black and based in slavery, see Marquez, "Black Model Minority."

25. For an example of Black parent engagement contradicting this racist trope, see Foubert, "'Damned If You Do, Damned If You Don't.'"

26. For a debate about culture, racial labels, and Anglos being of any race, see Klor de Alva, Shorris, and West, "Our Next Race Question."

27. For examples of valuing Black students' literacies in dual-language, see Presiado and Frieson, "'Make Sure You See This.'"

28. Smith, Lee, and Chang, "Characterizing Competing Tensions in Black Immigrant Literacies."

29. Goings, Bristol, and Walker, "Exploring the Transition Experiences."

30. These include some Latin American countries with larger Afro-descendent populations; Gómez, *Inventing Latinos*.

31. Bartlett and García, *Additive Schooling in Subtractive Times*; Chávez-Moreno, "Raciolinguistic and Racial Realist Critique."

32. A tension often emphasized in popular media, see, e.g., Johnson, *Spaces of Conflict, Sounds of Solidarity*; Kun and Pulido, *Black and Brown in Los Angeles*.

33. Dávila, *Latino Spin*.

34. A tension that is also present in other contexts, see Schnaiberg, "D.C. School Bilingual Plan Pits Black, Hispanic Parents."

35. Callahan and Gándara, *The Bilingual Advantage*; Chávez-Moreno, "Dual Language as White Property."

36. https://www.facinghistory.org/resource-library/video/little-things-are-big-jes-s-col-n.

37. For further theorization on the impossibility of humanness for Black folks, see, e.g., Dumas and Nelson, "(Re)Imagining Black Boyhood"; Wynter, "Unsettling the Coloniality of Being/Power/Truth/Freedom."
38. This book focuses on the dual-language program's teachings about race and other racial issues; it does not analyze student learning (i.e., how students made sense of the lesson or adopted/resisted hegemonic ideas).
39. Dávila, *Latino Spin*.
40. Gómez, *Manifest Destinies*; Gómez, *Inventing Latinos*.
41. Cioè-Peña, "Writing, Rioting and Righting Como Negra."

Chapter 5

1. Kim and Son, "What Is Visible and Invisible."
2. While bilingualism may bring a person employment opportunities, some quantitative research suggests Hispanic and Asian American workers' bilingualism does not lead to economic advantages—on the contrary, at times their wages are lower. See Shin and Alba, "The Economic Value of Bilingualism for Asians and Hispanics."
3. The biologically based intelligence argument has lived on, helped by the popularity of the book "The Bell Curve." For a critique, see Siegel, "The Real Problem with Charles Murray and 'The Bell Curve.'"
4. For other contexts with this pattern, see, e.g., López, *Hopeful Girls, Troubled Boys*.
5. Valenzuela et al., "Institutional and Structural Barriers to Latino/a Achievement."
6. For a cogent critique of academic language, see Flores and Rosa, "Undoing Appropriateness."
7. Flores and Rosa, "Undoing Appropriateness."
8. For information on Latinx education attainment, see Gándara and Contreras, *Latino Education Crisis*.
9. Román, Pastor, and Basaraba, "Internal Linguistic Discrimination."
10. Flores and Rosa, "Undoing Appropriateness."
11. Valdés, Poza, and Brooks, "Educating Students Who Do Not Speak the Societal Language."
12. For examples of this occurring in other contexts and a discussion of the Seal and interest convergence, see Chang-Bacon and Colomer, "Biliteracy as Property."
13. Chang-Bacon and Colomer, "Biliteracy as Property"; Subtirelu et al., "Recognizing Whose Bilingualism?"
14. Avni and Menken, "Expansion of Dual-Language Bilingual Education"; Freire, Valdez, and Delavan, "(Dis)Inclusion of Latina/o Interests."

Chapter 6

1. Trump's administration added to the history of separating families and formalized the practice in other ways; Abrego and Hernández, "Central American Family Separations."
2. Feinberg, Branton, and Martinez-Ebers, "Counties That Hosted a 2016 Trump Rally."
3. Ryan, "'This Was a Whitelash.'"
4. This election was a learning moment for me too. I later learned that the Electoral College indirectly gave more weight to White voters in slaveholding states through the Three-Fifths Compromise, which counted enslaved individuals as three-fifths of a person for determining a state's representation, thereby increasing the number of electoral votes of those states without granting voting rights to the slaves themselves. For more information,

see Codrington, "Electoral College's Racist Origins"; Kelkar, "Racial History of the Electoral College."

5. Brown and Brown, "Teaching K-8 Students About Race."
6. Kim and Son, "What Is Visible and Invisible."
7. Kim and Son, "What Is Visible and Invisible."
8. Montone and Loeb have identified various challenges in implementing secondary-level bilingual programs, such as program planning, curriculum and materials, and student scheduling. These challenges were also evident in my research sites. However, my discussion of these issues is limited to how they relate to my research questions, as an in-depth evaluation of program implementation falls outside the scope of my inquiry; Montone and Loeb, "Implementing Two-Way Immersion Programs in Secondary Schools."
9. For research problematizing charter schools, see Chapman and Donnor, "Critical Race Theory and the Proliferation of US Charter Schools."
10. Chávez-Moreno, "Dual Language as White Property."
11. State citations withheld to not identify the state.
12. Cross, "Teacher Shortage."
13. Alemán, "Situating Texas School Finance Policy"; Baker et al., "School Funding Disparities"; Jiménez-Castellanos, "English Language Learner Education Finance Scholarship"; Rodriguez, "Vertical Equity in School Finance."
14. Citation withheld for confidentiality purposes.
15. Alemán, "Situating Texas School Finance Policy"; Moses, *Embracing Race.*
16. McGhee, *Sum of Us.*

Conclusion

1. Also see, Chávez-Moreno, "Racist and Raciolinguistic Teacher Ideologies."
2. For educators interested in practitioner inquiry, I recommend e.g., Blackburn et al., *Acting Out!*; Campano, *Immigrant Students and Literacy*; Cochran-Smith and Lytle, *Inquiry as Stance*; Valdez et al., "We Are Victorious."
3. Love, *We Want to Do More.* See also Brown and Brown, "Teaching K-8 Students about Race"; Chávez-Moreno, "Continuum of Racial Literacies"; Hannah-Jones, "Creator of '1619 Project'"; López, "Antiracist Pedagogy and Empowerment in a Bilingual Classroom"; Wills, "Silencing Racism."
4. Leonardo, *Race Frameworks.*
5. Leonardo, *Race Frameworks.*
6. Leonardo, "Dialectics of Race Criticality."
7. Omi and Winant, "Resistance Is Futile?"
8. Nasir, *Racialized Identities.*
9. Baquedano-López, "Creating Social Identities."
10. Leonardo, *Race Frameworks.*
11. Leonardo, *Race Frameworks*; Omi and Winant, "Resistance Is Futile?"
12. Leonardo, *Race Frameworks.*
13. For "disidentification" and Latinx teachers, see Singh, "Refusing the Performance."
14. Haywood, "'Latino Spaces Have Always Been the Most Violent'"; López et al., "What's Your 'Street Race'?"
15. Irizarry, "Utilizing Multidimensional Measures of Race in Education Research"; Roth, "The Multiple Dimensions of Race."
16. Compare this with scholarship on science and math education: Lampert et al., "Keeping It Complex"; Rigby and Forman, "Leading for Justice, Leading for Learning"; Thompson,

Windschitl, and Braaten, "Developing a Theory of Ambitious Early-Career Teacher Practice."

17. I use lowercase "critical-race pedagogy" to broaden the concept rather than indicate pedagogy founded solely on CRT's tenets.

18. Leonardo and Manning, "White Historical Activity Theory."

19. For how this happens in other contexts, see Freire, Valdez, and Delavan, "(Dis)Inclusion of Latina/o Interests."

20. Bale, "Tongue-Tied"; DuBord, "Language Policy and the Drawing of Social Boundaries."

21. Del Valle, "Bilingual Education for Puerto Ricans"; Flores, "Tale of Two Visions."

22. de los Ríos, López, and Morrell, "Critical Ethnic Studies."

23. Darder, *Culture and Power in the Classroom*; Pacheco and Chávez-Moreno, "Bilingual Education for Self-Determination."

24. Rogers et al., "Educating Toward a Multiracial Democracy."

25. Bartlett and García, *Additive Schooling in Subtractive Times*; Degollado, Bell, and Salinas, "'No Había Bilingual Education.'"

26. Chávez-Moreno, "Review of Stamped"; Fields and Fields, *Racecraft*.

27. Compare how the teaching of race is banned in some states: Alexander et al., "CRT Forward"; Cammarota, "Race War in Arizona."

28. Certainly, the US census influences society's ideas of what racialized categories exist, but other societal institutions act as racial projects and also have made Latinx into a racialized group, see Caminero-Santangelo, "Latinidad"; Mora, *Making Hispanics*. While this book was in production, the US government announced changes to its racial categories; see Dowling, "Latinos Are Getting out of the 'Other' Box on the U.S. Census."

29. Kendi, *Stamped from the Beginning*.

30. For more on the clash of racial formation systems, Almaguer, "Race, Racialization, and Latino Populations."

31. Mignolo, *Idea of Latin America*.

32. Mora, *Making Hispanics*.

33. Aparicio et al., "Introduction."

34. Dache, Haywood, and Mislán, "Badge of Honor Not Shame"; López and Irizarry, "Somos Pero No Somos Iguales." For more on how Latinx is not a monolith, see Busey and Silva, "Troubling the Essentialist Discourse of Brown."

35. Barreto and Segura, *Latino America*; Johnson, *Spaces of Conflict*.

36. Almaguer, "Race, Racialization, and Latino Populations"; Kendi, *Stamped from the Beginning*. For more on the multiple dimensions to race, see, e.g. Irizarry, "Utilizing Multidimensional Measures of Race in Education Research"; Roth, "The Multiple Dimensions of Race."

37. Omi and Winant, *Racial Formation in the U.S.*, 247.

38. Omi and Winant, *Racial Formation in the U.S.*, 111.

39. Alim, Rickford, and Ball, *Raciolinguistics*; Aranda and Rebollo-Gil, "Ethnoracism and the 'Sandwiched' Minorities."

40. Gómez, *Manifest Destinies*; Molina, HoSang, and Gutiérrez, *Relational Formations of Race*; Omi and Winant, "Racial Formation Rules."

41. Consider the concepts "religious race" and "skin color race" in Leonardo, "Ideology and Its Modes of Existence." Also see López et al., "What's Your 'Street Race'?"

42. My claim is not to condone racial differentiation and boundaries, given the nefariousness of race. Of course, how a group is racially marked does not negate the effect of colorism on the experiences of individuals: Harris, "Toward a Critical Multiracial Theory in Education"; Haywood, "'Latino Spaces Have Always Been the Most Violent'"; López et al.,

"What's Your 'Street Race'?" Rather, my proposal concerns the dimension of group formation, not the individual experience of race.

43. I use the word "imagined" because, for one, not all Latinxs speak Spanish. See Chávez-Moreno, "The Problem with Latinx"; Chávez-Moreno, "Examining Race in LatCrit."

44. This includes imagining the Latinx racialized group as "you-should-know" Spanish, or perhaps more specifically, as bound by the idea that they should know Spanish due to familial ties to relevant regions. To complicate this racial logic and consider an alternative way of conceptualizing Latinx, see Chávez-Moreno, "The Problem with Latinx." Also, this does not exclude groups from non-Spanish-speaking Latin America, such as Brazilian Americans, who are at times heard/read/imagined as "Spanish speakers." Additionally, my claim does not suggest that other racial projects, such as religious institutions, make Spanish the signature boundary delineating the Latinx racialized group.

45. Alim, Rickford, and Ball, *Raciolinguistics*; Mora, *Making Hispanics*; Rosa, *Looking Like a Language*.

Appendix

1. Chávez-Moreno, "Critiquing Racial Literacy."
2. Alim, Rickford, and Ball, *Raciolinguistics*; Chávez-Moreno, "Racist and Raciolinguistic Teacher Ideologies"; Flores and Rosa, "Undoing Appropriateness."
3. LeCompte and Schensul, *Analysis and Interpretation of Ethnographic Data*.
4. Saldaña, *Coding Manual*, 91.
5. Saldaña, *Coding Manual*, 96.

Bibliography

Abrego, Leisy J., and Ester Hernández. "Central American Family Separations from the 1980s to 2019." In *Critical Dialogues in Latinx Studies: A Reader*. NYU Press, 2021.

Alberto, Lourdes. "Coming Out as Indian: On Being an Indigenous Latina in the U.S." *Latino Studies* 15, no. 2 (2017): 247–53. https://doi.org/10.1057/s41276-017-0058-y.

Alemán, Enrique. "Situating Texas School Finance Policy in a CRT Framework: How 'Substantially Equal' Yields Racial Inequity." *Educational Administration Quarterly* 43, no. 5 (2007): 525–58. https://doi.org/10.1177/0013161X07303276.

Alexander, Taifha, LaToya Baldwin Clark, Kyle Reinhard, and Noah Zatz. "CRT Forward: Tracking the Attack on Critical Race Theory." UCLA School of Law Critical Race Studies Program, 2023. https://crtforward.law.ucla.edu/wp-content/uploads/2023/04/UCLA-Law_CRT-Report_Final.pdf.

Alim, H. Samy, John R. Rickford, and Arnetha F. Ball, eds. *Raciolinguistics: How Language Shapes Our Ideas About Race*. New York: Oxford University Press, 2016.

Almaguer, Tomás. "Race, Racialization, and Latino Populations in the United States." *Racial Formation in the Twenty-First Century* (2012): 143–61.

Annamma, Subini Ancy, Yolanda Anyon, Nicole M. Joseph, Jordan Farrar, Eldridge Greer, Barbara Downing, and John Simmons. "Black Girls and School Discipline: The Complexities of Being Overrepresented and Understudied." *Urban Education* 54, no. 2 (2019): 211–42.

Aparicio, Ana, Andrea Bolivar, Alex Chávez, Sherina Feliciano-Santos, Santiago Guerra, Gina Pérez, Jonathan Rosa, Gilberto Rosas, Aimee Villarreal, and Patricia Zavella. "Introduction." In *Ethnographic Refusals, Unruly Latinidades*, edited by Alex Chávez and Gina Pérez, xiii–xxxv. Albuquerque: University of New Mexico Press, 2022.

Aranda, Elizabeth M., and Guillermo Rebollo-Gil. "Ethnoracism and the 'Sandwiched' Minorities." *American Behavioral Scientist* 47, no. 7 (2004): 910–27.

Avni, Sharon, and Kate Menken. "The Expansion of Dual-Language Bilingual Education into New Communities and Languages: The Case of Hebrew in a New York City Public Middle School." *Theory into Practice* 58, no. 2 (April 3, 2019): 154–63. https://doi.org/10.1080/00405841.2019.1569378.

Babino, Alexandra, and Mary Amanda Stewart. "Remodeling Dual-Language Programs: Teachers Enact Agency as Critically Conscious Language Policy Makers." *Bilingual Research Journal* 41, no. 3 (July 2018): 272–97. https://doi.org/10.1080/15235882.2018.1489313.

Baker, Bruce, Ajay Srikanth, Preston Green, and Robert Cotto. "School Funding Disparities and the Plight of Latinx Children." *Education Policy Analysis Archives* 28, no. 135 (2020): 1–22.

Bale, Jeff. "Tongue-Tied: Imperialism and Second Language Education in the United States." *Critical Education* 2, no. 8 (2011): 1–25.

Bang, Megan, Ananda Marin, Sandi Wemigwase, Preeti Nayak, and Fikile Nxumalo. "Undoing Human Supremacy and White Supremacy to Transform Relationships: An Interview with Megan Bang and Ananda Marin." *Curriculum Inquiry* 52, no. 2 (2022): 150–61.

Baquedano-López, Patricia. "Creating Social Identities through Doctrina Narratives." *Linguistic Anthropology: A Reader* (2001): 343–58.

Barreto, Matt, and Gary Segura. *Latino America: How America's Most Dynamic Population Is Poised to Transform the Politics of the Nation.* New York: PublicAffairs, 2014.

Bartlett, Lesley, and Bryan McKinley Jones Brayboy. "Race and Schooling: Theories and Ethnographies." *Urban Review* 37, no. 5 (2005): 361–74. https://doi.org/10.1007/s11256-005 -0021-3.

Bartlett, Lesley, and Ofelia García. *Additive Schooling in Subtractive Times: Bilingual Education and Dominican Immigrant Youth in the Heights.* Nashville, TN: Vanderbilt University Press, 2011.

Beltrán, Cristina. *The Trouble with Unity: Latino Politics and the Creation of Identity.* New York: Oxford University Press, 2010.

Blackburn, Mollie V., Caroline T. Clark, Lauren M. Kenney, and Jill M. Smith. *Acting Out!: Combating Homophobia Through Teacher Activism.* New York: Teachers College Press, 2010.

Blackwell, Maylei, Floridalma Boj Lopez, and Luis Urrieta. "Critical Latinx Indigeneities." *Latino Studies* 15, no. 2 (2017): 126–37. https://doi.org/10.1057/s41276-017-0064-0.

Brah, Avtah. "Thinking Through the Concept of Diaspora." In *The Post-Colonial Studies Reader*, edited by Bill Ashcroft and Gareth Griffiths, 2nd ed., 443–46. New York: Routledge, 2006.

Brayboy, Bryan McKinley Jones, Angelina E. Castagno, and Emma Maughan. "Equality and Justice for All? Examining Race in Education Scholarship." *Review of Research in Education* 31, no. 1 (2007): 159–94. https://doi.org/doi:10.3102/0091732X07300046159.

Briceño, Allison, Claudia Rodríguez-Mojica, and Eduardo Muñoz-Muñoz. "From English Learner to Spanish Learner: Raciolinguistic Beliefs That Influence Heritage Spanish Speaking Teacher Candidates." *Language & Education* 32, no. 3 (May 4, 2018): 212–26. https://doi.org/10.1080/09500782.2018.1429464.

Brown, Keffrelyn, and Anthony L. Brown. "Teaching K-8 Students about Race: African Americans, Racism, & the Struggle for Social Justice in the US." *Multicultural Education* 19, no. 1 (2011): 9.

Busey, Christopher L., and Carolyn Silva. "Troubling the Essentialist Discourse of Brown in Education: The Anti-Black Sociopolitical and Sociohistorical Etymology of Latinxs as a Brown Monolith." *Educational Researcher* 50, no. 3 (2021): 176–86. https://doi.org/10.3102 /0013189X20963582.

Cabán, Pedro A. "Moving from the Margins to Where? Three Decades of Latino/a Studies." *Latino Studies* 1, no. 1 (2003): 5–35.

Cabrera, Nolan L. "Where Is the Racial Theory in Critical Race Theory?: A Constructive Criticism of the Crits." *Review of Higher Education* 42, no. 1 (2018): 209–33. https://doi.org/10 .1353/rhe.2018.0038.

Cabrera, Nolan L., Jeffrey F. Milem, Ozan Jaquette, and Ronald W. Marx. "Missing the (Student Achievement) Forest for All the (Political) Trees: Empiricism and the Mexican American Studies Controversy in Tucson." *American Educational Research Journal* 51, no. 6 (2014): 1084–1118. https://doi.org/10.3102/0002831214553705.

Calderón, Dolores, and Luis Urrieta. "Studying in Relation: Critical Latinx Indigeneities and Education." *Equity & Excellence in Education* 52, no. 2–3 (2019): 219–38. https://doi.org /10.1080/10665684.2019.1672591.

Callahan, Rebecca M., and Patricia Gándara. *The Bilingual Advantage: Language, Literacy and the U.S. Labor Market*, Vol. 99. Bristol, UK: Multilingual Matters, 2014.

Caminero-Santangelo, Marta. "Latinidad." In *The Routledge Companion to Latino/a Literature*, edited by Suzanne Bost and Frances R. Aparicio, 29–40. Routledge, 2012.

Cammarota, Julio. "Race War in Arizona: Reflections on the Ethnic Studies Ban and White Hegemony." *Latino Studies* 15, no. 4 (2017): 522–31. https://doi.org/10.1057/s41276-017 -0094-7.

Campano, Gerald. *Immigrant Students and Literacy: Reading, Writing, and Remembering.* New York: Teachers College Press, 2007.

Carbado, Devon W. "Racial Naturalization." *American Quarterly* 57, no. 3 (2005): 633–58.

Carpio, Genevieve. *Collisions at the Crossroads: How Place and Mobility Make Race.* Oakland: University of California Press, 2019.

Carter, Prudence L., Russell Skiba, Mariella I. Arredondo, and Mica Pollock. "You Can't Fix What You Don't Look At: Acknowledging Race in Addressing Racial Discipline Disparities." *Urban Education* 52, no. 2 (2017): 207–35.

Castillo-Montoya, Milagros, and Daisy Verduzco Reyes. "Learning Latinidad: The Role of a Latino Cultural Center Service-Learning Course in Latino Identity Inquiry and Sociopolitical Capacity." *Journal of Latinos and Education* 19, no. 2 (April 2020): 132–47. https://doi .org/10.1080/15348431.2018.1480374.

Center for Applied Linguistics. "Growth of Two-Way Immersion Programs, 1962-Present." TWI directory tables, 2011. http://www.cal.org/twi/directory/twigrow.htm.

Chang, Benjamin Johnson, and Wayne Au. "You're Asian, How Could You Fail Math?: Unmasking the Myth of the Model Minority." *Rethinking Schools* 22, no. 2 (2008): 15–19.

Chang-Bacon, Chris K., and Soria E. Colomer. "Biliteracy as Property: Promises and Perils of the Seal of Biliteracy." *Journal of Literacy Research* 54, no. 2 (2022): 182–207.

Chapman, Thandeka K., and Jamel K. Donnor. "Critical Race Theory and the Proliferation of US Charter Schools." *Equity & Excellence in Education* 48, no. 1 (2015): 137–57.

Chávez-Moreno, Laura C. "The Continuum of Racial Literacies: Teacher Practices Countering Whitestream Bilingual Education." *Research in the Teaching of English* 57, no. 2 (2022): 108–32. https://doi.org/10.58680/rte202232151.

———. "Critiquing Racial Literacy: Presenting a Continuum of Racial Literacies." *Educational Researcher* 51, no. 7 (2022): 481–88. https://doi.org/10.3102/0013189X221093365.

———. "Dual Language as White Property: Examining a Secondary Bilingual-Education Program and Latinx Equity." *American Educational Research Journal* 58, no. 6 (2021): 1107–41. https://doi.org/10.3102/00028312211052508.

———. "Examining Race in LatCrit: A Systematic Review of Latinx Critical Race Theory in Education." *Review of Educational Research* (2023): 1–38. https://doi.org/10.3102/0034 6543231192685.

———. "A Literature Review of Raciolinguistics in Dual-Language Bilingual Education: A Call for Conceptualizing Racialization." In *The Handbook of Dual Language Bilingual Education*, edited by Juan Friere, Cristina Alfaro, and Ester de Jong, 254–65. Routledge, 2024. 10.4324/9781003269076-20.

———. "The Problem with Latinx as a Racial Construct Vis-à-Vis Language and Bilingualism: Toward Recognizing Multiple Colonialisms in the Racialization of Latinidad." In *Handbook of Latinos & Education: Theory, Research, and Practice*, edited by Enrique G. Murillo Jr. et al., 2nd ed., 164–80. New York: Routledge, 2021.

———. "Race Reflexivity: Examining the Unconscious for a Critical Race Ethnography." In *Critical Ethnography, Language, Race/ism and Education*, edited by Stephen May and Blanca Caldas, 91–107. Bristol, UK: Multilingual Matters, 2022.

———. "A Raciolinguistic and Racial Realist Critique of Dual Language's Racial Integration." *Journal of Latinos and Education* 22, no. 5 (2023): 2085–2101. https://doi.org/10.1080 /15348431.2022.2086555.

———. "Racist and Raciolinguistic Teacher Ideologies: When Bilingual Education Is 'Inherently Culturally Relevant' for Latinxs." *Urban Review* 54, no. 4 (2022): 554–75. https://doi .org/10.1007/s11256-021-00628-9.

———. "Researching Latinxs, Racism, and White Supremacy in Bilingual Education: A Literature Review." *Critical Inquiry in Language Studies* 17, no. 2 (2020): 101–20. https://doi.org /10.1080/15427587.2019.1624966.

———. "Review of Stamped from the Beginning: The Definitive History of Racist Ideas in America." *Education Review* 25 (2018): 1–5. https://doi.org/10.14507/er.v25.2407.

———. "U.S. Empire and an Immigrant's Counternarrative: Conceptualizing Imperial Privilege." *Journal of Teacher Education* 72, no. 2 (2021): 209–22. https://doi.org/10.1177 /0022487120919928.

Cheng, Wendy. *The Changs Next Door to the Díazes: Remapping Race in Suburban California*. Minneapolis: University of Minnesota Press, 2013.

Christian, Donna, Elizabeth R. Howard, and Michael I. Loeb. "Bilingualism for All: Two-Way Immersion Education in the United States." *Theory into Practice* 39, no. 4 (2000): 258–66. https://doi.org/10.1207/s15430421tip3904_9.

Cioè-Peña, María. "Writing, Rioting and Righting Como Negra: A Testimonio of Black Latinx Erasure in Bilingual Education." *Harvard Educational Review* 94, no. 4 (2024): 1–24.

Clemetson, Lynette. "Hispanics Now Largest Minority, Census Shows." *New York Times*, January 22, 2003. https://www.nytimes.com/2003/01/22/us/hispanics-now-largest-minority -census-shows.html.

Cobas, José A., Jorge Duany, and Joe R. Feagin. "Racializing Latinos: Historical Background and Current Form." In *How the United States Racializes Latinos: White Hegemony and Its Consequences*, edited by José A. Cobas, Jorge Duany, and Joe R. Feagin, 1–14. Boulder, CO: Paradigm, 2009.

Cochran-Smith, Marilyn, and Susan L. Lytle. *Inquiry as Stance: Practitioner Research for the Next Generation*. New York: Teachers College Press, 2009.

Codrington, Wilfred. "The Electoral College's Racist Origins." *The Atlantic*, November 17, 2019. https://www.theatlantic.com/ideas/archive/2019/11/electoral-college-racist-origins/601918/.

Collier, Virginia P., and Wayne P. Thomas. "The Astounding Effectiveness of Dual-Language Education for All." *NABE Journal of Research & Practice* 2 (2004): 1–20.

Combs, Mary Carol, Carol Evans, Todd Fletcher, Elena Parra, and Alicia Jiménez. "Bilingualism for the Children: Implementing a Dual-Language Program in an English-Only State." *Educational Policy* 19, no. 5 (2005): 701–28.

Cross, Freddie. "Teacher Shortage Areas Nationwide Listing 1990–1991 through 2016–2017." Report. U.S. Department of Education; Office of Postsecondary Education, 2016.

Dache, Amalia, Jasmine Marie Haywood, and Cristina Mislán. "A Badge of Honor Not Shame: An AfroLatina Theory of Black-Imiento for US Higher Education Research." *Journal of Negro Education* 88, no. 2 (2019): 130–45.

Darder, Antonia. *Culture and Power in the Classroom: A Critical Foundation for Bicultural Education*. New York: Greenwood Publishing Group, 1991.

Dávila, Arlene M. *Latino Spin: Public Image and the Whitewashing of Race*. New York: NYU Press, 2008.

Degollado, Enrique David, Randy Clinton Bell, and Cinthia S. Salinas. "'No Había Bilingual Education:' Stories of Negotiation, Educación, y Sacrificios from South Texas Escuelitas."

Journal of Latinos and Education, April 26, 2019, 1–15. https://doi.org/10.1080/15348431 .2019.1604351.

de los Ríos, Cati V., Jorge López, and Ernest Morrell. "Critical Ethnic Studies in High School Classrooms: Academic Achievement via Social Action." In *Race, Equity, & Education: Sixty Years from Brown*, edited by Pedro Noguera, Jill Pierce, and Roey Ahram, 177–98. Cham, Switzerland: Springer International Publishing, 2016.

Del Valle, Sandra. "Bilingual Education for Puerto Ricans in New York City: From Hope to Compromise." *Harvard Educational Review* 68, no. 2 (1998): 193–218.

Desmond, Matthew. "Relational Ethnography." *Theory and Society* 43, no. 5 (2014): 547–79.

Dixson, Adrienne D., and Celia K. Rousseau. "And We Are Still Not Saved: Critical Race Theory in Education Ten Years Later." *Race Ethnicity & Education* 8, no. 1 (2005): 7–27. https:// doi.org/10.1080/1361332052000340971.

Donato, Rubén, and Jarrod Hanson. "'In These Towns, Mexicans Are Classified as Negroes': The Politics of Unofficial Segregation in the Kansas Public Schools, 1915–1935." *American Educational Research Journal* 54, no. S1 (2017): 53S–74S. https://doi.org/10.3102 /0002831216669781.

Dondero, Molly, and Chandra Muller. "School Stratification in New and Established Latino Destinations." *Social Forces* 91, no. 2 (2012): 477–502. https://doi.org/10.1093/sf/sos127.

Dowling, Julie A. "Opinion: Latinos Are Getting out of the 'Other' Box on the U.S. Census." *Los Angeles Times*, April 3, 2024. https://www.latimes.com/opinion/story/2024-04-03/census -latino-hispanic-race-ethnicity.

DuBord, Elise. "Language Policy and the Drawing of Social Boundaries: Public and Private Schools in Territorial Tucson." *Spanish in Context* 7, no. 1 (2010): 25–45.

Dumas, Michael, and Joseph Derrick Nelson. "(Re)Imagining Black Boyhood: Toward a Critical Framework for Educational Research." *Harvard Educational Review* 86, no. 1 (2016): 27–47. https://doi.org/10.17763/0017-8055.86.1.27.

Dunn, Alyssa Hadley. "Global Village versus Culture Shock: The Recruitment and Preparation of Foreign Teachers for U.S. Urban Schools." *Urban Education* 46, no. 6 (2011): 1379–1410. https://doi.org/10.1177/0042085911413152.

Enriquez, Laura E. "Border-Hopping Mexicans, Law-Abiding Asians, and Racialized Illegality: Analyzing Undocumented College Students Experiences through a Relational Lens." In *Relational Formations of Race*, edited by Daniel HoSang and Natalia Molina, 257–77. Berkeley: University of California Press, 2019.

Fallas-Escobar, Christian, and Matthew R. Deroo. "Latina/o Bilingual Teacher Candidates' Meaning-Making of Space and Place: Attending to Raciolinguistic Landscapes in Bilingual Teacher Education." *Multimodality & Society*, 3, no. 3 (2023). https://doi.org/10 .26349795231182481.

Feinberg, Ayal, Regina Branton, and Valerie Martinez-Ebers. "Counties That Hosted a 2016 Trump Rally Saw a 226 Percent Increase in Hate Crimes." *Washington Post*, March 22, 2019. https://www.washingtonpost.com/politics/2019/03/22/trumps-rhetoric-does-inspire-more -hate-crimes/.

Fergus, Edward, Pedro Noguera, and Margary Martin. "Construction of Race and Ethnicity for and by Latinos." In *Handbook of Latinos and Education: Theory, Research, and Practice*, edited by Enrique G. Murillo, Jr., Sofia A. Villenas, Ruth Trinidad Galván, Juan Sánchez Muñoz, Corinne Martínez, and Margarita Machado-Casas, 170–81. New York: Routledge, 2010.

Fields, Karen E., and Barbara J. Fields. *Racecraft: The Soul of Inequality in American Life*. London: Verso, 2014.

Flores, Antonio. "How the U.S. Hispanic Population Is Changing," 2017. http://www.pew research.org/fact-tank/2017/09/18/how-the-u-s-hispanic-population-is-changing/.

Flores, Glenda M. "Controlling Images of Space: Latina Teachers and Racial Positioning in Multiracial Schools." *City & Community* 14, no. 4 (2015): 410–32.

Flores, Nelson. "Deficit Perspectives and Bilingual Education in a Post-Civil Rights Era." *Journal of Language and Literacy Education*, November 2016.

———. "A Tale of Two Visions: Hegemonic Whiteness and Bilingual Education." *Educational Policy* 30, no. 1 (2016): 13–38. https://doi.org/10.1177/0895904815616482.

Flores, Nelson, and Jonathan Rosa. "Undoing Appropriateness: Raciolinguistic Ideologies and Language Diversity in Education." *Harvard Educational Review* 85, no. 2 (2015): 149–71.

Flores, Tatiana. "'Latinidad Is Cancelled': Confronting an Anti-Black Construct." *Latin American and Latinx Visual Culture* 3, no. 3 (2021): 58–79. https://doi.org/10.1525/lavc.2021.3 .3.58.

Foubert, Jennifer L. M. "'Damned If You Do, Damned If You Don't:' Black Parents' Racial Realist School Engagement." *Race Ethnicity & Education*, 2019, 1–18.

Freire, Juan, Verónica Valdez, and M. Delavan. "The (Dis)Inclusion of Latina/o Interests from Utah's Dual-Language Education Boom." *Journal of Latinos & Education* 16, no. 4 (2017): 276–89. https://doi.org/10.1080/15348431.2016.1229617.

Freire, Paulo. *Education for Critical Consciousness.* New York: Continuum, 1973.

Gamez, Rebeca, and Timothy Monreal. "'We Have That Opportunity Now': Black and Latinx Geographies, (Latinx) Racialization, and 'New Latinx South.'" *Journal of Leadership, Equity, and Research* 7, no. 2 (2021).

Gándara, Patricia, and Frances Contreras. *The Latino Education Crisis: The Consequences of Failed Social Policies.* Cambridge, MA: Harvard University Press, 2009.

Gándara, Patricia, and Megan Hopkins, eds. *Forbidden Language: English Learners and Restrictive Language Policies.* New York: Teachers College Press, 2010.

García, Ofelia, and Kenzo K. Sung. "Critically Assessing the 1968 Bilingual Education Act at 50 Years: Taming Tongues and Latinx Communities." *Bilingual Research Journal* 41, no. 4 (October 15, 2018): 318–33. https://doi.org/10.1080/15235882.2018.1529642.

Goings, Ramon B., Travis J. Bristol, and Larry J. Walker. "Exploring the Transition Experiences of One Black Male Refugee Pre-Service Teacher at a HBCU." *Journal for Multicultural Education* 12, no. 2 (2018): 126–43. https://doi.org/10.1108/JME-01-2017-0004.

Golash-Boza, Tanya, and William Darity. "Latino Racial Choices: The Effects of Skin Colour and Discrimination on Latinos' and Latinas' Racial Self-Identifications." *Ethnic & Racial Studies* 31, no. 5 (2008): 899–934. https://doi.org/10.1080/01419870701568858.

Goldberg, David Theo. "Racial Comparisons, Relational Racisms: Some Thoughts on Method." *Ethnic & Racial Studies* 32, no. 7 (2009): 1271–82.

Gómez, Laura E. *Inventing Latinos: A New Story of American Racism.* New York: The New Press, 2020.

———. *Manifest Destinies: The Making of the Mexican American Race.* New York: NYU Press, 2018.

González, Juan. *Harvest of Empire: A History of Latinos in America.* New York: Penguin, 2011.

Hall, Stuart. "Race, the Floating Signifier: What More Is There to Say about 'Race'?" In *Selected Writings on Race and Difference: Stuart Hall*, edited by Paul Gilroy and Ruth Wilson Gilmore, 359–73. Durham, NC: Duke University Press, 2021.

Hamann, Edmund, Stanton Wortham, and Enrique G. Murillo, eds. *Revisiting Education in the New Latino Diaspora.* Charlotte, NC: Information Age Publishing, 2015.

Haney López, Ian. "Race, Ethnicity, Erasure: The Salience of Race to LatCrit Theory." *California Law Review* 85, no. 5 (1997): 1143–1211. https://doi.org/10.2307/3481058.

Hannah-Jones, Nikole. "Creator of '1619 Project' on Trump's 'Patriotic Education.'" Interview by Audie Cornish. *All Things Considered*. NPR, September 18, 2020. https://www.npr.org /2020/09/18/914519531/creator-of-1619-project-on-trumps-patriotic-education.

Harper, Shaun R. "Race without Racism: How Higher Education Researchers Minimize Racist Institutional Norms." *Review of Higher Education* 36, no. 1 (2012): 9–29.

Harris, Cherise A., and Nikki Khanna. "Black Is, Black Ain't: Biracials, Middle-Class Blacks, and the Social Construction of Blackness." *Sociological Spectrum* 30, no. 6 (2010): 639–70.

Harris, Jessica C. "Toward a Critical Multiracial Theory in Education." *International Journal of Qualitative Studies in Education* 29, no. 6 (2016): 795–813.

Haywood, Jasmine M. "'Latino Spaces Have Always Been the Most Violent': Afro-Latino Collegians' Perceptions of Colorism and Latino Intragroup Marginalization." *International Journal of Qualitative Studies in Education* 30, no. 8 (September 14, 2017): 759–82. https://doi .org/10.1080/09518398.2017.1350298.

Hernandez, Sera J. "Are They All Language Learners?: Educational Labeling and Raciolinguistic Identifying in a California Middle School Dual-Language Program." *CATESOL Journal* 29, no. 1 (2017): 133–54.

Hernández, Tanya. *Racial Innocence: Unmasking Latino Anti-Black Bias and the Struggle for Equality*. Boston: Beacon Press, 2022.

Hochman, Adam. "Racialization: A Defense of the Concept." *Ethnic & Racial Studies* 42, no. 8 (2019): 1245–62. https://doi.org/10.1080/01419870.2018.1527937.

HoSang, Daniel, and Natalia Molina. "Introduction: Toward a Relational Consciousness of Race." In *Relational Formations of Race: Theory, Method, and Practice*, edited by Natalia Molina, Daniel Martinez HoSang, and Ramón A. Gutiérrez, 1–18. Oakland: University of California Press, 2019.

Howard, Tyrone C. *Why Race and Culture Matter in Schools: Closing the Achievement Gap in America's Classrooms*. Multicultural Education Series. New York: Teachers College Press, 2010.

Hurie, Andrew H., and Rebecca M. Callahan. "Integration as Perpetuation: Learning from Race Evasive Approaches to ESL Program Reform." *Teachers College Record* 121, no. 9 (2019): 1.

Irizarry, Yasmiyn. "Utilizing Multidimensional Measures of Race in Education Research: The Case of Teacher Perceptions." *Sociology of Race and Ethnicity* 1, no. 4 (2015): 564–83.

Jiménez-Castellanos, Oscar. "English Language Learner Education Finance Scholarship: An Introduction to the Special Issue." *Education Policy Analysis Archives* 25, no. 1 (2017): 26.

Johnson, Gaye Theresa. *Spaces of Conflict, Sounds of Solidarity: Music, Race, and Spatial Entitlement in Los Angeles*. Berkeley: University of California Press, 2013.

Johnston-Guerrero, Marc P., and Vu Tran. "Born This Way?: U.S. College Students Make Sense of the Biosocial Underpinnings of Race and Other Identities." *International Journal of Multicultural Education* 18, no. 2 (2016): 107–24.

Jong, Ester de, and Carol Bearse. "The Same Outcomes for All?: High School Students Reflect on Their Two-Way Immersion Program Experiences." In *Immersion Education: Practices, Policies, Possibilities*, edited by Diane J. Tedick, Donna Christian, and Tara Williams Fortune, 104–22. Washington, DC: Center for Applied Linguistics, 2011.

Kelkar, Kamala. "The Racial History of the Electoral College—and Why Efforts to Change It Have Stalled." *PBS NewsHour*, January 21, 2018. https://www.pbs.org/newshour/nation/the -racial-history-of-the-electoral-college-and-why-efforts-to-change-it-have-stalled.

Kendi, Ibram X. *Stamped from the Beginning: The Definitive History of Racist Ideas in America*. New York: Nation Books, 2016.

Kim, Elisabeth, and Minhye Son. "What Is Visible and Invisible: The Portrayal of Dual Language Programs on School Websites." *Language and Education*, 2023, 1–19. DOI:10.1080 /09500782.2023.2223165.

Klor de Alva, Jorge, Earl Shorris, and Cornel West. "Our Next Race Question: The Uneasiness Between Blacks and Latinos." In *Critical Race Theory: The Cutting Edge*, edited by Richard Delgado and Jean Stefancic, 3rd ed., 574–79. Philadelphia: Temple University Press, 2013.

Kohli, Rita, Marcos Pizarro, and Arturo Nevárez. "The 'New Racism' of K–12 Schools: Centering Critical Research on Racism." *Review of Research in Education* 41, no. 1 (2017): 182–202.

Kun, Josh, and Laura Pulido, eds. *Black and Brown in Los Angeles: Beyond Conflict and Coalition*. Berkeley: University of California Press, 2013.

Lacayo, Celia O. "Perpetual Inferiority: Whites' Racial Ideology toward Latinos." *Sociology of Race and Ethnicity* 3, no. 4 (2017): 566–79.

Ladson-Billings, Gloria, and William F. Tate. "Toward a Critical Race Theory of Education." *Teachers College Record* 97, no. 1 (1995): 47–68.

Lampert, Magdalene, Megan L. Franke, Elham Kazemi, Hala Ghousseini, Angela Chan Turrou, Heather Beasley, Adrian Cunard, and Kathleen Crowe. "Keeping It Complex: Using Rehearsals to Support Novice Teacher Learning of Ambitious Teaching." *Journal of Teacher Education* 64, no. 3 (2013): 226–43. https://doi.org/10.1177/0022487112473837.

Lau v. Nichols, 414 US 563 (U.S. Supreme Court 1974).

LeBaron, Alan. "When Latinos Are Not Latinos: The Case of Guatemalan Maya in the United States, the Southeast and Georgia." *Latino Studies* 10, no. 1 (2012): 179–95. https://doi.org /10.1057/lst.2012.8.

LeCompte, Margaret Diane, and Jean J. Schensul. *Analysis and Interpretation of Ethnographic Data: A Mixed Methods Approach*. 2nd ed. Lanham, MD: AltaMira, 2013.

Lee, Stacey J. *Unraveling the "Model Minority" Stereotype: Listening to Asian American Youth*. 2nd ed. New York: Teachers College Press, 2009.

Leonardo, Zeus. "Dialectics of Race Criticality: Studies in Racial Stratification and Education." *A Companion to Research in Education*, 2014, 247–57.

———. "Ideology and Its Modes of Existence: Toward an Althusserian Theory of Race and Racism." In *Handbook of Cultural Politics and Education*, edited by Zeus Leonardo, 193–217. Leiden, Netherlands: Brill, 2010.

———. *Race Frameworks: A Multidimensional Theory of Racism and Education*. New York: Teachers College Press, 2013.

Leonardo, Zeus, and Logan Manning. "White Historical Activity Theory: Toward a Critical Understanding of White Zones of Proximal Development." *Race Ethnicity & Education* 20, no. 1 (January 2, 2017): 15–29. https://doi.org/10.1080/13613324.2015.1100988.

Leonardo, Zeus, and Michalinos Zembylas. "Whiteness as Technology of Affect: Implications for Educational Praxis." *Equity & Excellence in Education* 46, no. 1 (2013): 150–65. https:// doi.org/10.1080/10665684.2013.750539.

Lewis, Amanda E. *Race in the Schoolyard: Negotiating the Color Line in Classrooms and Communities*. Piscataway, NJ: Rutgers University Press, 2011.

Lewis, Amanda E., John B. Diamond, and Tyrone A. Forman. "Conundrums of Integration: Desegregation in the Context of Racialized Hierarchy." *Sociology of Race and Ethnicity* 1, no. 1 (2015): 22–36.

Lewis, Amanda E., Margaret A. Hagerman, and Tyrone A. Forman. "The Sociology of Race and Racism: Key Concepts, Contributions & Debates." *Equity & Excellence in Education* 52, no. 1 (2019): 29–46.

Lima Becker, Mariana, and Gabrielle Oliveira. "'This Is a Very Sensitive Point': Bilingual Teachers' Interactions with Neo-Nationalism in a Two-Way Immersion Program in the United States." *TESOL Quarterly* 57, no. 3 (2023): 890–917. https://doi.org/10.1002/tesq.3244.

Lipsky, Michael. *Street-Level Bureaucracy: Dilemmas of the Individual in Public Service.* 30th anniversary. New York: Russell Sage Foundation, 2010.

López, Josué, and Jason Irizarry. "Somos Pero No Somos Iguales/We Are but We Are Not the Same: Unpacking Latinx Indigeneity and the Implications for Urban Schools." *Urban Education* 57, no. 9 (2022): 1539–64. https://doi.org/10.1177/0042085919835292.

López, Nancy. "Antiracist Pedagogy and Empowerment in a Bilingual Classroom in the U.S., circa 2006." *Theory into Practice* 47, no. 1 (2008): 43–50. https://doi.org/10.1080/00405840701764755.

———. *Hopeful Girls, Troubled Boys: Race and Gender Disparity in Urban Education.* New York: Routledge, 2002.

Love, Bettina L. *We Want to Do More Than Survive: Abolitionist Teaching and the Pursuit of Educational Freedom.* Boston: Beacon Press, 2019.

Lowenhaupt, Rebecca. "Bilingual Education Policy in Wisconsin's New Latino Diaspora." In *Revisiting Education in the New Latino Diaspora*, edited by Edmund Hamann, Stanton Wortham, and Enrique G. Murillo, 245–62. Charlotte, NC: Information Age Publishing, 2015.

Lozano, Rosina. *An American Language: The History of Spanish in the United States.* Oakland: University of California Press, 2018. https://doi.org/10.1525/california/9780520297067.001.0001.

Lynn, Marvin, and Laurence Parker. "Critical Race Studies in Education: Examining a Decade of Research on US Schools." *Urban Review* 38, no. 4 (2006): 257–90.

Macías, Reynaldo Flores, Carolyn Webb de Macías, William de La Torre, and Mario Vásquez. *Educación Alternativa: On the Development of Chicano Bilingual Schools.* Hayward, CA: Southwest Network, 1975.

Marquez, Bayley J. "The Black Model Minority: Slavery, Settlement, and the Genealogy of the Model Minority." *Du Bois Review: Social Science Research on Race* 19, no. 1 (2022): 129–45. https://doi.org/10.1017/S1742058X21000345.

Marquez, Bayley J., and Juliet Rose Kunkel. "The Domestication Genocide of Settler Colonial–Language Ideologies." *American Quarterly* 73, no. 3 (2021): 461–82. https://doi.org/10.1353/aq.2021.0046.

Martinez, George A. "The Legal Construction of Race: Mexican-Americans and Whiteness." *Harvard Latino Law Review* 2 (1997): 321–48.

Martínez, Ramón Antonio. "Dual-Language Education and the Erasure of Chicanx, Latinx, and Indigenous Mexican Children: A Call to Re-Imagine (and Imagine beyond) Bilingualism." *Texas Education Review* 5, no. 1 (2017): 81–92.

Massey, Douglas S. "Racial Formation in Theory and Practice: The Case of Mexicans in the United States." *Race and Social Problems* 1, no. 1 (2009): 12–26.

McCormick, Jennifer, and César J. Ayala. "Felícita 'La Prieta' Méndez (1916–1998) and the End of Latino School Segregation in California." *Centro Journal* 19, no. 2 (2007): 13–35.

McGhee, Heather. *The Sum of Us: What Racism Costs Everyone and How We Can Prosper Together.* New York: One World, 2021.

Merseth, Julie Lee. "The Relational Positioning of Arab and Muslim Americans in Post-9/11 Racial Politics." In *Relational Formations of Race*, edited by Daniel HoSang and Natalia Molina, 296–324. Berkeley: University of California Press, 2019.

Mignolo, Walter D. *The Idea of Latin America*. Durham, NC: Duke University Press, 2005.

Milian, Claudia. *LatinX*. Minneapolis: University of Minnesota Press, 2019.

Milner, H. Richard. "Disrupting Punitive Practices and Policies: Rac(e)Ing Back to Teaching, Teacher Preparation, and Brown." *Educational Researcher* 49, no.3 (2020): 1–14.

Molina, Natalia. "Examining Chicana/o History through a Relational Lens." *Pacific Historical Review* 82, no. 4 (2013): 520–41.

———. *How Race Is Made in America: Immigration, Citizenship, and the Historical Power of Racial Scripts*. Berkeley: University of California Press, 2014.

Molina, Natalia, Daniel HoSang, and Ramón Gutiérrez, eds. *Relational Formations of Race: Theory, Method, and Practice*. Oakland: University of California Press, 2019.

Montone, Chris, and Michael I. Loeb. "Implementing Two-Way Immersion Programs in Secondary Schools." Santa Cruz, CA: Center for Research on Education, Diversity & Excellence, 2000. https://escholarship.org/uc/item/23d3c1bm.

Mora, G. Cristina. *Making Hispanics: How Activists, Bureaucrats, and Media Constructed a New American*. Chicago: University of Chicago Press, 2014.

Morales, P. Zitlali, and Joanna V. Maravilla. "The Problems and Possibilities of Interest Convergence in a Dual Language School." *Theory into Practice* 58, no. 2 (April 2019): 145–53. https://doi.org/10.1080/00405841.2019.1569377.

Moses, Michele S. *Embracing Race: Why We Need Race-Conscious Education Policy*. New York: Teachers College Press, 2002.

Nasir, Na'ilah. *Racialized Identities: Race and Achievement among African American Youth*. Stanford, CA: Stanford University Press, 2011.

National Center for Education Statistics. "Racial/Ethnic Enrollment in Public Schools," 2021. https://nces.ed.gov/programs/coe/indicator/cge.

Nuñez, Idalia, Jiadi Zhang, Dalia Hernandez Farias, and Maria Elizabeth Becerra. "'They Are. Bilingual.': Manifestations of Bilanguaging Love in a Dual Language Bilingual Classroom." Bilingual Research Journal 46, no. 1–2 (2023): 47–63. DOI: 10.1080/15235882.2023.2189174.

Okamoto, Dina, and G. Cristina Mora. "Panethnicity." *Annual Review of Sociology* 40, no. 1 (2014): 219–39. https://doi.org/10.1146/annurev-soc-071913-043201.

Omi, Michael, and Howard Winant. *Racial Formation in the United States*. 3rd ed. New York: Routledge, 2015.

———. "Racial Formation Rules: Continuity, Instability, and Change." In *Racial Formation in the Twenty-First Century*, edited by Daniel Martinez HoSang, Oneka LaBennett, and Laura Pulido, 302–31. Berkeley: University of California Press, 2012.

———. "Resistance Is Futile?: A Response to Feagin and Elias." *Ethnic and Racial Studies* 36, no. 6 (2013): 961–73.

Orellana, Marjorie Faulstich, and Kris D. Gutiérrez. "At Last: What's the Problem? Constructing Different Genres for the Study of English Learners." *Research in the Teaching of English* 41, no. 1 (2006): 118–23.

Orfield, G., and E. Frankenberg. "Brown at 60: Great Progress, a Long Retreat, and an Uncertain Future." Los Angeles: The Civil Rights Project, 2014.

Orozco, Richard A., and Francesca López. "Impacts of Arizona's SB 1070 on Mexican American Students' Stress, School Attachment, and Grades." *Education Policy Analysis Archives* 23 (2015): 42–42.

Pacheco, Mariana, and Laura C. Chávez-Moreno. "Bilingual Education for Self-Determination: Re-Centering Chicana/o/x and Latina/o/x Student Voices." *Bilingual Research Journal* 4, no. 4 (2021): 522–38. https://doi.org/10.1080/15235882.2022.2052203.

Palacios, Agustín. "Multicultural Vasconcelos: The Optimistic, and at Times Willful, Misreading of 'La Raza Cósmica.'" *Latino Studies* 15, no. 4 (2017): 416–38. https://doi.org/10.1057/s41276-017-0095-6.

Palmer, Deborah. "Race, Power, and Equity in a Multiethnic Urban Elementary School with a Dual-Language 'Strand' Program." *Anthropology & Education Quarterly* 41, no. 1 (2010): 94–114. https://doi.org/10.1111/j.1548-1492.2010.01069.x.

Palmer, Deborah, Claudia Cervantes-Soon, Lisa Dorner, and Daniel Heiman. "Bilingualism, Biliteracy, Biculturalism, and Critical Consciousness for All: Proposing a Fourth Fundamental Goal for Two-Way Dual-Language Education." *Theory into Practice* 58, no. 2 (April 3, 2019): 121–33. https://doi.org/10.1080/00405841.2019.1569376.

Patel, L. *Decolonizing Educational Research: From Ownership to Answerability*. New York: Routledge, 2016.

Pérez Huber, Lindsay, Corina Lopez, Maria Malagon, Veronica Velez, and Daniel Solórzano. "Theorizing Racist Nativism." *Contemporary Justice Review* 11, no. 1 (2008): 39–51. https://doi.org/10.1080/10282580701850397.

Philip, Thomas M. "Asian American as a Political-Racial Identity: Implications for Teacher Education." *Race, Ethnicity and Education* 17, no. 2 (2014): 219–41.

Pirtle, Whitney N., Breanna Brock, Nonzenzele Aldonza, Kaline Leke, and Dallas Edge. "'I Didn't Know What Anti-Blackness Was Until I Got Here': The Unmet Needs of Black Students at Hispanic-Serving Institutions." *Urban Education* 59, no. 1 (2021). 00420859211044948.

Pollock, Mica. *Colormute: Race Talk Dilemmas in an American School*. Princeton, NJ: Princeton University Press, 2009.

Presiado, Vivian E., and Brittany L. Frieson. "'Make Sure You See This': Counternarratives of Multilingual Black Girls' Language and Literacy Practices." *Literacy Research: Theory, Method, and Practice* 70, no. 1 (2021): 388–407. https://doi.org/10.1177/23813377211038264.

Quijano, Aníbal. "Coloniality of Power and Eurocentrism in Latin America." *International Sociology* 15, no. 2 (June 1, 2000): 215–32. https://doi.org/10.1177/0268580900015002005.

Rigby, Jessica G., and Stephanie Forman. "Leading for Justice, Leading for Learning: Conceptualizing Urban School Leadership for Antiracist Mathematics Teaching and Learning." *Urban Education*, March 29, 2023, 00420859231162907. https://doi.org/10.1177/00420859231162907.

Ríos, Gabriela Raquel. "Mestizaje." In *Decolonizing Rhetoric and Composition Studies: New Latinx Keywords for Theory and Pedagogy*, edited by Iris D. Ruiz and Raúl Sánchez, 109–24. New York: Palgrave Macmillan, 2016. https://doi.org/10.1057/978-1-137-52724-0_8.

Rodriguez, Gloria M. "Vertical Equity in School Finance & the Potential for Increasing School Responsiveness to Student and Staff Needs." *Peabody Journal of Education* 79, no. 3 (2004): 7–30.

Rodríguez, Néstor. "Theoretical and Methodological Issues of Latina/o Research." In *Latinas/os in the United States: Changing the Face of América*, edited by Havidán Rodríguez, Rogelio Sáenz, and Cecilia Menjívar, 3–15. Boston: Springer, 2008.

Rodríguez, Sophia, and Gilberto Q. Conchas. *Race Frames in Education: Structuring Inequality and Opportunity in a Changing Society*. New York: Teachers College Press, 2022.

Rogers, John, Erica Hodgin, Joseph Kahne, and Veronica Terriquez. "Educating Toward a Multiracial Democracy in California." UCLA's Institute for Democracy, Education, and Access, 2022.

Román, Diego, Alberto Pastor, and Deni Basaraba. "Internal Linguistic Discrimination: A Survey of Bilingual Teachers' Language Attitudes toward Their Heritage Students' Spanish." *Bilingual Research Journal* 42, no. 1 (January 2, 2019): 6–30. https://doi.org/10.1080/15235882.2018.1563006.

Romero, Robert Chao, and Kevin Escudero. "'Asian Latinos' and the U.S. Census." *AAPI Nexus: Policy, Practice and Community* 10, no. 2 (2012): 119–38.

Rosa, Jonathan. *Looking Like a Language, Sounding Like a Race: Raciolinguistic Ideologies and the Learning of Latinidad.* New York: Oxford University Press, 2019.

Roth, Wendy D. "The Multiple Dimensions of Race." *Ethnic & Racial Studies* 39, no. 8 (2016): 1310–38. https://doi.org/10.1080/01419870.2016.1140793.

———. *Race Migrations: Latinos and the Cultural Transformation of Race.* Stanford, CA: Stanford University Press, 2012.

Roth, Wendy D., Şule Yaylacı, Kaitlyn Jaffe, and Lindsey Richardson. "Do Genetic Ancestry Tests Increase Racial Essentialism? Findings from a Randomized Controlled Trial." *PLOS ONE* 15, no. 1 (2020): e0227399. https://doi.org/10.1371/journal.pone.0227399.

Ryan, Josiah. "'This Was a Whitelash': Van Jones' Take on the Election Results." CNN, November 9, 2016. https://www.cnn.com/2016/11/09/politics/van-jones-results-disappointment-cnntv/index.html.

Saldaña, Johnny. *The Coding Manual for Qualitative Researchers.* 2nd ed. Thousand Oaks, CA: Sage Publications, 2013.

Sánchez, MaríaTeresa, Ofelia García, and Cristian Solorza. "Reframing Language Allocation Policy in Dual Language Bilingual Education." *Bilingual Research Journal* 41, no. 1 (2018): 37–51. https://doi.org/10.1080/15235882.2017.1405098.

San Miguel, Guadalupe. *Chicana/o Struggles for Education: Activism in the Community.* College Station: Texas A&M University Press, 2013.

Santiago, Maribel. "Diluting Mexican American History for Public Consumption: How 'Mendez' Became the 'Mexican American "Brown."'" *Teachers College Record* 122, no. 8 (2020): n8.

Santos, Carlos, Cecilia Menjívar, and Erin Godfrey. "Effects of SB 1070 on Children." In *Latino Politics and Arizona's Immigration Law SB 1070,* edited by Lisa Magaña and Erik Lee, 79–92. New York: Springer, 2013.

Schnaiberg, Lynn. "D.C. School Bilingual Plan Pits Black, Hispanic Parents." *Education Week,* November 9, 1994. https://www.edweek.org/teaching-learning/d-c-school-bilingual-plan-pits-black-hispanic-parents/1994/11.

Scott, Janelle, and Monisha Bajaj. "Introduction: Racialization and Educational Inequality in Transnational Perspective." In *World Yearbook of Education 2023,* 1–13. Routledge, 2023.

Shin, Hyoung-jin, and Richard Alba. "The Economic Value of Bilingualism for Asians and Hispanics." *Sociological Forum* 24, no. 2 (2009): 254–75. https://doi.org/10.1111/j.1573-7861.2009.01099.x.

Siegel, Eric. "The Real Problem with Charles Murray and 'The Bell Curve.'" Scientific American Blog Network. Accessed October 16, 2023. https://blogs.scientificamerican.com/voices/the-real-problem-with-charles-murray-and-the-bell-curve/.

Singh, Michael V. "Negotiating Antiblackness as Non-Black Latino Men Teachers: Relational Race Politics in the Discourse on Men of Color Teachers." *Urban Education* (2023): 1–29. https://doi.org/00420859231162901.

———. "Refusing the Performance: Disrupting Popular Discourses Surrounding Latino Male Teachers and the Possibility of Disidentification." *Educational Studies* 55, no. 1 (2019): 28–45.

Skerrett, Allison. "English Teachers' Racial Literacy Knowledge and Practice." *Race Ethnicity & Education* 14, no. 3 (2011): 313–30. https://doi.org/10.1080/13613324.2010.543391.

Sleeter, Christine E., and Dolores Delgado Bernal. "Critical Pedagogy, Critical Race Theory, and Antiracist Education: Implications for Multicultural Education." In *Handbook of Research on Multicultural Education*, edited by James A. Banks and Cherry A. McGee Banks, 2nd ed., 240–58. San Francisco: Jossey Bass, 2004.

Smedley, Audrey, and Brian D. Smedley. "Race as Biology Is Fiction, Racism as a Social Problem Is Real: Anthropological and Historical Perspectives on the Social Construction of Race." *American Psychologist* 60, no. 1 (2005): 16–26. https://doi.org/10.1037/0003-066X.60.1.16.

Smith, Patriann, Jaehoon Lee, and Rong Chang. "Characterizing Competing Tensions in Black Immigrant Literacies: Beyond Partial Representations of Success." *Reading Research Quarterly*, 2020.

Stone, Theresa Burruel. "Centering Place in Ethnographies of 'Latinx' Schooling: The Utility of a Multi-Sited Place Project for Revealing Emplaced Narratives." *International Review of Qualitative Research* 15, no. 3 (2022): 399–425.

Stovall, David. "Killing You Is Justice." In *Trayvon Martin, Race, and American Justice: Writing Wrong*, edited by Kenneth J. Fasching-Varner, Rema E. Reynolds, Katrice A. Albert, and Lori L. Martin, 9–13. Boston: Sense Publishers, 2014.

Subtirelu, Nicholas, Margaret Borowczyk, Rachel Thorson Hernández, and Francesca Venezia. "Recognizing Whose Bilingualism? A Critical Policy Analysis of the Seal of Biliteracy." *Modern Language Journal* 103, no. 2 (2019): 371–90.

Sung, Kenzo K. "'Accentuate the Positive; Eliminate the Negative': Hegemonic Interest Convergence, Racialization of Latino Poverty, and the 1968 Bilingual Education Act." *Peabody Journal of Education* 92, no. 3 (2017): 302–21. https://doi.org/10.1080/0161956X.2017.1324657.

———. "Raciolinguistic Ideology of Antiblackness: Bilingual Education, Tracking, and the Multiracial Imaginary in Urban Schools." *International Journal of Qualitative Studies in Education* 31, no. 8 (2018): 667–83. https://doi.org/10.1080/09518398.2018.1479047.

Thompson, Jessica, Mark Windschitl, and Melissa Braaten. "Developing a Theory of Ambitious Early-Career Teacher Practice." *American Educational Research Journal* 50, no. 3 (2013): 574–615.

Torres-Saillant, Silvio. "Inventing the Race: Latinos and the Ethnoracial Pentagon." *Latino Studies* 1, no. 1 (2003): 123–51.

Urciuoli, Bonnie. *Exposing Prejudice: Puerto Rican Experiences of Language, Race, and Class*. Boulder, CO: Westview Press, 1996.

US Department of Education. "Our Nation's English Learners," 2017. https://www2.ed.gov/datastory/el-characteristics/index.html.

Valdés, Guadalupe, Luis Poza, and Maneka Deanna Brooks. "Educating Students Who Do Not Speak the Societal Language: The Social Construction of Language Learner Categories." *Profession*, 2014. https://profession.mla.org/educating-students-who-do-not-speak-the-societal-language-the-social-construction-of-language-learner-categories/

Valdez, Carolina, Edward Curammeng, Farima Pour-Khorshid, Rita Kohli, Thomas Nikundiwe, Bree Picower, Carla Shalaby, and David Stovall. "We Are Victorious: Educator Activism as a Shared Struggle for Human Being." *Educational Forum* 82, no. 3 (2018): 244–58.

Valenzuela, Angela, Emmanuel Garcia, Harriett Romo, and Beatrix Perez. "Institutional and Structural Barriers to Latino/a Achievement." *Association of Mexican American Educators Journal* 6, no. 3 (2012): 22–29.

Vásquez, Manuel A., Chad E. Seales, and Marie Friedmann Marquardt. "New Latino Destinations." In *Latinas/os in the United States: Changing the Face of América*, edited by Havidán Rodríguez, Rogelio Sáenz, and Cecilia Menjívar, 19–35. Boston: Springer, 2008.

Wallace, Derron. *The Culture Trap: Ethnic Expectations and Unequal Schooling for Black Youth*. New York: Oxford University Press, 2023.

Warmington, Paul. "Taking Race out of Scare Quotes: Race-Conscious Social Analysis in an Ostensibly Post-Racial World." *Race Ethnicity & Education* 12, no. 3 (2009): 281–96. https://doi.org/10.1080/13613320903178253.

Wills, John S. "Silencing Racism: Remembering and Forgetting Race and Racism in 11th-Grade U.S. History Classes." *Teachers College Record* 121, no. 6 (2019): 1–44.

Winn, Maisha T. *Girl Time: Literacy, Justice, and the School-to-Prison Pipeline*. New York: Teachers College Press, 2011.

Wolfe, Patrick. *Traces of History: Elementary Structures of Race*. Brooklyn, NY: Verso, 2016.

Wortham, Stanton, Katherine Mortimer, and Elaine Allard. "Mexicans as Model Minorities in the New Latino Diaspora." *Anthropology & Education Quarterly* 40, no. 4 (2009): 388–404.

Wynter, Sylvia. "Unsettling the Coloniality of Being/Power/Truth/Freedom: Towards the Human, After Man, Its Overrepresentation—An Argument." *Centennial Review* 3, no. 3 (2003): 257–337.

Zamora, Sylvia. *Racial Baggage: Mexican Immigrants and Race Across the Border*. Stanford, CA: Stanford University Press, 2022.

Zentella, Ana. "'Limpia, Fija y Da Esplendor': Challenging the Symbolic Violence of the Royal Spanish Academy." *Chiricú Journal: Latina/o Literatures, Arts, and Cultures* 1, no. 2 (2017): 21–42. https://doi.org/10.2979/chiricu.1.2.04.

Zepeda-Millán, Chris, and Sophia Wallace. "Racialization in Times of Contention: How Social Movements Influence Latino Racial Identity." *Politics, Groups, and Identities* 1, no. 4 (2013): 510–27.

Acknowledgments

The most cherished gifts for me are receiving honest and constructive feedback that not only stimulates my thinking but also fosters my learning and growth. I'm sincerely grateful to the volunteer anonymous reviewers who generously accepted reading and providing reviews on the book proposal and the entire manuscript. I'm also deeply grateful to the reader-participants of my book manuscript workshop:

Zeus Leonardo, for recommending readings and ways of thinking, for asking probing questions to clarify my ideas and address tensions and contradictions, and for enthusiastically supporting this work;

Daniel Martinez HoSang, for providing critical and generative questions and comments that enhanced my thinking;

Pedro Noguera, for supporting me, especially when I was a postdoctoral scholar at UCLA GSEIS; and

Floridalma Boj Lopez, Genevieve Carpio, and Ananda Marin, for sharing insightful conversations, suggestions, and generous feedback before, during, and after my manuscript workshop that significantly helped me refine my ideas and improve this book.

Others outside of the workshop also read and offered pivotal comments. My heartfelt gratitude extends to Laura E. Gómez, who read and provided detailed page-by-page commentary on the entire manuscript, demonstrating her support for my work.

I'm thankful to Enrique Alemán, Jr., Renee Moreno, Tasha Hauff, and Amato Nocera for their helpful insights on the prospectus and/or various sections of the manuscript.

To all these scholars: your feedback has been an intellectual gift of immeasurable worth. I thank you for helping me be thoughtful about the words I write and share with the world.

Special thanks to Karen Adler for her thorough reading of the manuscript and for offering insightful questions and suggestions, guiding me in presenting the book that I envisioned. I also extend my gratitude to Monica Jainschigg for her meticulous and thoughtful copyediting, which significantly enhanced the book's message. Thank you to the editorial and production team at Harvard Education Press, including Jessica

Fiorillo, Michael Higgins, Anne Noonan, Emma Struebing, and Helen Wheeler at Westchester Publishing Services, for your dedication and expertise in bringing this book to life.

I'm blessed to have inspiring colleagues in the Department of Chicana/o & Central American Studies, and I especially thank Charlene Black-Villaseñor, Genevieve Carpio, Floridalma Boj Lopez, Leisy Abrego, Eric Avila, Chris Zepeda-Millán, Robert Chao Romero, Veronica Terriquez, Maylei Blackwell, and Abel Valenzuela. I also thank the CCAS staff Sandy García, Janeth Ruvalcaba, Ellie Hernández, Valeria Moedano, and Alain de Vera.

I thank the UCLA Department of Education for sponsoring my postdoctoral fellowship. Since arriving at UCLA, I've been blessed to have many people support me through conversations over lunch, caring advice, and institutional support: Celia Lacayo, Marissa López, J.Ed Araiza, Pedro Noguera, Ananda Marin, Anne Pebley, Mike Prelip, Gilbert Gee, Steve Wallace, Jerry Kang, Scott Waugh, Chris Dunkel Schetter, Christina Christie, Marjorie Elaine, Otto Santa Ana, Tyrone Howard, Teresa McCarty, Daniel Solórzano, Ozan Jaquette, Eddie Cole, Jessica Harris, Lucrecia Santibañez, and Inmaculada García-Sánchez.

I'm grateful to the scholars and mentors who have supported me on this journey, particularly Gloria Ladson-Billings and Mariana Pacheco. I also thank: Carl Grant, Lesley Bartlett, Marilyn Cochran-Smith, Leigh Patel, Gabrielle Oliveira, Ofelia García, Jonathan Rosa, Nelson Flores, Gilbert Conchas, Nancy Acevedo-Gil, Eligio Martinez, Samy Alim, Bianca Baldridge, Nolan Cabrera, Dave Stovall, Rich Milner, Jayne Fargnoli, Camika Royal, Decoteau Irby, Chezare Warren, Tonya Perry, Angela Valenzuela, Rita Kohli, Katy Swalwell, David García, Thomas Philip, Cati de los Ríos, Juan González, Eleni Schirmer, Erica Turner, Annalee Good, Mary Klehr, Ayşe Yolcu, Stephanie R. Miller, Jennifer Foubert, Taucia González, and Carrie Sampson. Each of the individuals named has provided invaluable mentorship, friendship, accountability, critical dialogue, resources, materials, advice, and/or answered "cold-call" emails; regardless of the level of interaction, I'm sincerely grateful for your support.

I won't be able to name all the scholars who influence my thinking, but they include the authors I cite in this book, and I thank them for their scholarship. I also extend my thanks to you, the reader, for engaging with the ideas in this book. Additionally, I owe a special acknowledgment to Kay Andres and Sunny Chan. Their diligent editing, insightful suggestions, and commitment to refining my prose in other work have been instrumental in my development as a writer, particularly in communicating complex ideas more effectively.

I extend my thanks to the study participants and the community of Oakville for their honesty and contribution to my inquiry, and for inspiring me with their dedication to improving education for all students.

I'm grateful to the National Academy of Education (NAEd) and the Spencer Foundation Postdoctoral Fellowship for supporting this project by providing me with the time needed to reflect and write. I thank the NAEd members and fellows of the Fall 2023 Annual Retreat for their questions and feedback on my book manuscript presentation.

I thank the University of Arizona's College of Education for inviting me to their Advancing Justice Seminar, where I explored questions about Latinx racialization with teachers, staff, students, community members, and scholars.

I'm grateful to the UCLA Faculty Development Academic Personnel Office, the Social Sciences Division, the Chicano Studies Research Center, and the Department of CCAS for sponsoring my book manuscript workshop. I also thank the UCLA Society of Hellman Fellows Program and the UCLA Institute of American Cultures and the Chicano Studies Research Center for research grants to support this book's dissemination.

I thank the University of Wisconsin-Madison School of Education for the Carrie R. Barton Memorial Scholarship, the Arvil S. Barr Fellowship, and the Ed-GRS Fellowship. Their generous financial support during my dissertation years enabled me to delve into this work.

For their invaluable support during the writing period, offering encouragement, laughter, cariño, and much-needed distractions, I am deeply thankful to my friends: Hiram; Ankur Mehta; Tejas Parasher; Huijun and Kevin; Navid Bavi; Shohini Kundu; Mirea Sharifi; Rebecca Vinsonhaler; Jorge Nasser; Inma; Ananda and Mike; Anne and Barry; Zoraida and Oscar; Mary and Allen; Thiago and Fabio; Debora Sobreira; Taifha Alexander; Heeju and James; Veronica Castro Sabbaghi; and to the Levering Book Club: Priyanka, Emily, Mariya, and Thai.

A los antepasados, gracias por persistir y plantar sus semillas.

A mis padres, Myrna y Silvestre, a mis hermanas, Raquel y Myrnita, y a mis abuelites, tíes, primes, cuñades, sobrines, y familia, gracias por su cariño y apoyo.

A Hiram Beltrán-Sánchez, gracias por todo lo que he mencionado y por acompañarme durante todo este proceso y aventura, y gracias por amarme y hacerme mejor persona.

About the Author

Laura C. Chávez-Moreno is an award-winning researcher, qualitative social scientist, and assistant professor in the César E. Chávez Department of Chicana/o and Central American Studies and the Department of Education at the University of California, Los Angeles. Her research has been published in top-tier journals such as *Review of Educational Research*, *Educational Researcher*, *American Educational Research Journal*, *Research in the Teaching of English*, and *Journal of Teacher Education*. Dr. Chávez-Moreno was an awardee of the 2022 National Academy of Education/Spencer Foundation Postdoctoral Fellowship and was a member of the 2020–2022 NCTE Research Foundation's Cultivating New Voices Among Scholars of Color cohort. She received her PhD in curriculum and instruction from the University of Wisconsin–Madison. Before obtaining her PhD, she was a teacher of high school Spanish in the School District of Philadelphia. She grew up in Douglas, Arizona, and Agua Prieta, Sonora, México.

Index